CDPSE™ Review Manual

About ISACA

For more than 50 years, ISACA® (*www.isaca.org*) has advanced the best talent, expertise and learning in technology. ISACA equips individuals with knowledge, credentials, education and community to progress their careers and transform their organizations, and enables enterprises to train and build quality teams. Among those credentials, ISACA advances and validates business-critical skills and knowledge through the globally respected Certified Information Systems Auditor® (CISA®), Certified in Risk and Information Systems Control™ (CRISC™), Certified Information Security Manager® (CISM®), Certified in the Governance of Enterprise IT® (CGEIT®) and Certified Data Privacy Solutions Engineer™ (CDPSE™) credentials. ISACA is a global professional association and learning organization that leverages the expertise of its 145,000 members who work in information security, governance, assurance, risk and privacy to drive innovation through technology. It has a presence in 188 countries, including more than 220 chapters worldwide.

Disclaimer

ISACA has designed and created *CDPSE™ Review Manual* primarily as an educational resource to assist individuals preparing to take the CDPSE™ certification exam. It was produced independently from the CDPSE exam and the CDPSE Certification Working Group, which has had no responsibility for its content. Copies of past exams are not released to the public and were not made available to ISACA for preparation of this publication. ISACA makes no representations or warranties whatsoever with regard to these or other ISACA publications assuring candidates' passage of the CDPSE exam.

ISACA
1700 E. Golf Road, Suite 400
Schaumburg, IL 60173, USA
Phone: +1.847.660.5505
Fax: +1.847.253.1755
Contact us: https://support.isaca.org
Website: www.isaca.org

Participate in the ISACA Online Forums: https://engage.isaca.org/onlineforums

Twitter: http://twitter.com/ISACANews
LinkedIn: www.linkedin.com/company/isaca
Facebook: www.facebook.com/ISACAGlobal
Instagram: www.instagram.com/isacanews/

ISBN 978-1-60420-830-6
CDPSE™ Review Manual
Printed in the United States of America

CDPSE™ Review Manual

ISACA is pleased to offer the *CDPSE™ Review Manual*. The purpose of the manual is to provide CDPSE™ candidates with technical information and references to prepare and study for the Certified Data Privacy Solutions Engineer™ (CDPSE) exam.

The *CDPSE™ Review Manual* is the result of contributions of volunteers across the globe who are actively involved in data privacy and who have generously contributed their time and expertise. The *CDPSE™ Review Manual* will be updated to keep pace with rapid changes in the field of data privacy. As such, your comments and suggestions regarding this manual are welcome.

No representations or warranties are made by ISACA in regard to these or other ISACA/IT Governance Institute® (ITGI®) publications that ensure candidates' passing the CDPSE exam. This publication was produced independently of the CDPSE Certification Working Group, which has no responsibility for the content of this manual.

Copies of the CDPSE exam are not released to the public. The sample practice questions in this manual are designed to provide further clarity to the content presented in the manual and to depict the type of questions typically found on the CDPSE exam. The CDPSE exam is a practice-based exam. Simply reading the reference material in this manual will not properly prepare candidates for the exam. The sample questions are included for guidance only. Your scoring results do not indicate future individual exam success.

Certification has resulted in a positive impact on many careers, including worldwide recognition for professional experience and enhanced knowledge and skills. We wish you success with the CDPSE exam.

Page intentionally left blank

Acknowledgments

The *CDPSE™ Review Manual* is the result of the collective efforts of many volunteers. ISACA members from throughout the global data privacy profession participated, generously offering their talent and expertise. This international team exhibited a spirit and selflessness that has become the hallmark of contributors to ISACA manuals. Their participation and insight are truly appreciated.

Authors

David Bowden, CISM, CDPSE, CIPT, CSM, PMP, Zwift, Inc., USA
James L. Halcomb, Jr., EDME, Elucidate Consulting, LLC, USA
Rebecca Herold, CISA, CISM, CIPM, CIPP/US, CIPT, CISSP, FIP, FLMI, Ponemon Institute Fellow, The Privacy Professor/Privacy Security Brainiacs SaaS Services, USA

Reviewers

Sanjiv Agarwala, CISA, CISM, CGEIT, CDPSE, CISSP, FBCI, LA(ISO27001,22301), Oxygen Consulting Services Pvt Ltd, India
Ashief Ahmed, CISA, CDPSE, SSI, Canada
Richi Aktorian, CISA, CISM, CGEIT, CRISC, CDPSE, Indonesia
Ecrument Ari, CISA, CISM, CGEIT, CRISC, CDPSE, CEH, CIPM, CIPP/E, CRMA, FIP, ISO 27001/22301/20000 Lead Auditor, Surprise Consultancy, Turkey
Januarius Asongu, Ph.D., CISA, CISM, CGEIT, CRISC, CDPSE, JPMorgan Chase & Co., USA
C. Patrick F. Brown, CISM, CDPSE, CIPM, CIPP/E, CIPP/US, CIPT, FIP, NCSB Privacy and Information Security Law Specialist, PLS, Lawyers Mutual Liability Insurance Company of North Carolina, USA
Deepinder Singh Chhabra, CISA, CISM, CGEIT, CRISC, CDPSE, C|CISO, CISSP, Verizon, United Kingdom
Ramon Codina, CISM, CDPSE, Spain
Francisco Garcia Dayo, CISA, CDPSE, Vestiga Consultores, Mexico
Pascal Fortin, CISA, CISM, CRISC, CDPSE, CPIP, CRMA, KPMG, Canada
Shigeto Fukuda, CISA, CDPSE, Japan
Chandrasekhar Sarma Garimella, CISA, CRISC, CDPSE, CtrlS Datacenters Ltd, India
Peter Gwee, CISA, CISM, CRISC, CDPSE, ST Engineering Electronics (Cyber Security Systems Group), Singapore
Hideko Igarashi, CISA, CISM, CRISC, CDPSE, CISSP, Japan
Anand M. Jha, CISA, CDPSE, Azur Solutions Architect Expert, CCSK, CISSP, GCIH, GPEN, ISO27001 LA, OPSE, Ernst & Young LLP, India
Leighton Johnson, CISA, CISM, CGEIT, CRISC, CDPSE, ISFMT, Inc., USA
Christian Kengne, CSX-P, CDPSE, ISO.27001 LA, Accenture, Canada
John Krogulski, CISA, CISM, CDPSE, WIDA, USA
Carol Lee, CISM, CRISC, CDPSE, CCSP, CEH, CIPM, CSSLP, Johnson Electric Group, Hong Kong
Cher Lee Leow, CISA, CISM, CDPSE, Grab Taxi Holding Pte Ltd, Singapore
Dimitris Maketas, CISA, CDPSE, CCSK, CICA, GRCA, GRCP, ISO 27001 Internal Auditor, ISO 273032 Senior Lead Cyber Security Manager, ITIL, PRINCE 2 Practitioner, Switzerland
Adel Abdel Moneim, CISA, CISM, CGEIT, CRISC, CDPSE, CCFP-EU, CCISO, CCSK, CCSP, CDPO, CEH, CFR, CHFI, CISSP, CLSSP, CND, CSA, CTIA, ECES, ECIH, ECSA, EDRP, IoTSP, ISO 22301 SLA/SLI, ISO24762 LDRM, ISO27005 LRM, ISO27032, ISO27035 LIM, ISO27701 SLI/SLA, ISO29100 SLPI, ISO38500 LITCGM, LCM, LPT, Master ISO27001, MCCT, PECB MS Auditor, SABSA-SCF, TOGAF, ITU-RCC, Egypt
Scott Morgan, CISM, CDPSE, Florida Department of Highway Safety and Motor Vehicles, USA
Akira Muranaka, CISA, CISM, CGEIT, CRISC, CDPSE, FIP, Equifax, USA
Chintan Parekh, CISA, CRISC, CDPSE, USA
Vaibhav Patkar, CISA, CISM, CRISC, CGEIT, CDPSE, CISSP, India
Santosh Putchala, CISM, CDPSE, USA

Acknowledgments *(cont.)*

Derrick A. Richardson, CISM, CDPSE, HQ USAREUR G6, USA
Claude K. Sam-Foh, CISA, CISM, CDPSE, Ryerson University, Canada
Loren Saxton II, CISM, CRISC, CDPSE, T-Mobile, USA, Inc., USA
Prathyush Reddy Veluru, CISA, CISM, CRISC, CPDSE, India

ISACA has begun planning the 2nd edition of the *CDPSE™ Review Manual*. Volunteer participation drives the success of the manual. If you are interested in becoming a member of the select group of professionals involved in this global project, we want to hear from you. Please email us at *studymaterials@isaca.org*.

Table of Contents

CDPSE
Certified Data Privacy Solutions Engineer.
An ISACA Certification

CDPSE
Certified Data Privacy Solutions Engineer.
An ISACA Certification

Page intentionally left blank

About This Manual

Overview

The *CDPSE™ Review Manual* is intended to assist candidates preparing for the CDPSE exam.

Note: This manual is one source of preparation for the exam and should not be thought of as the only source, nor should it be viewed as a comprehensive collection of all the information and experience that is required to pass the exam. No single publication offers such coverage and detail.

A candidate who has little or no knowledge and experience with respect to any topics encountered in this manual should consult additional references. The exam is composed of questions testing the candidate's technical and practical knowledge and ability to apply experience in given situations.

The *CDPSE™ Review Manual* covers the knowledge and tasks associated with the domains detailed in the CDPSE job practice. You can find the domain information on the ISACA website at *www.isaca.org/credentialing/certified-data-privacy-solutions-engineer/cdpse-exam-content-outline.*

A job practice is the basis for the exam and experience requirements to earn the CDPSE certification. The job practice is organized by domains and tasks that define the knowledge, roles and responsibilities needed for the data privacy engineer.

For purposes of the job practice, the terms "enterprise" and "organization" or "organizational" are synonyms. This manual uses the term "enterprise."

There are three domains in the CDPSE job practice, and each is tested on the exam in the percentages listed below:

Privacy Governance	34%
Privacy Architecture	36%
Data Life Cycle	30%

The objectives of each domain appear at the beginning of each chapter with the corresponding knowledge subdomains and task statements that are tested on the exam. Exam candidates should evaluate their strengths, based on knowledge and experience, in each of these domains.

Format of This Manual

Each chapter of the *CDPSE™ Review Manual* follows the same format:

- The Overview section summarizes the chapter's focus and provides the following:
  - The domain exam content outline
  - Related task statements
  - Suggested resources for further study
  - Self-assessment questions
- The Content section includes:
  - Content to support the different areas of the job practice
  - Definitions of terms commonly found on the exam

This manual is written in standard American English, with the exception of material imported from publications written in International English.

Submit suggestions to enhance the *CDPSE™ Review Manual* or suggested reference materials to *studymaterials@isaca.org.*

Preparing for the CDPSE Exam

The CDPSE exam evaluates a candidate's practical knowledge, experience, and ability to apply it to the job practice domains described in this review manual. The exam candidate should look to multiple resources to prepare for the exam, including this review manual and external publications. This section offers some tips for studying for the exam.

Candidates should read this manual to identify areas where they need more knowledge, and then consult reference sources to expand their knowledge and gain relevant experience.

Actual exam questions test the candidate's practical application of this knowledge.

Sample self-assessment questions and answers, with explanations, are provided at the end of each chapter. Remember that the sample questions may not be similar to questions appearing on the actual exam. Candidates should consult the cited references to locate publications with more detailed information on the topics addressed in this manual.

Getting Started

Having adequate time to prepare for the CDPSE exam is critical. Most candidates spend between three and six months studying prior to taking the exam. Candidates should set aside a designated time each week to study, and perhaps increase study time as the exam date approaches.

It helps to develop a plan for studying to prepare for the exam.

Using the CDPSE Review Manual

The *CDPSE™ Review Manual* is divided into three chapters, each corresponding to a domain in the CDPSE job practice. While the review manual does not include every concept that could be tested on the CDPSE exam, it does cover a breadth of knowledge to provide a solid base for the exam candidate. The manual is one source of preparation for the exam and should not be considered the only source. Nor should candidates view it as a comprehensive collection of all the information and experience required to pass the exam.

Features in the Review Manual

The *CDPSE™ Review Manual* includes several features to help candidates navigate the job practice and enhance their ability to learn and retain the material.

Review Manual Feature	Description
Overview	The Overview provides the context of the domain, including the job practice areas and applicable learning objectives and task statements.

Suggested Resources for Further Study	Because many of the concepts presented within the review manual are complex, candidates may find it useful to refer to external sources to supplement their understanding of those concepts. The suggested references for each chapter are resources to help enhance study efforts.
Self-assessment Questions and Answers	The self-assessment questions in each chapter are not intended to measure the candidate's ability to answer questions correctly on the CDPSE exam for that area. The questions are intended to familiarize the candidate with question structure, and they may or may not be similar to questions that appear on the actual examination.
Glossary	The glossary included at the end of the manual contains terms that apply to: • The material included in the chapters • Related areas not specifically discussed in the manual Since the glossary is an extension of the manual text, it can point to areas the candidate may want to explore further using additional references.

Types of Questions on the CDPSE Exam

CDPSE exam questions are developed with the intent of measuring and testing practical knowledge and the application of data privacy principles and standards. All questions are presented in a multiple-choice format and are designed for one best answer.

The candidate is cautioned to read each question carefully. Knowing that these types of questions are asked, and learning how to study to answer them will go a long way toward responding correctly. Candidates should select the best answer from the choices provided. There can be many potential solutions to the problems posed in the question scenarios, depending on industry, geographical location, etc. It is advisable to consider the information provided in the question and to determine which of the options provided is the best answer.

Each CDPSE question has a stem (question) and four options (answer choices). The candidate is asked to choose the correct or best answer from the options. The stem may be in the form of a question or an incomplete statement.

A helpful approach to these questions includes the following:

- Candidates should read the entire stem and determine what the question is asking, looking for keywords such as "BEST," "MOST," "FIRST," etc., and key terms that may indicate what domain or concept is being tested.
- Candidates should read all the options, and then read the stem again to try to eliminate some options based on their immediate understanding of the question.
- Candidates should reread the remaining options and apply personal experience to determine the best answer to the question.

When preparing for the exam, candidates should recognize that data privacy is a global profession, and that their perceptions and experiences may not reflect a global position. Because the exam and CDPSE manuals are written for the international data privacy community, candidates must be flexible when reading about conditions that may contradict their experiences.

The CDPSE exam questions are written by experienced privacy professionals from around the world. Each question on the exam is reviewed by ISACA's CDPSE Exam Item Development Working Group, which consists of international members. This geographic representation ensures that all exam questions are understood equally well in every country and language.

Note: Candidates using the CDPSE review materials to prepare for the exam should remember that it covers a broad spectrum of privacy issues. Candidates should not assume that reading this or other manuals and answering review questions will fully prepare them for the examination. Since actual exam questions often relate to practical experiences, candidates should refer to their own experiences and other reference sources, and draw upon the experiences of colleagues and others who have earned the CDPSE designation.

Page intentionally left blank

Chapter 1:

Privacy Governance

Overview

Part A: Governance

Part B: Management

Part C: Risk Management

Overview

Privacy governance includes the areas of privacy management and risk management. Privacy governance practices ensure that all personal information within the enterprise is identified and managed in accordance with legal requirements for personal information use and protection, governing policies, procedures and guidelines, and data subject rights.

Privacy management practice areas include establishing privacy roles and responsibilities related to data; fostering privacy training, and awareness communications and activities; monitoring vendor and third-party management practices; developing a privacy audit process; and implementing a privacy incident management capability.

Privacy risk management practices should include establishing a privacy risk management process, performing privacy impact assessments (PIAs), and identifying privacy threats, attacks and vulnerabilities.

This domain represents 34 percent (approximately 41 questions) of the exam.

Domain 1: Exam Content Outline

Part A: Governance

1. Personal Data and Information
2. Privacy Laws and Standards
3. Privacy Documentation
4. Legal Purpose, Content and Legitimate Interest
5. Data Subject Rights

Part B: Management

1. Roles and Responsibilities Related to Data
2. Privacy Training and Awareness
3. Vendor and Third-Party Management
4. Audit Process
5. Privacy Incident Management

Part C: Risk Management

1. Risk Management Process
2. Privacy Impact Assessment
3. Threats, Attacks and Vulnerabilities Related to Privacy

Learning Objectives/Task Statements

Within this domain, the data privacy engineer/practitioner should be able to:

- Identify the internal and external requirements for the organization's privacy programs and practices.
- Participate in the evaluation of privacy policies, programs and policies for their alignment with legal requirements, regulatory requirements and industry best practices.
- Coordinate and perform privacy impact assessments (PIAs) and other privacy-focused assessments.
- Participate in developing procedures that align with privacy policies and business needs.

- Implement procedures that align with privacy policies.
- Participate in the management and evaluation of contracts, service level agreements, and practices of vendors and other external parties.
- Participate in the privacy incident management process.
- Collaborate with cybersecurity personnel on the security risk assessment process to address privacy compliance and risk mitigation.
- Collaborate with other practitioners to ensure that privacy programs and practices are followed during the design, development and implementation of systems, applications and infrastructure.
- Evaluate the enterprise architecture and information architecture to ensure support for privacy by design principles and considerations.
- Evaluate advancements in privacy-enhancing technologies and changes in the regulatory landscape.
- Identify, validate and implement appropriate privacy and security controls according to data classification procedures.
- Design, implement, and monitor processes and procedures to keep inventory and dataflow records current.
- Develop and implement a prioritization process for privacy practices.
- Develop, monitor and report performance metrics and trends related to privacy practices.
- Report on the status and outcomes of privacy programs and practices to relevant stakeholders.
- Participate in privacy training and promote awareness of privacy practices.
- Identify issues requiring remediation and opportunities for process improvement.

Suggested Resources for Further Study

European Union Parliament, Council of the European Union, *General Data Protection Regulation, https://eur-lex.europa.eu/legal-content/EN/TXT/HTML/?uri=CELEX:32016R0679&qid=1499881815698&from=EN,* 27 April 2016

Herold, Rebecca; *Managing an Information Security and Privacy Awareness and Training Program, 2nd Edition,* CRC Press, USA, 2010

International Organization for Standardization, *ISO/IEC TR 27550:2019: Information technology—Security techniques—Privacy engineering for system life cycle processes*, Switzerland, 2019

International Organization for Standardization, *ISO/IEC 27701:2019: Security techniques—Extension to ISO/IEC 27001 and ISO/IEC 27002 for privacy information management—Requirements and guidelines*, Switzerland, 2019

International Organization for Standardization, *ISO/IEC 29100:2011: Information technology—Security techniques—Privacy framework*, Switzerland, 2011

ISACA, *Continuous Oversight in the Cloud: How to Improve Cloud Security, Privacy and Compliance,* USA, 2019

ISACA, *Implementing a Privacy Protection Program: Using COBIT 5 Enablers with the ISACA Privacy Principles,* USA, 2017

ISACA, *ISACA Privacy Principles and Program Management Guide,* USA, 2016

National Institute of Standards and Technology, *NIST Internal Report 8062: An Introduction to Privacy Engineering and Risk Management in Federal Systems,* USA, 2017

National Institute of Standards and Technology, *NIST Privacy Framework: A Tool for Improving Privacy through Enterprise Risk Management, Version 1.0*, USA, 2020, *www.nist.gov/privacy-framework/privacy-framework*

National Institute of Standards and Technology, *NIST Privacy Risk Assessment Methodology (PRAM),* 28 October 2018, *www.nist.gov/itl/applied-cybersecurity/privacy-engineering/collaboration-space/browse/risk-assessment-tools*

Page intentionally left blank

Self-assessment Questions

CDPSE self-assessment questions support the content in this manual and provide an understanding of the type and structure of questions that typically appear on the exam. Often a question will require the candidate to choose the **MOST** likely or **BEST** answer among the options provided. Please note that these questions are not actual or retired exam items. Please see the section, "About This Manual," for more guidance regarding practice questions.

1. Which of the following privacy threats is also used as a tool in data security?

   A. Content unawareness
   B. Information disclosure
   C. Non-repudiation
   D. Identifiability

2. Which of the following is a benefit of adopting privacy standards?

   A. Ensure that products and services perform consistently.
   B. Provide information for the potential data subject's current and future reference.
   C. Assist the enterprise in achieving its objectives.
   D. Enable individuals to have more control over how their data are used.

3. Which of the following **BEST** describes a type of privacy harm?

   A. Malicious intent from insiders
   B. Malicious websites
   C. Policy and consent noncompliance
   D. Unwarranted restriction

4. Which of the following is a **PRIMARY** role and responsibility of a privacy incident response team?

   A. Work closely with the information security department and other organizational key stakeholders to coordinate privacy incident response activities and data collection.
   B. Document and support privacy principles and support privacy protections throughout the enterprise privacy management program.
   C. Create and design the requirements for privacy protections within the enterprise's products and services.
   D. Set the framework for how to collect, assess, control, optimize, finance, share, store and monitor privacy risk.

Answers on page 22

Chapter 1 Answer Key

Self-Assessment Questions

1. A. Content unawareness means that an entity providing information is unaware of what information is being disclosed. This is a privacy threat only.

   B. Information disclosure occurs when personal information is exposed to unauthorized individuals. This is a privacy threat only.

   C. Non-repudiation is used in data security to prove that a sender in fact sent a particular message. However, non-repudiation can pose a privacy threat when used to gather evidence to counter the claims of a repudiating party.

   D. Identifiability is the condition that results in a personally identifiable information (PII) principal being identified, directly or indirectly, on the basis of a given set of PII.

2. **A. Privacy standards help to ensure that products and services perform consistently, as intended.**

   B. Provide information for the potential data subject's current and future reference describes the purpose of an information consent form.

   C. A privacy framework assists an enterprise in achieving its objectives.

   D. Data privacy laws help to enable individuals to have more control over how their data are used.

3. A. Malicious intent from insiders is an example of a privacy threat.

   B. Malicious websites are examples of privacy threats.

   C. Policy and consent noncompliance is an example of a privacy threat.

   D. Unwarranted restriction includes not only blocking access to data or services, but also limiting awareness of the existence of data or its uses in ways that are disproportionate to operational purposes. This is an example of a privacy harm.

4. **A. This describes the primary role and responsibility of a privacy incident response team.**

   B. This describes a vital requirement of an enterprise's privacy and data protection roles.

   C. This describes a primary responsibility of a privacy engineer.

   D. This describes a responsibility of the enterprise risk management committee.

Part A: Governance

Enterprises must consider, implement and support appropriate controls to protect and manage an individual's privacy throughout the full life cycle of personal and associated sensitive information. To accomplish this, enterprises need to determine the internal and external requirements for the enterprise's privacy programs and practices. Key requirements are described in **figure 1.1**.

Figure 1.1—Key Privacy Program Requirements

Type of Requirement	Consideration
Internal requirements	• Assigning privacy roles and responsibilities • Defining and inventorying personal information • Implementing enterprise employee privacy policies, procedures and training • Establishing vendor management programs • Providing privacy incident management • Performing privacy audits and assessments
External requirements	• Documenting applicable laws, regulations, standards and contractual obligations • Choosing privacy principles and frameworks • Posting a privacy notice that reflects actual enterprise practices and meets legal requirements • Maintaining third-party oversight • Addressing data subject rights

Enterprises should establish and implement an executive-supported privacy risk management strategy. This strategy should:

- Consider privacy risk during the design phase of the enterprise's business processes, applications and systems.
- Identify and implement mitigating controls for risks to the privacy and security of personal and sensitive information.
- Inventory the circumstances in which data are processed.
- Understand the privacy interests of individuals directly or indirectly served or affected by an enterprise.
- Conduct risk assessments for an enterprise to understand its business environment, and to identify and prioritize privacy risks.

When planning a privacy risk strategy, a useful resource is the National Institute for Standards and Technology (NIST) Privacy Framework.

After the initial implementation of the privacy program, enterprises need to identify the additional necessary controls, as applicable, throughout the entire development and implementation life cycle. Finally, privacy costs and resources should be included in project budgets so that the costs are associated with the privacy controls.

Per the NIST Privacy Framework, enterprises should develop and implement their governance structure based on the enterprise's risk management priorities to minimize privacy risk. Specifically, the Govern-P function focuses on enterprise-level activities such as the following:

- Establishing enterprise privacy values and policies
- Identifying legal/regulatory requirements
- Using the enterprise's risk tolerance focus and prioritizing its efforts consistent with its risk management strategy and business needs

Privacy engineers and other privacy practitioners play an important role in ensuring these actions are comprehensively, sufficiently and effectively used in all enterprise processes, including by service providers that support business processes. To track and determine the enterprise's levels of compliance, privacy practitioners can develop, implement, monitor and report privacy performance metrics and trends to key stakeholders. Privacy metrics support prioritizing privacy governance activities and projects.

An enterprise must protect all individuals' personal information. All rules, procedures and processes that protect individuals' data within the enterprise are referred to as governance practice. To create, implement and manage a governance practice, the enterprise must:

- Identify all the individuals' information in the enterprise that falls under the privacy guidelines.
- Identify legal and regulatory requirements that protect users of the enterprise data.
- Create enterprise governance policies, procedures and guidelines.
- Implement the policies, procedures and guidelines.

1.1 Personal Data and Information

The term "data" has historically been used to mean digital forms of information, and the broader term "information" has been used to reference all forms—such as hard copy media, audio, visual, insights derived from analysis, and the subset of digital data.

The concepts of "personal information" and "personal data" have evolved and may differ, sometimes greatly, from one location, law, regulation, standard or enterprise to the next. There is no single international definition of personal data or personal information.

Different laws, regulations, standards and industries define personal data differently. The terms "personal information" and "personal data" are used interchangeably in some locations, but elsewhere personal data is defined as a subset of personal information.

For example, legal professionals often use personal data to refer to information about a specific individual, whom they typically refer to as the data subject. The term personal information is often used by information assurance practitioners to mean the same thing. ISACA established a common terminology to avoid using differing terms for the same idea.[1]

Enterprises should consider defining the terms and sharing the terms with privacy engineers to help them understand how any differences between definitions of terms can affect their decisions. See section 3.1 Data Inventory and Classification for more information.

Note: The terms in this section represent most terms used to mean some type of personal information throughout the world; however, they may not be all-inclusive of the terms and definitions used globally. Data privacy engineers should be familiar with the terms used in the jurisdictions where they work.

1.1.1 Defining Personal Data and Personal Information

A list of definitions for common personal data and personal information terms is provided in **figure 1.2**.

Figure 1.2—Personal Data and Personal Information Definitions

Term	Definition	Example
Personal data	Digital-only information that can be associated with a specific individual.	• A user ID for website account authentication
Personal information	Any type of information, in any form (digital and non-digital), that can be associated with a specific individual. More inclusive than PII.	• A person's full name used on a mail-in hard copy ballot, or the mailing address printed on an envelope
Personal datum	Any type of information, in any form (digital and non-digital) that can indirectly point to an identifiable individual.	• Metadata, which often reveal a clear view of the activities of an individual, although personal data are not specifically included
Data subject	An individual who is the subject of personal information; the individual to whom particular personal information applies. In some locations, a data subject can only be a living individual. In other locations, deceased individuals may also be data subjects. Enterprises need to determine with their legal counsel any limitations that may exist for a data subject.	• An enterprise's client
Sensitive personal data or sensitive data	As per the General Data Protection Regulation, special categories of personal data that merit higher protection than other types of personal data.	• Racial or ethnic origin, genetic or biometric data • Sexual orientation or health-related data
Personally identifiable information (PII)	Any information that can be used to establish a link between the information and the natural person to whom such information relates, or that might be directly or indirectly linked to a natural person. **Note:** This term is being phased out in the United States. In some specific industries and in other geographic locations other terms are being adopted that mean basically the same thing.	• Social security number • Address • Phone number

Source: ISACA, *Privacy Principles and Program Management Guide*, USA, 2016

1.2 Privacy Laws and Standards Across Jurisdictions

Multiple privacy principles, frameworks, laws, regulations, standards and self-regulation frameworks exist across many jurisdictions. Privacy professionals need to identify and understand the legal requirements that apply to their

enterprises and document an inventory of the terms. This inventory should be maintained and kept current. Privacy engineers should use these inventories to learn, understand and create appropriate plans for services and products involving personal information to comply with the applicable legal requirements.

1.2.1 Application of Privacy Laws and Regulations

Privacy laws and regulations have changed dramatically throughout thetwentieth and twenty-first centuries as privacy concerns have also changed and evolved. In 1902, in one of the first privacy court cases of the century, Abigail Roberson sued the Franklin Mills Flour company for using an image of her in a product advertisement without her consent.[2] In her lawsuit, Roberson alleged that she had been "greatly humiliated by the scoffs and jeers of persons who have recognized her face and picture on this advertisement, and her good name [was] attacked, causing her great distress and suffering, both in body and mind."[3] While this may seem like a clear-cut violation of privacy today, there were no precedents to base a judgment on in 1902. The judge found no legal foundation to issue a definitive ruling in the case and advised that it would be necessary for lawmakers to create laws against such actions to establish a basis for judgment.

Lawsuits are still brought to court when images are used without permission. However, with the wide range of applicable data protection laws, the person suing for unauthorized use of a photo can be someone other than the subject of the photo. For example, in May 2020, the mother of three underage children in the Netherlands took the children's grandmother to court for violating the EU General Data Protection Regulation (GDPR) by posting the children's photos to Facebook without the mother's consent. The court found the grandmother guilty.[4]

Laws and regulations have been enacted that govern a range of privacy issues much broader than unauthorized use of images. Legal considerations for privacy and personal information now apply to every industry in all developed countries. Legal considerations erase the boundaries of local jurisdictions as application of the laws extends beyond geographic boundaries to digital space.

The expansion of the enterprise environment to include outsourced third parties, often in different countries, and the consideration of new and emerging technologies have added to concerns about privacy and personal information issues. Consider the potential effect on privacy of new technologies such as Internet of Things (IoT) devices, artificial intelligence (AI), robotics process automation (RPA), blockchain and facial recognition.

The focus on ensuring privacy has expanded to include concerns about a multitude of consumer services and products. A chief concern is how to safeguard information that can point to specific individuals or groups of individuals, revealing insights about their lives, whereabouts, likes and dislikes, and an endless number of other personal aspects.

1.2.2 Privacy Protection Legal Models

Some parts of the world do not have legal privacy protections. In other parts, it is implied that privacy is a human right. For countries and regions that have privacy protections in place, four privacy protection legal models are used:

- Comprehensive model
- Sectoral model
- Co-regulatory model
- Self-regulatory model

It is important to understand the legal implications for the enterprise when using each privacy protection model. Information security and assurance practitioners should speak with their legal counsel to determine the legal privacy protection models that apply, and the impacts these models can have on the current or planned privacy protection program. The high-level descriptions of each model can help guide discussions with legal counsel.

The information about the four models is provided in **figure 1.3.**

Figure 1.3—Privacy Protection Legal Models

Model	Description
Comprehensive Model	This model defines the laws that govern actions for all industries in the private and public sector and are enforced by an official agency. The actions that are covered in this model include: • Collection • Use • Storage • Sharing • Destruction of personal information This model is used by countries and regions (e.g., EU, Canada) that generally have an
Sectoral Model	This model consists of laws, regulations and standards that cover specific industries or specific types of personal information. The industries and countries that use this model generally have different official agencies enforcing privacy protection. It is used by countries and regions that generally have a different official or agency sector to enforce the privacy protections within each industry. The result is that multiple agencies are responsible for enforcing the privacy requirements for each industry. This model can be considered inadequate in some jurisdictions that use the comprehensive model. **Note**: Some countries that use the comprehensive model also use the sectoral model. For example, financial and healthcare information in Spain and France are subject to stringent sectoral requirements in addition to the national data protection requirements.
Co-regulatory Model	In this model, government and private parties share responsibility for establishing and enforcing privacy protections. Although co-regulation can be accomplished in a number of ways, the privacy protection actions generally are divided between the parties. For example, the federal government might establish a set of privacy goals but then rely on each industry to establish the details for how to accomplish those goals. The details may be set out in standards, guidelines or enforceable rules. Typically, the government and the industries work together on enforcement. Examples of countries using the co-regulatory model for privacy protections are Australia, New Zealand and the Netherlands.

Figure 1.3—Privacy Protection Legal Models

Model	Description
Self-regulatory Model	This model does not have privacy or data protection laws but expects enterprises to create their own rules. An industry, group, government, or other type of association with many members agrees to a specified set of guidelines, actions and restrictions for the use and handling of personal information. For example, a group determines that the best way to secure consumer privacy in cyberspace is to follow a set of privacy guidelines within the virtual marketplace and not by government regulations. A wide range of industries throughout the world consider self-regulation to be the preferred alternative to laws and regulations. Self-regulation establishes the expectation that those who say they are following a specific set of self-regulated rules or guidelines are actually implementing them. Self-regulation is subject to change over time.

1.2.3 Privacy Laws and Regulations

Data protection (privacy) laws and regulations now cover requirements for enterprises to reveal why they are collecting information that could be linked to an individual or group, and how that information is used, including giving the associated individuals choices and controls over how their information is used, shared, retained, protected and destroyed.

Every enterprise must identify and then keep track of all the privacy laws and regulations that apply not only to the enterprise, but also to the service providers the enterprise has contracted. A few of the most commonly known privacy laws and regulations are shown in **figure 1.4**.

Figure 1.4—Common Privacy Laws and Regulations

Law or Regulation	Topics Covered
US Health Insurance Portability and Accountability Act (HIPAA)	HIPAA establishes national standards to protect individuals' medical records and other personal health information. It applies to health plans, healthcare clearinghouses, and healthcare providers that conduct certain healthcare transactions electronically.
EU General Data Protection Regulation (GDPR)	GDPR requirements apply to the processing of the personal data of citizens or residents of each member state of the European Union. They aim to create more consistent protection of consumer and personal data across EU nations.
US California Consumer Privacy Act (CCPA)	CCPA grants California consumers a wide range of data privacy rights and control over their personal information, including the right to know, the right to delete, and the right to opt out of the sale of personal information that enterprises collect. It includes additional protections for minors.
54 US State and Territory Privacy Breach Notice Laws	All 50 states and the District of Columbia, Guam, Puerto Rico and the Virgin Islands have enacted legislation requiring private or governmental entities to notify individuals of security breaches involving personal information.
US Gramm-Leach-Bliley Act (GLBA)	Financial institutions covered by the GLBA must tell their customers about their information-sharing practices and explain to customers their right to opt out if they do not want their information shared with certain third parties.
Australian Privacy Act	The Privacy Act is the principal piece of Australian legislation protecting the handling of personal information about individuals. It covers the collection, use, storage and disclosure of personal information, and requirements following privacy breaches.
Canadian Personal Information Protection and Electronic Documents Act (PIPEDA)	PIPEDA applies to the private sector to address enterprise collection, storage and use of personal information.
Japan Act on the Protection of Personal Information	This act aims to protect an individual's rights and interests while considering the utility of personal information—including recognition that the proper and effective application of personal information contributes to the creation of new industries, a vital economic society, and an enriched quality of life for the people of Japan. The act includes setting an overall vision for the proper handling of personal information, creating a basic governmental policy for handling personal information, and establishing other measures to protect personal information, while considering the significantly expanded utilization of personal information.
Brazil Lei Geral de Proteção de Dados (LGPD)	The LGPD unifies more than 40 different personal data statutes within Brazil, applicable both online and offline, by replacing certain regulations and supplementing others. The LGPD applies to any enterprise that processes the personal data of people in Brazil, regardless of where that enterprise might be located.

Note: Specific privacy laws and regulations will not be directly tested on the CDPSE exam; however, the CDPSE candidate will need to understand how laws and regulations affect privacy programs and privacy controls.

Enterprises that do not implement privacy protections to meet legal and regulatory requirements face huge fines—such as tens of millions of dollars as applied under Section 5 of the US Federal Trade Commission Act (FTC Act), up to 4 percent of the enterprise's income for the previous year under the EU GDPR,[5] and up to 20-year penalties[6] for noncompliance with the US Health Insurance Portability and Accountability Act (HIPAA).

Each enterprise must know the full range of all the laws and regulations that apply to them, from local to international. Applicability is based on where the corporate offices are located, where employees work, the residency of customers and patients, where data are stored and other factors. Legal analysis should be done initially to identify the applicable laws and regulations, and then the list should be kept up to date on an ongoing basis.

1.2.4 Privacy Standards

Privacy standards help to ensure that products and services perform consistently, as intended. Standards also support interoperability, create uniform design, installation and testing methods, protect users and their environment, enable a comprehensive privacy management approach, and improve quality of life for communities and individuals wherever they are used worldwide.

With advances in hardware and software located in multiple geographic areas, privacy standards help create uniform practices. Privacy standards support uniformity through detailed descriptions of each activity. New technology creates new types of personal information and new uses for that information, resulting in an ongoing need to develop new privacy standards.

Privacy standards can be used to establish requirements or recommendations for privacy engineers and enterprises to use within a wide range of services and products. The requirements then help privacy engineers and enterprises to:

- Establish consistently implemented data security and privacy capabilities
- Create controls to protect personal information
- Ensure individuals are consistently given rights to access their personal information
- Provide similar controls for how that information is used, shared and retained
- Reduce a wide range of privacy risks

Some industries mandate the use of specific privacy standards and data security standards that support privacy protections. One example is the Payment Card Industry Data Security Standard (PCI-DSS), which requires specified credit card processors to use PCI-DSS to process payments for associated credit cards.

Other industries provide, but do not mandate, privacy standards for enterprises to use for the greater good of consumers. For example, the Digital Advertising Alliance (DAA) provides the DAA Self-Regulatory Principles[7] to establish and enforce specific privacy practices across the industry for digital advertising. There are increasingly more technically focused privacy standards being established for technology engineers, information security professionals and privacy practitioners to follow.

Some common privacy standards include:

- **IEEE**:
  - P802E - IEEE Draft Recommended Practice for Privacy Considerations for IEEE 802 Technologies
  - P802.1AEdk - Standard for Local and metropolitan area networks-Media Access Control (MAC) Security Amendment 4: MAC Privacy protection
  - P7002 - Data Privacy Process

- P1912 - Standard for Privacy and Security Framework for Consumer Wireless Devices
- P2876 - Recommended Practice for Inclusion, Dignity and Privacy in Online Gaming
- P7012 - Standard for Machine Readable Personal Privacy Terms
- P2049.2 - Standard for Human Augmentation: Privacy and Security
- P2410 - Standard for Biometric Privacy

- **International Organization for Standardization (ISO)/International Electrotechnical Commission (IEC)**:
  - ISO/IEC 27701:2019: Security techniques—Extension to ISO/IEC 27001 and ISO/IEC 27002 for privacy information management—Requirements and guidelines
  - ISO/IEC TR 27550:2019: Information technology—Security techniques—Privacy engineering for system life cycle processes
  - ISO/IEC 27030—Information technology—Security techniques—Guidelines for security and privacy in Internet of Things (IoT)
- **NIST Privacy Standards and Guidelines**:
  - NISTIR 8062 Introduction to Privacy Engineering and Risk Management
  - NIST Privacy Framework: A Tool for Improving Privacy Through Enterprise Risk Management
  - NISTIR 7628 Guidelines for Smart Grid Cybersecurity
- **OASIS Privacy Standards**:
  - OASIS Privacy Management Reference Model and Methodology (PMRM)
  - OASIS Privacy by Design Documentation for Software Engineers Version 1.0 (PbD-SE)-a Committee Specification
  - OASIS Annex Guide to Privacy by Design: Documentation for Software Engineers Version 1.0
- **PCI-DSS:** Standards to establish the actions necessary to secure credit cardholder data, which also supports privacy protections and principles and the prevention of privacy breaches.

1.2.5 Privacy Principles and Frameworks

Privacy principles applied within an established privacy framework enable an enterprise to apply privacy controls comprehensively and consistently to all aspects of its business activities, in all locations. A few examples of popularly used privacy principles include:

- ISO/TS 17975:2015 Health Informatics —Principles and Data Requirements for Consent in the Collection, Use or Disclosure of Personal Health Information
- OECD Privacy Principles 2013
- Generally Accepted Privacy Principles
- ISACA Privacy Principles

According to the *ISACA Privacy Principles and Program Management Guide,*[8] a framework is a comprehensive structure that assists enterprises in achieving their objectives for the governance and management of enterprise IT, and all other types of information processing. Its organized and holistic approach supports the creation of optimal value from IT and physical systems by maintaining a balance between realizing benefits and optimizing risk levels and resource use.

Often the same enterprises that create standards also create management frameworks that support defining the most beneficial times, areas and ways to use the standards. The enterprises then reference them as standard frameworks, techniques or principles. A few examples of privacy frameworks include:

- APEC Privacy Framework
- ISO/IEC 29100:2011: Information technology—Security techniques—Privacy framework
- ISO/IEC 29187-1:2013 Information Technology—Identification of Privacy Protection Requirements Pertaining to Learning, Education and Training (LET)—Part 1: Framework and Reference Model
- MITRE Privacy Engineering Framework
- NIST Privacy Framework
- NIST PII Inventory Dashboard
- Privacy by Design

1.2.6 Privacy Self-Regulation Standards

Creating privacy self-regulation frameworks has become more common in all types of industries due to increased privacy laws and regulations, and in response to breaches and risks created by new and emerging technologies.

For example, various global enterprises are creating self-regulation standards to address the increasing variations in online behavioral advertising:

- The Advertising Standards Authority, an independent UK regulator for advertising in all types of media, enforces the Online Behavioral Advertising (OBA) rules.
- In the United States, the White House and Federal Trade Commission have called for the creation of industry privacy standards.
- In the EU, member states are considering the use of privacy standards in addition to GDPR to protect the personal information of their citizens.
- The Asia-Pacific Economic Cooperative (APEC) Privacy Framework outlines consumer expectations as to how their privacy interests should be protected. APEC economies can use the framework to share best practices and harmonize legal standards so that sharing consumer information across borders does not become a source of risk to consumers, enterprises or governments.

In general, most industries prefer creating their own self-regulating standards rather than having to follow laws and regulations established by government organizations. Following are some self-regulatory privacy standards currently in use:

- **US Energy Industry**—The North American Energy Standards Board (NAESB) developed model business practices for third-party access to consumer smart grid data based on existing reports and laws. NAESB has published the following nonbinding privacy standards for the energy industry:
  - **NAESB REQ.22, Third Party Access to Smart Meter□Based Information**—This standard provides voluntary model business practices for third-party access to smart meter-based information. The NAESB based the privacy recommendations within this standard largely on NISTIR 7628 Rev. 1.
  - **NAESB REQ.21, Energy Services Provider Interface**[9]—According to the NAESB, the "purpose of the NAESB Energy Services Provider Interface (ESPI) standard (REQ.21) is to create a standardized process and interface for the exchange of a retail customer's energy usage information between their designated data custodian (i.e., distribution company) and an authorized third-party service provider." REQ.21 includes some recommendations for mitigating the associated privacy risk.
- **US Agricultural Industry**—The Privacy and Security Principles for Farm Data[10] are aimed at reassuring farmers that data they share with big data service providers will not be misused. The nonbinding principles

provide guidelines to enterprises that collect, store and analyze farm data. The guidelines can be used in crafting service contracts and marketing tools that use farm data to boost crop yields or reduce costs for farmers.

- **Mobile Applications Industry**—The Digital Advertising Alliance (DAA) issued the "Application of Self-Regulatory Principles to the Mobile Environment," to provide guidance for advertisers, agencies, media and technology enterprises on how to give consumers control over the use of cross-app (i.e., behavioral advertising), personal directory and precise location data in mobile applications. The Network Advertising Initiative (NAI) released a self-regulatory "Mobile Application Code" for NAI members, which governs behaviorally targeted ads on mobile devices.
- **Advertising Industry**—The NAI Code of Conduct is a set of self-regulatory principles that require NAI member enterprises to provide notice and choice with respect to interest-based advertising via HTTP cookies. The code limits the types of data member enterprises can use for advertising purposes, and it imposes a host of substantive restrictions on member enterprise collection, use and transfer of data used for interest-based advertising. The DAA, which has established a separate set of self-regulatory principles for digital advertising, enforces privacy practices through the use of the DAA Principles of Transparency and Accountability.
- **Social Media Industry**—The Safer Social Networking Principles self-regulatory agreement is signed by the major active EU social networking service providers that have committed to implementation of measures to ensure the safety of minors on their services.
- **Mobile Computing Industry**—The European Framework for Safer Mobile Use by Younger Teenagers and Children[11] was signed by leading European mobile providers and content providers. It sets out a series of national and corporate measures to ensure safer use of mobile computing devices, including by teenagers and children.
- **Personal Information Processors**—APEC Privacy Recognition for Processors (PRP) System Governance[12] documents on PRP were endorsed by APEC in August 2015. Baseline requirements of the PRP are set out in an intake questionnaire designed to help personal information controllers identify qualified and accountable personal information processors to provide assistance in complying with relevant privacy obligations.
- **Customer Data Protection and use of Bring Your Own Device (BYOD)**—The Hong Kong Monetary Authority issued a circular offering guidance to banks on implementing layers of security controls for prevention and detection of customer data loss and leakage. The circular requires banks to comply with a standard of stringent minimum controls developed by the Hong Kong Association of Banks if BYOD is allowed.
- **Code of Practice on Consumer Credit Data**—The code of practice was issued by the Privacy Commissioner for Personal Data in Hong Kong, which provides practical guidance in handling consumer credit data. The code applies to the practices of credit reference agencies, and to credit providers' dealings with credit reference agencies and debt collection agencies.
- **Advisory Guidelines for the Telecommunication Sector**—The advisory guidelines issued by the Personal Data Protection Commission in Singapore were designed to help address the unique data privacy requirements of the telecommunications sector for compliance with the Personal Data Protection Act 2012. The scope covers circumstances in the telecommunications sector including roaming, advertisements in bills, display of personal data in itemized bills, and the do-not-call provision.
- **Banking Industry**—The Code of Banking Practice clarifies practices for banks in New Zealand with respect to data protection legislation and regulations, and to efforts to treat customers fairly and reasonably.
- **Human Biomedical Research Industry**—The Ethics Guidelines for Human Biomedical Research[13] is a consolidation of past recommendations of the Bioethics Advisory Committee (BAC). It establishes a framework for research ethics governance in Singapore to ensure that research participants' privacy is properly protected. It also serves as an ethical resource for researchers and members of ethics committees or institutional review boards (IRBs) concerned with data protection rules and regulations.

1.3 Privacy Documentation

An effective privacy governance program is not possible without documentation. Maintaining various types of documentation is critical to clearly demonstrate enterprise data management practices and objectives, to meet obligations under applicable privacy laws, to build trust among key stakeholders, and to demonstrate a standard of due care in the management of the privacy program.

Privacy practitioners need to:

- Ensure that internal policies and procedures, external privacy notices, and other related documents are aligned with the enterprise's applicable privacy laws, regulations, contractual obligations and other legal requirements.
- Ensure that any required or enterprise-adopted industry standards are reflected in the enterprise's privacy documentation and practices.
- Regularly review and evaluate both inward-facing policies, procedures and related documentation and outward-facing privacy notices, websites, social media pages and related documentation to ensure alignment with privacy requirements.

1.3.1 Types of Documentation

A wide variety of documentation is necessary to support and demonstrate a comprehensive privacy management program and meet a wide variety of privacy legal requirements. The common types of documentation that privacy practitioners must understand—and typically create, maintain, evaluate and communicate to others—are discussed in this section.

This is not an exhaustive list of all types of documentation necessary for supporting all types of privacy management programs. Also, the types of documentation are not listed in any implied order of importance or use. Each enterprise should use this list as a starting point for determining the documentation necessary to meet its own legal requirements and privacy risks.

Privacy Notice

A privacy notice is an outward-facing statement that is written for data subjects and data protection authorities. It describes how the enterprise collects, uses, retains, safeguards and discloses personal information. A privacy notice is often referred to as a privacy policy or a privacy statement.

The privacy notice establishes the legal accountability for the associated enterprise to follow the practices listed in the privacy notice. Regulators, auditors and lawyers judge the enterprise privacy management program and managers against the enterprise's practices as they relate to the privacy notice. It is important for enterprises to understand that the data controller and the data processor are responsible for complying with the privacy notice. See section 1.6 Roles and Responsibilities Related to Data for more information.

Note: For the purposes of this manual, a privacy notice means the outward-facing statement, and privacy policy means the inward-facing document for employees and other workers to know and follow.

Privacy notices serve the following primary purposes:

- Establish accountability for the enterprise use and protection of personal information
- Educate data subjects, using language that is as easily understood as possible, on the following:
  - The personal data collected
  - How the personal data are used

    - With whom the personal data are shared
    - How long the personal data are retained
- Inform data subjects about procedures to exercise their rights over their associated personal information
- Support data subjects' consent or other legal authorization permitting the data controller to use the personal information as intended or planned
- Build and maintain data subjects' trust

Privacy notices are presented to data subjects in many ways. For example:

- A page on the enterprise website is dedicated to describing privacy-related activities.
- Forms that ask for personal information indicate how the personal information will be used and safeguarded.
- Brochures, such as those sent out each year in the United States by payment card companies, describe privacy protections and rights.
- Documents that are provided at the enterprise facility, such as a healthcare clinic or hospital, explain how personal information is collected, used and shared, and set forth individuals' rights to access their associated personal information.
- Contracts, such as those for loans or other financial services, describe how the enterprise collects, uses, stores, shares and safeguards personal information.
- Signs on buildings or interior walls, such as those warning that closed-circuit television (CCTV) cameras are in use, can serve as privacy notices.

Terms-of-use statements commonly include descriptions of the rules governing how the enterprise will use personal information, and the associated enterprises point to those statements as their privacy notices.[14] While this is a common practice, it is best to maintain separate privacy notices and terms-of-use statements.

Consent Form

Among the intended uses of a consent form are 1) to provide information for the potential data subject's current and future reference, and 2) to document the interaction between the subject and the entity obtaining the consent.

A signed consent form on its own may not establish an adequate consent process. The informed consent process is an ongoing exchange of information between the enterprise and the data subject. It could include the use of question-and-answer sessions, emails, community meetings and videotape presentations.[15]

Obtaining documented consent is a separate activity from fulfilling requirements that data controllers inform data subjects about how to make inquiries or notify the enterprise of various types of decisions, e.g., withdrawal of consent or request to delete personal data.

Privacy Policies

A privacy policy is management's formally expressed document that describes the overall intention and direction for data processor employees to follow in protecting personal information. The privacy policy is an inward-facing document and is not meant for use outside the enterprise (data controller). For the purposes of this publication, the term inward-facing document is used to establish the rules that employees and others who are associated with the enterprise must follow to support privacy protections.[16]

Note: In some parts of the world and under some laws, regulations and contractual agreements, employees and contractors are considered data processors. However, some EU GDPR enforcement agencies and other regulators do not consider employees to be data processors. Each privacy manager and privacy engineer needs to engage with legal counsel for clarification.

Privacy Procedures

While policies establish the overall intentions and goals of privacy activities within an enterprise, procedures provide the how-to instructions for implementing and effectively meeting the end goals of the policy in specific circumstances. Privacy practitioners need to participate, in a way that's appropriate to the business culture, in the development of privacy procedures created throughout the enterprise. Privacy practitioners can then ensure that privacy procedures are aligned with and support corresponding enterprise privacy policies and associated business needs.

Procedures inform personnel how to consistently perform daily work activities to meet the requirements established by the policies.

Documented procedures are necessary to support compliance with privacy policies and legal requirements for personal data protection. They are also necessary to support an understanding from one employee to the next, of how to consistently perform actions to meet privacy policy requirements. According to Herold[17],

> *If your personnel do not know or understand how to maintain confidentiality of information, or how to secure it appropriately, not only do you risk having one of your most valuable business assets (information) mishandled, inappropriately used, or obtained by unauthorized persons, but you also risk being in noncompliance of a growing number of laws and regulations that require certain types of information security and privacy awareness and training activities.*

It is especially important for privacy engineers and other privacy practitioners to collaborate with other practitioners throughout the enterprise to ensure that:

- Privacy programs and practices are followed during the design, development and implementation of systems, applications and infrastructure
- Enterprise and information architectures support privacy-by-design principles and considerations
- New and emerging privacy-enhancing technologies are used appropriately
- Privacy engineering practices are changed appropriately and consistently to align with changes in legal requirements
- Privacy and security controls can be appropriately identified, validated and implemented according to established data classification policies

Procedures should be documented, maintained and made available to all workers who need them to support their job responsibilities. Privacy practitioners should assist in implementing privacy procedures throughout the enterprise, or have some type of oversight. Practitioners' participation not only ensures the enterprise is meeting the associated privacy policy intents, but also gives practitioners better insights into how privacy practices affect business activities in actual application and use.

Records of Processing

Records of processing are most commonly associated with GDPR Article 30, which describes the records of processing documentation required for compliance. The documentation mentioned previously should be maintained in order to keep the records of processing activities. Records of processing include the following:[18]

1. *Each controller and, where applicable, the controller's representative, shall maintain a record of processing activities under its responsibility. That record shall contain all of the following information:*
    a. *the name and contact details of the controller and, where applicable, the joint controller, the controller's representative and the data protection officer;*
    b. *the purposes of the processing;*
    c. *a description of the categories of data subjects and of the categories of personal data;*

   d. *the categories of recipients to whom the personal data have been or will be disclosed including recipients in third countries or international organizations;*
   e. *where applicable, transfers of personal data to a third country or an international organization, including the identification of that third country or international organization and, in the case of transfers referred to in the second subparagraph of Article 49(1), the documentation of suitable safeguards;*
   f. *where possible, the envisaged time limits for erasure of the different categories of data;*
   g. *where possible, a general description of the technical and organizational security measures referred to in Article 32(1).*

2. *Each processor and, where applicable, the processor's representative shall maintain a record of all categories of processing activities carried out on behalf of a controller, containing:*
   a. *the name and contact details of the processor or processors and of each controller on behalf of which the processor is acting, and, where applicable, of the controller's or the processor's representative, and the data protection officer;*
   b. *the categories of processing carried out on behalf of each controller;*
   c. *where applicable, transfers of personal data to a third country or an international organization, including the identification of that third country or international organization and, in the case of transfers referred to in the second subparagraph of Article 49(1), the documentation of suitable safeguards;*
   d. *where possible, a general description of the technical and organizational security measures referred to in Article 32(1).*
3. *The records referred to in paragraphs 1 and 2 shall be in writing, including in electronic form.*
4. *The controller or the processor and, where applicable, the controller's or the processor's representative, shall make the record available to the supervisory authority on request.*
5. *The obligations referred to in paragraphs 1 and 2 shall not apply to an enterprise or an organization employing fewer than 250 persons unless the processing it carries out is likely to result in a risk to the rights and freedoms of data subjects, the processing is not occasional, or the processing includes special categories of data as referred to in Article 9(1) or personal data relating to criminal convictions and offences referred to in Article 10.*

Corrective Action Plan

A corrective action plan (CAP) is a formally documented plan to mitigate and remediate identified privacy issues and noncompliance risks discovered during audits and risk assessments. A CAP is also a good place to document opportunities to improve enterprise processes while improving privacy practices. A CAP is often required to meet the enforcement actions specifically required by regulatory agencies. For example, the US Department of Health and Human Services (HHS) Office for Civil Rights (OCR) has issued hundreds of HIPAA noncompliance penalties[19] that include requirements for the associated enterprises to establish CAPs to correct HIPAA compliance violations.

In the HHS OCR cases, the purpose of the CAP is to correct the underlying noncompliance practices that led to the HIPAA violations. The HHS OCR develops and enforces a CAP after an investigation, resolution agreement and fines.

CAPs are also used by other regulatory agencies throughout the world. Regulatory CAPs may span a year, or multiple decades, depending upon the discovered deficiencies and violations. Auditors (external and internal) and information security and privacy practitioners use CAPs to support program management.

Data Protection Impact Assessment

A data protection impact assessment (DPIA) is a type of privacy assessment that has a more specific scope than a generally termed privacy impact assessment (PIA). The GDPR's Article 35 describes the required content for DPIA documentation as follows:[20]

The assessment shall contain at least:

1. *a systematic description of the envisaged processing operations and the purposes of the processing, including, where applicable, the legitimate interest pursued by the controller;*
2. *an assessment of the necessity and proportionality of the processing operations in relation to the purposes;*
3. *an assessment of the risks to the rights and freedoms of data subjects referred to in paragraph 1; and*
4. *the measures envisaged to address the risks, including safeguards, security measures and mechanisms to ensure the protection of personal data and to demonstrate compliance with this Regulation taking into account the rights and legitimate interests of data subjects and other persons concerned.*

See section 1.13.1 Established PIA Methodologies for more information.

System of Record Notice

In accordance with Section (e)(3) of the Privacy Act of 1974,[21] as amended, every US federal agency must create documented system of record notices (SORNs) to appear on the documents enterprises use to collect PII from individuals, which are to be maintained in a Privacy Act System of Records. A SORN is a formal notice to the public that identifies the purpose of collecting PII, from whom, what type is collected, how the PII is shared externally (routine uses), and how to access and correct any PII maintained by each federal agency. Agencies must publish SORNs in the *Federal Register*. Some federal agencies have responsibility for one or more systems of records that are applicable to all agencies, government-wide. Privacy engineers in federal agencies, or who contract with federal agencies, need to be aware of the SORNs and the described PII.

Personal Information Inventory

A personal information inventory is a documented repository of the personal data assets collected, derived, processed, stored or otherwise handled by an enterprise. Inclusion of data flow mappings with data inventories provides valuable insights, and is recommended whenever possible.

Because there is no universal definition of personal information, each enterprise must determine the specific information items to document in its enterprise's PII. The specific information items should reflect the established definition of personal information related to the enterprise's services, products, locations, customers, patients, employees and vendors, and other determining factors. Privacy practitioners need to ensure that procedures exist to keep inventories and existing dataflow diagrams, if they exist, updated and current.

Often used with IT, security or governance manuals or automated tools, personal information inventories include details about the enterprise's network, applications, systems, storage areas, and physical forms of information. Personal information inventories support the efforts of privacy management program initiatives to record detailed information about the enterprise's personal information (e.g., human resources data, customer data or marketing data). Because every enterprise is unique, the personal information inventory items will vary from one enterprise to the next. Personal information inventories can be documented within hard copy media, spreadsheets, word processing documents, databases, or other types of tools. See section 3.1 Data Inventory and Classification for more information.

Other Types of Documentation

There are many other types of documentation that support enterprises in managing their privacy programs and meeting a wide range of specific legal requirements. The format and content of such documentation often varies greatly between, and often within, enterprises. Some important but not rigidly defined types of documentation include:

- **Activity logs**: Activity logs documenting privacy management activities can be manually created, generated by applications and systems, or automatically created through a wide range of vendor- or in-house created tools. Logs can detail information such as the names of individuals who have attended privacy training, the number of unsuccessful identity-verification attempts, the locations of people using employee-issued vehicles, and the identities of those who have access to personal information records.
- **Data protection legal requirements**: Enterprises should identify and document all privacy legal requirements applicable to their operations. This documentation should be provided to key stakeholders throughout the enterprise—notably to privacy engineers, to help them ensure that systems, applications, networks and other services and products they design appropriately support the legal requirements.
- **Privacy risk assessment reports**: A privacy risk report reflects the findings from a systematic evaluation of how personal information is collected, used, shared, maintained and destroyed by an enterprise. A privacy risk assessment report is important documentation that provides an overview of the enterprise's privacy risk status. It is useful not only to meet legal requirements, including those from privacy regulations such as GDPR and CCPA, but also to manage risks that may accompany new and emerging technologies, and to address privacy risks not covered by legal requirements. See more about privacy risk assessments in section 1.13 Privacy Impact Assessments.
- **PIA reports**: A PIA generally is a process used to determine if personal information is being appropriately safeguarded, used, shared, made available to the individuals associated with it, and destroyed. A PIA report details the findings of a PIA and includes associated documentation detailing how the discovered privacy risks will be appropriately mitigated. See more about PIAs in section 1.13 Privacy Impact Assessments.
- **Privacy governance reports**: This is a report to communicate to key stakeholders the current levels of privacy compliance throughout the enterprise; improvements made since the last privacy governance report was published; risks, incidents and problems encountered since the last privacy governance report was published; and the status and outcomes of privacy programs and practices changes. Such a report is necessary for multiple reasons, the primary being:
  - To demonstrate the value of the privacy department and governance program
  - To make key stakeholders aware of privacy problems and risks throughout the enterprise
  - To communicate successes and improvements within the privacy program
  - To engage key stakeholders with the privacy practitioners and learn the areas of concern to the key stakeholders
- **Training activities**: It is important to document when training occurs, along with the topic of the training, those who attended the training, and the date and time of the training. In addition, it is important to document how the training was delivered, and the results of any quizzes or tests provided to the training attendees. Such documentation provides important evidence to prove a standard of due care for training activities to any auditor or regulator. Documentation also provides a historical record of the training activities that have occurred, supports better understanding of the training's effectiveness, and can provide insights for how to improve the training program.
- **Awareness communications:**[22] Awareness is not the same as training. Awareness campaigns can occur simultaneously at various locations and on a continuous basis. Privacy awareness activities promote ongoing compliance and keep key issues at the top of employees' minds. Compliance needs and awareness activities should change with the needs of the enterprise. Awareness is typically the "what" component of the education strategy for influencing behavior and practice. Training is typically the "how" component to implement security

and privacy. To make awareness activities effective, it is important to understand the needs of the audience. Awareness audiences are very broad, comprising everyone who works with an enterprise, including third parties, customers and consumers. Awareness audiences have diverse experiences, backgrounds and job responsibilities. The awareness goals, at the decision-making level, are to convince the audience that security and privacy risk reduction is achievable, and to ensure that enterprises leaders are aware of their legal and regulatory obligations. Documentation of all awareness activities demonstrates a standard of due care and supports a wide range of legal requirements for privacy.

1.4 Legal Purpose, Consent and Legitimate Interest

Legal purpose, consent and legitimate interest relate to the ways personal information is used, shared, processed, made available to the associated individuals (the data subjects), retained, and accessed for other types of activities.

While these terms and concepts have been used and understood for decades in a subjective sense, their explicit use within the EU GDPR has increased interest and heightened the need to understand their associated meanings and requirements. Understanding the terms and concepts is particularly necessary for privacy engineers, because a large portion of the systems, applications, networks, services and procedures engineered must conform with legal requirements defined by these terms.

1.4.1 Legal Purpose

A long-held privacy principle[23] is that when enterprises collect and use personal information, the data controller should:

- When the request for personal information is made, describe and specify in the privacy notice or other means of communication the purpose for which personal information and any associated sensitive information is collected, ensuring that the purpose complies with applicable law and relies on a permissible legal basis.
- Align subsequent use of the personal information and sensitive information with the purpose provided and the consents obtained, and comply with associated legal requirements for use limitation.
- When necessary, communicate with applicable data protection legal authorities about legitimate purpose and use limitations.

The purposes for which personal information is collected, used and shared must be consistent with associated legal requirements. An example of a regulation that codifies how to determine if such purposes are legal is found within the GDPR,[24] Article 6 requires that processing of personal data is "lawful" only if at least one of the following situations applies:

- *The data subject has given consent to the processing of his or her personal data for one or more specific purposes.*
- *Processing is necessary for the performance of a contract to which the data subject is party or to take steps at the request of the data subject prior to entering into a contract.*
- *Processing is necessary for compliance with a legal obligation to which the controller is subject.*
- *Processing is necessary in order to protect the vital interests of the data subject or of another natural person.*
- *Processing is necessary for the performance of a task carried out in the public interest or in the exercise of official authority vested in the controller.*
- *Processing is necessary for the purposes of the legitimate interests pursued by the controller (other than a public authority) or by a third party, except where such interests are overridden by the interests or fundamental rights and freedoms of the data subject which require protection of personal data, in particular where the data subject is a child.*

While EU member states must meet these minimum requirements, each may establish additional, more specific requirements. Therefore, it is important for each enterprise to know the requirements of all the countries from which personal information is collected and processed, and not assume that the GDPR covers all requirements.

1.4.2 Consent

When collecting personal information from individuals, enterprises should:[25]

- Obtain appropriate consent, implicit or explicit, according to what any corresponding regulation mandates with respect to the collection, use and disclosure of personal information.
- Ensure that appropriate and necessary consents have been obtained:
  - Prior to commencing collection activities
  - Prior to using the personal information for purposes beyond those for which it was originally collected
  - Prior to the transfer of personal information to third parties or other jurisdictions

If obtaining consents through a fax machine, or through use of any other electronic transmission method, it is a good security practice to include a cover sheet notifying recipients that enclosed documents may contain privileged information that must be safeguarded from unauthorized disclosure.

Privacy engineers are needed to ensure that consents are provided to individuals appropriately and consistently. The privacy engineers should also ensure that associated consents and denials of consent are appropriately recorded. For denials of consent, since the individual may not provide any documentation for a denial, the privacy engineer needs to establish a method to document, either digitally or manually, that the denial occurred.

Going forward, services and products must be engineered to support:

- Decisions regarding the use or non-use of personal information
- Compliance with associated legal requirements for use limitation

Multiple regulations throughout the world have specific requirements for how and when consents should be collected and used.

Following are two examples:

1. **GDPR:**[26] Two articles specifically detail the times when a consent must be obtained from the associated data subject:
   - **a.** Article 7 details four distinct conditions for consent:
     - **i.** When processing is based on consent, the data subject's consent must be explicit.
     - **ii.** If the data subject's consent is given in the context of a written declaration that also concerns other matters, the request for consent shall be presented in a manner that is clearly distinguishable from the other matters.
     - **iii.** The data subject has the right to withdraw consent at any time, and withdrawing consent must be as easy as giving consent.
     - **iv.** The consent must be freely given and not conditional to personal data processing that is not necessary, or to the performance of a contract or the provision of a service.
   - **b.** Article 8 details three conditions of children's consent:
     - **i.** When a child is at least 16 years old, the child's own consent to processing is considered lawful. However, when a child is younger than 16 years old, consent must be authorized by the child's legal guardian. A caveat is that EU countries can establish laws requiring a younger age than 16, but not younger than 13 years old, for provision of direct consent.

ii. When a child is younger than 16, the data controller must make efforts to verify that the person who gives consent as the legal guardian actually does have such authority.

iii. These requirements do not supersede the applicable general contract laws within each of the EU countries.

2. **HIPAA:**[27] HIPAA allows uses and disclosures of protected health information (PHI), a type of personal data very specific to healthcare, to perform treatment, facilitate payment, or enable other healthcare activities by covered entities (healthcare providers, insurers and clearinghouses) and their business associates without requiring consents. However, those covered entities are given the option of using consents in these situations to demonstrate trust, to maintain the documentation, or for a variety of other reasons. However, there are other situations when consent, referenced as authorization in the HIPAA regulatory text, is required, including the sharing of psychotherapy notes, marketing purposes, sale of PHI, public health purposes or research.

1.4.3 Legitimate Interest

The legitimate interests of an enterprise that collects personal information from consumers or employees, derives personal information from IoT device data or AI activities, or is given personal information from another enterprise to perform an activity on its behalf may establish the legal basis for performing various processing activities without the associated individuals' consent. Such a situation may occur if the interests or legal rights of the associated individuals do not override the enterprise's legal rights for processing, when considering the reasonable expectations of individuals based on their relationship with the enterprise.

In general, there is a relevant and appropriate relationship between the individual (data subject) and the enterprise (data controller) when the individual is a client, customer or patient, or is employed by or otherwise in some type of relationship with the enterprise. For example:

- When an enterprise needs to use employee personal information to create stakeholder annual statements or to file country tax return reports
- When in the interest of national security, such as obtaining summary patient infection statistical data when determining the total number of individuals infected with COVID-19 in each geographic area of a country to support controlling the spread
- When doing forensic analysis to determine the source of a network hacking incident

Determining if legitimate interest applies depends upon the assessment of the situation, including whether the involved individuals could have reasonably expected, when their personal information was collected, that analysis of their personal data could reasonably take place. The interests and legal rights of the individuals could supersede the interest of the enterprise if the individuals did not reasonably expect further processing. It is important for privacy engineers to be aware of such legitimate interest rights when they are establishing services and products involving the use of personal information. Because of the need for assessment to determine legal interest, privacy engineers should involve their legal counsel, information security officer and privacy officer in making such decisions.

The GDPR is commonly referenced as the predominant regulation that requires legitimate interest assessment. However, other local, state and national laws and regulations may also allow consideration of legitimate interest prior to using personal information for purposes that were not explicit when the personal information was collected.

1.5 Data Subject Rights

The issue of data subject rights (i.e., the rights of the individuals associated with the personal information) is a topic of ongoing debate. Laws and regulations have established a wide range of diverse data subject rights over the past several decades. Privacy engineers and other privacy practitioners need to identify, document and understand the rights that apply to the data subjects whose personal information they collect, derive, store, transmit, share, access or otherwise process.

The NIST Privacy Framework,[28] which is a voluntary tool that enterprises can use to build a privacy management program, includes two specific functions supporting data subject rights for access, control and communications about their personal information:

- **Control-P**: Develop and implement appropriate activities to enable enterprises or individuals to process data with sufficient granularity to manage privacy risks. The Control-P function considers data processing management from the standpoint of both enterprises and individuals.
- **Communicate-P**: Develop and implement appropriate activities to enable enterprises and individuals to have a reliable understanding and engage in a dialog about data processing methods and associated privacy risks. The Communicate-P function recognizes that both enterprises and individuals may need to know how data are processed in order to manage privacy risk effectively.

Privacy engineers can use the controls described within the categories and subcategories of the Control-P and Communicate-P functions to guide the engineering of services and products that allow individuals to access their own associated personal information. These include the following categories:

- **Control-P categories**:
  - Data processing policies, processes and procedures (CT.PO-P): Policies, processes and procedures are maintained and used to manage data processing (e.g., purpose, scope, roles and responsibilities in the data processing ecosystem, and management commitment) consistent with the enterprise's risk strategy to protect individuals' privacy.
  - Data processing management (CT.DM-P): Data are managed consistent with the enterprise's risk strategy to protect individuals' privacy, increase manageability, and enable the implementation of privacy principles (e.g., individual participation, data quality, data minimization).
  - Disassociated processing (CT.DP-P): Data processing solutions increase disassociability consistent with the enterprise's risk strategy to protect individuals' privacy and enable implementation of privacy principles (e.g., data minimization).
- **Communicate-P categories**:
  - Communication policies, processes and procedures (CM.PO-P): Policies, processes and procedures are maintained and used to increase transparency of the enterprise's data processing practices (e.g., purpose, scope, roles and responsibilities in the data processing ecosystem; management commitment) and associated privacy risks.
  - Data processing awareness (CM.AW-P): Individuals and enterprises have reliable knowledge about data processing practices and associated privacy risks, and effective mechanisms are used and maintained to increase predictability consistent with the enterprise's risk strategy to protect individuals' privacy.

Subcategories, and their associated details, for each category previously listed are found in the NIST Privacy Framework.[29] The subcategories give privacy engineers specific types of guidance, capabilities, and controls to consider to support data subject rights.

Part B: Management

Management practices include establishing privacy roles and responsibilities related to data, privacy training, and awareness communications and activities; vendor and third-party management practices; a privacy audit process; and a privacy incident management capability.

An effective enterprise privacy management strategy should strive to address current and emerging privacy issues, be appropriate for the business ecosystem, address the enterprise's legal requirements for data protection, and ideally be based upon objectively established privacy principles that fit the enterprise culture and environment. Without these basics in place, an enterprise risks having gaps in its privacy management program or failing to use an efficient and repeatable management strategy, which can lead to privacy risks, inappropriate use of personal information, and privacy breaches.

The privacy management strategy should align with the overall enterprise architecture and risk management processes. It should be comprehensive and complete for all enterprise activities and types of information, and contain all required documentation at the appropriate level of detail to be actionable. Privacy practitioners need to collaborate with IT and information security practitioners and other key stakeholders throughout the enterprise. This approach will help support actions that result in privacy policies and practices being followed during the design, development and implementation of enterprise-wide systems, applications and infrastructure.

The enterprise privacy management strategy should be accessible to and used by every role within the enterprise that has responsibilities supporting privacy management. While an enterprise should communicate the overall concepts and goals of the privacy management strategy to all employees, every employee does not need access to the details supporting the privacy management strategy. The privacy management strategy should be accessible only to those who need access, such as those accountable for the privacy practices throughout the enterprise, those responsible for maintaining the various components of the enterprise privacy management strategy, and key stakeholders supporting the privacy management strategy. The privacy strategy should be unique to each enterprise, based upon the enterprise's unique organizational environment, industry, location, and other applicable factors.

While enterprises may determine that additional components are necessary for their own unique business environments, the common components of a strong privacy strategy include:

- Roles and responsibilities related to data
- Privacy training and awareness
- Vendor and third-party management
- Audit process
- Privacy incident management

1.6 Roles and Responsibilities Related to Data

To maintain a successful and up-to-date privacy program, an enterprise must:

- Identify the roles that are responsible for addressing privacy protections.
- Secure personal data and associated data.
- Uphold the program at all levels throughout the enterprise.
- Support the program throughout the full data, system and application life cycles.

Historically, addressing privacy was the sole responsibility of the legal department and occasionally the marketing department. As more types of privacy breaches occurred and emerging technologies created more types of personal data, having only the legal and marketing departments handle the data privacy issues was viewed as shortsighted. Addressing privacy issues solely in the legal department left many areas of the enterprise vulnerable.

In many enterprises, the people who are responsible for privacy are separated from the people who are responsible for information security. Often, these departments do not understand the relationship that should exist between them.[30]

Privacy is the responsibility of the whole enterprise. To successfully address privacy issues, enterprise privacy management strategies and information security management architecture must be effectively and actively integrated. Those responsible for data privacy and those responsible for information security must be in close contact and communication. Otherwise, damaging conflicts in practices and technologies could emerge. For example:

- Changes in security controls or in IT architecture can affect privacy risk levels.
- When privacy controls are implemented, they often require the implementation of information security technologies and controls.
- Gaps in compliance can exist when one area assumes the other is taking care of a compliance issue.

Functions such as HR, legal, IT, data management, software development and change management play key roles in supporting the primary privacy efforts for their own departments. Those responsible for their department's privacy issues need to understand and identify the applicable personal information and privacy protection legal requirements for their scope of responsibility.

Stakeholders throughout an enterprise business unit must be included when reviewing and creating both information security and privacy policies. There are roles at the corporate level that are responsible for corporate privacy management, data protection and legal issues.

All of these enterprise groups need to work together so the corporate-level roles understand the privacy management, data protection and legal needs for the entire enterprise. The corporate roles can then determine how to address the privacy and information security requirements for the enterprise.

Vital requirements for the enterprise privacy and data protection roles include:[31]

- Understanding how to identify privacy risk, privacy harms and relevant legal requirements
- Understanding the enterprise's privacy and data protection policies
- Understanding and creating procedures within the scope of the roles' responsibilities to comply with privacy policies
- Using the enterprise's chosen privacy principles and frameworks to implement privacy policies and create associated supporting privacy protections
- Documenting and supporting privacy principles and supporting privacy protections throughout the enterprise privacy management program

A wide variety of roles and responsibilities that are specific to data protection and privacy have emerged over the past few decades. Some of the more commonly used roles and responsibilities are shown in **figure 1.5**.

Figure 1.5—Privacy Roles and Responsibilities

Role	Responsibilities
Data controller	The data controller controls and is ultimately responsible for the appropriate use, sharing and security of personal information. Typically, the data controller is responsible for the legal business/enterprise structure as a whole. The enterprise data controller's responsibilities include: • Establishing appropriate and consistent monitoring, measuring and reporting of the effectiveness of the privacy management program and tools. • Establishing a framework for measuring and monitoring the following: • Effectiveness of the privacy management program • Level of compliance with applicable policies, standards and legal requirements • Use and implementation of privacy tools • Types and numbers of privacy bréaches that occur • Privacy risk areas within the data controller's responsibilities • Third parties that have access to personal information, sensitive information and the associated risk levels • Reporting compliance with privacy policies, applicable standards and laws to key stakeholders. • Integrating internationally accepted privacy practices, such as those from ISO, NIST and ISACA, into the enterprise's business practices. • Establishing procedures that cover the use of personal data in investigating, monitoring, continuous auditing, analytics, etc., completed by internal and/or external auditors. • Anonymizing personal data if the local/national law is not allowed to monitor pure personal data for fraud/crime prevention, etc.
Chief privacy officer (CPO) or data protection officer (DPO)	The CPO or DPO has overall responsibility for the enterprise privacy management program. Smaller enterprises may not have the CPO as part of the C-suite; instead, this role may report to another C-level position. In some parts of the world, there may be a requirement for an enterprise to have a position responsible for an enterprise's overall operational privacy management program. The GDPR requires that the enterprise's DPO must comply with its requirements. Also, US federal agencies have established a senior agency official for privacy roles to fulfill CPO types of responsibilities.
Privacy steering committee	The privacy steering committee is responsible for monitoring and reviewing to ensure that good privacy practices are identified, prioritized, and applied effectively and consistently throughout the enterprise. The steering committee also considers the related ethical considerations for the derivation, collection, use and sharing of personal data, and provides input on how the CPOs, DPOs, privacy engineers, privacy management architects and privacy managers should address those considerations. The privacy steering committee is responsible for monitoring and reviewing to ensure that good privacy practices are identified, prioritized, and applied effectively and consistently throughout the enterprise. The steering committee also considers the related ethical considerations for the derivation, collection, use and sharing of personal data, and provides input on how the CPOs, DPOs, privacy engineers, privacy management architects and privacy managers should address those considerations.

Figure 1.5—Privacy Roles and Responsibilities (cont.)

Role	Responsibilities
Privacy engineer	The privacy engineer is responsible for creating and designing the requirements for privacy protections within the enterprise's products and services.
Privacy management architect	The privacy management architect is responsible for creating the plans used to build the processes that support effective and efficient privacy management within products and services and throughout the enterprise.
Privacy manager	The privacy manager is responsible for managing specifically assigned scopes of privacy management program activities and supporting efforts. In some parts of the world, a privacy manager is part of the CPO's or DPO's team.
Enterprise risk management committee	The enterprise risk management committee is responsible for enterprise decision-making; for setting the framework for how to collect, assess, control, optimize, finance, share and store data; and for monitoring privacy risk from all sources. The purpose for managing the decision-making and the framework is to increase the enterprise's short- and long-term value to its stakeholders from the privacy management program.
Data processor	A data processor is a natural or legal person, public authority, agency or any other body that processes personal information on behalf of a data controller. In some parts of the world (e.g., the EU), this term does not apply to a data controller's employees. In other parts of the world (e.g., the US), an enterprise's employees are data processors for the enterprise. Examples of data processors include payroll clerks, accountants, market research teams, customer service representatives, IT administrators and any other position with a job responsibility that involves personal information access of some sort on behalf of the data controller.
Business unit manager	A business unit manager is an enterprise member who is responsible for ensuring that privacy is appropriately addressed and mitigated by their direct reports. The business manager ensures that employees address privacy issues according to enterprise privacy policies and procedures related to their business area's activities. Business unit managers may also have privacy manager responsibilities.
Information custodian/Service owner	These individuals are in charge of certain processes or business applications that involve personal information. They are also responsible for communicating business initiatives that may affect privacy management practices that in turn may affect the user community and data subjects. These roles may understand business/operational risk, costs and benefits, and specific privacy management requirements for their business area.
Third party/vendor management team	This team is responsible for overseeing the data protection, privacy and compliance activities that third parties follow within their organizations. For example, the third party/vendor management team ensures that the vendor has an adequate privacy incident management procedure to follow for suspected or actual breaches of personal information.

Source: Data from *ISACA Privacy Practices and Program Management Guide*, USA, 2016; and *Implementing a Privacy Protection Program Using COBIT 5 Enablers With ISACA Privacy Principles*, USA, 2017

Enterprises may need to establish additional privacy-specific roles depending on their enterprise services, products, industries and locations. Examples of other privacy roles:

- Product privacy officers: Work with the acquisitions team to ensure necessary privacy requirements are addressed in the products and services purchased by the enterprise
- Privacy administrators: Follow procedures to support meeting requirements to implement privacy protections
- Privacy compliance and auditing officers: Ensure that privacy requirements are implemented and consistently used

In smaller enterprises, the tasks these different roles cover can, and often must, be carried out by the privacy manager or some other role appropriate to the particular type of enterprise.

The privacy roles and structures previously listed are appropriate for an enterprise that has reached a certain size and organizational complexity; handles personal information or manages information that can reveal insights into specific individuals' lives; or uses big data analytics, AI, or data from smart devices.

For larger enterprises or enterprises that need a stronger focus on privacy, a more elaborate privacy department structure is appropriate, and additional privacy groups and roles can be added to the roles listed.

To increase accountability and motivation for personnel to know and follow security and privacy requirements, data protection and privacy responsibilities for the associated roles should be incorporated into:

- Formally documented job descriptions
- Employment agreements
- Privacy policy awareness acknowledgment documents

Business unit managers can communicate general and specific privacy security roles and responsibilities for personnel in their formal job descriptions. All employees, officers and contractors should be held accountable for compliance with privacy, security, and acceptable use policies, and to protect the institution's information and network assets.[32]

Job descriptions for personnel whose primary job responsibilities are not strictly information security and privacy, but who handle, access or otherwise use personal information, should include specific directives regarding their responsibilities for maintaining security and privacy in their job function. All contractor and consultant contracts should include information security and privacy responsibilities, and enterprises should consider basing financial rewards or penalties on compliance with the listed responsibilities and requirements.[33]

1.7 Privacy Training and Awareness

Providing personnel with the security and privacy information they need, while ensuring that they understand and follow the requirements, is an important component of an enterprise's success. If personnel do not know or understand how to maintain confidentiality of information, or how to secure it appropriately, the enterprise not only risks having one of the most valuable business assets (information) mishandled, but also risks being in noncompliance with laws and regulations that require information security and privacy awareness and training activities. Enterprises also risk damaging another valuable asset, corporate reputation. Data protection and privacy education are important for many reasons, including the following:[34]

- **Regulatory requirements compliance**—An increasing number of laws and regulations require some form of training and awareness activities to occur within the enterprises subject to their jurisdiction. Penalties and sanctions for noncompliance with associated laws and regulations, and following breaches, generally increase when investigators and auditors determine that no, or insufficient, privacy training and awareness activities were provided to employees.

- **Compliance with published privacy notices and policies**—Enterprises are obligated to comply with their own information security and privacy policies and with their own privacy notices. If compliance is not enforced, such policies are worthless, and noncompliance can lead to monetary and regulatory penalties. Enterprises need to educate personnel about their information security and privacy roles and responsibilities, especially in support of published notices, policies, standards and procedures. Awareness and training should be designed to support compliance with security and privacy policies and notices. Executives should act as role models for personnel; their actions heavily influence employee awareness levels, and privacy notice and policy compliance.
- **Customer trust and satisfaction**—Respect for customer security and privacy is one of the most important issues facing enterprises today. Customers want to know that the enterprises they do business with are doing everything reasonable and responsible to safeguard their PII and all other types of personal information.
- **Due diligence**—In general, due diligence means demonstrating that management has ensured adequate protection of enterprise assets, such as information, and compliance with legal and contractual obligations. This is a powerful motivator for implementing a training and awareness program. To have a program that effectively conforms to the guidelines, an enterprise must demonstrate that it exercises due diligence in meeting compliance requirements, and also promotes an organizational culture that encourages ethical conduct and a commitment to compliance with the law.

Privacy practitioners must devote sufficient time and resources to identifying and developing effective privacy training, and the important supporting awareness communications, activities and events. Lack of awareness and understanding of privacy issues, risks and requirements will leave the enterprise vulnerable to privacy breaches and noncompliance consequences.

1.7.1 Content and Delivery

Privacy training materials, awareness content and communications should be accurate and contain correct and realistic statements on risk, harms and practices. Training content and awareness materials must be understandable and tailored to job functions to the extent possible. General and role-based training and periodic awareness reminders are required for all employees, and employee incentives should be tied to privacy management awareness. Additional privacy training and targeted awareness communications should be provided to all relevant target groups and employees with job responsibilities that involve unique personal information risk and harms.

For example, employees in the following areas should have customized privacy training and awareness communications to target privacy risk and harms:[35]

- Call centers
- Marketing and sales
- HR
- Application development and support teams

Figure 1.6 provides an overview of enterprise privacy training and awareness program components, possible delivery methods and supporting technologies, and associated benefits.

Figure 1.6—Attributes of Privacy Training and Awareness Services		
Service Capability	Supporting Technology	Benefit
Establish a formal privacy education program	• Online technologies • In-person activities • Classroom delivery	• Compliance with legal requirements • More effective privacy protections • Fewer privacy breaches
Provide formal privacy training to increase privacy awareness and understanding of the enterprise's privacy policies, procedures and principles, resulting in better protection of personal information and compliance with a variety of laws and compliance requirements	• Training courses (internal and external) • Webinars • Classroom • Video • Conferences/seminars • Provided by associations (e.g., ISACA)	• Compliance with legal requirements to provide privacy training • Increased privacy awareness throughout the enterprise • Reduced risk of social engineering attacks (e.g., phishing, identity theft) • Privacy breaches identified and responded to more quickly • Fewer privacy-related mistakes • Fewer malicious activities related to personal information
Provide ongoing privacy communications to enable increased privacy awareness and understanding, resulting in better protection of personal information	• Newsletters • Events (e.g., privacy fairs, contests, guest speakers) • Posters • Privacy reminders/news on ticker/crawler messages on intranet sites • News feeds • Knowledge bases • Social media • Email • Dedicated intranet sites • Collaboration tools • Vendor and industry advisories • Notices of privacy sanctions and penalties	• Compliance with legal requirements to provide reminders about privacy requirements • Privacy awareness maintained throughout the enterprise • Reduced risk of social engineering attacks (e.g., phishing, identity theft) • Faster identification of and response to privacy breaches • Fewer privacy-related mistakes • Fewer malicious activities related to personal information
Source: ISACA, *Implementing a Privacy Protection Program: Using COBIT® 5 Enablers With ISACA Privacy Principles*, USA, 2017		

1.7.2 Training Frequency

There are many times when privacy training and privacy awareness communications and activities should be provided. Privacy training should be provided to employees when hired, and to all data processors (employees or specific groups of employees) periodically, e.g., annually, and when a significant event or organizational change occurs.

Training and awareness activities, including role-based training, situational training and professional certifications for key workforce members, should be provided at a frequency based on responsibilities and associated privacy risks.

Privacy awareness communications should cover all internal privacy policies, the enterprise privacy notices, communications with data subjects, and any other activity that involves personal information or sensitive information.

All privacy training events and offerings, and all privacy awareness communications and activities should be documented to demonstrate due diligence. All employees who satisfactorily complete privacy training should be tracked and documented. The documentation should be retained for an appropriate period of time, based on the enterprise's legal retention compliance requirements.

1.7.3 Measuring Training and Awareness

Privacy training and privacy awareness activities and events should be measured for their educational impact, effectiveness, and how they influenced the job activities of those taking the training and receiving the awareness materials.

A few example metrics for these goals:

- Number of updates to privacy management awareness communications materials
- Number of different privacy training offerings
- Percentage of employees participating in privacy training
- Percentage of employees passing established levels in tests
- Percentage of employees with performance plans incorporating privacy management goals
- Number of participant postings providing answers to quizzes within awareness communications
- Number of employees observed following privacy policies during work area audits performed after training
- Number of breaches that occurred prior to training compared with after training

Feedback from trainees and trainers can help the enterprise determine the efficacy of the training and awareness programs.

These metrics should be used for administrative purposes, and as evidence to support due diligence. Privacy awareness can be measured only through behavior and the consequences of behavior. For example, if privacy breaches and privacy complaints occur, then privacy awareness can be assessed.

1.8 Vendor and Third-Party Management

Using vendors and third parties presents a major privacy risk for enterprises. If an enterprise does not have appropriate oversight into its vendors' data protection and privacy practices, security incidents and privacy breaches involving the enterprise's data and systems can be catastrophic.

Privacy and data protection controls are only as strong as the weakest link, which could be a vendor with poor privacy practices. The third-party landscape has become increasingly complex, and reliance on third-party services has increased. As a result, enterprise oversight of how a vendor manages privacy and data may be lacking.

1.8.1 Legal Requirements

When an enterprise accesses contracted third parties' and vendors' systems, the enterprise is still responsible and liable for the privacy and protection of its data. Enterprises can be held accountable and be subject to fines and penalties for breaches caused by their vendors.

Some enterprises believe that a "hold harmless" clause protects them from such responsibility. However, the enterprise must ensure that its vendors are meeting the same legal commitment that the enterprise has established within its own posted or published privacy notices.

Many privacy regulations and government requirements require some level of vendor oversight. Enterprises often must comply with more than one privacy regulation and government requirement. Literally hundreds of regulations throughout the world include some level of vendor oversight requirements. A few are shown in **figure 1.7**.

Figure 1.7—Examples of Third-Party Management Requirements

Regulation or Government Program	Third-Party Management Requirements
EU GDPR	Article 28 details a long list of requirements for data processors, the term used for third parties. The overarching requirement: "Where processing is to be carried out on behalf of a controller, the controller shall use only processors providing sufficient guarantees to implement appropriate technical and organizational measures in such a manner that processing will meet the requirements of this Regulation and ensure the protection of the rights of the data subject." Privacy engineers need to review this entire section and the full regulation, which has third-party requirements listed in various places throughout, to ensure privacy programs include all necessary processes, technologies and controls.
US HIPAA	HIPAA uses the term "business associates" for contracted third parties engaged to perform treatment, payment or operations activities that involve access to the covered entity's PHI. Business associates must comply with all HIPAA Security Rule requirements, HITECH Act breach response requirements, and any Privacy Rule requirements that apply to the business associate to support contracted services and products. Covered entities not only must have a contract signed by each business associate, but also must obtain reasonable assurances from business associates that they are complying with HIPAA requirements for securing all applicable information.
US GLBA	Financial institutions must enter into contractual agreements that prohibit third parties with access to consumers' nonpublic personal information (NPPI) from disclosing or using the NPPI other than to perform services for the institutions, or functions on the institutions' behalf in the ordinary course of business to carry out those services.

Figure 1.7—Examples of Third-Party Management Requirements (cont.)

Regulation or Government Program	Third-Party Management Requirements
US Family Educational Rights and Privacy Act (FERPA)	When PII from education records is disclosed to a third-party provider, FERPA still governs its use, and the school or district is responsible for ensuring its protection. Providers must comply with any established transparency required by each school or district that uses their services or products. The school or district directly controls the third-party provider's protection of the PII entrusted to the provider.
US Federal Information Security Management Act of 2002 (FISMA)	FISMA requires US federal government agencies to manage contracted entities in accordance with *NIST SP 800-53 Security and Privacy Controls for Information Systems and Organizations*, Section 3.20, Supply Chain Risk Management.
US Department of Defense Cybersecurity Maturity Model Certification (CMMC) Program	The purpose of the CMMC is to improve and make consistent the ways the US Department of Defense and military vet and provide oversight to their contractors and provide requirements for assessing and enhancing the cybersecurity posture of the Defense Industrial Base (DIB). The CMMC is meant to serve as a verification mechanism to ensure that appropriate levels of cybersecurity practices and processes are in place to maintain basic cyber-hygiene and to protect controlled unclassified information (CUI) residing on the Defense Department's industry partner (third-party) networks.
Australian Privacy Principles (APP)	APP 6 outlines when an APP-covered entity may use or disclose personal information, which generally is only when use or disclosure is for a purpose for which it was collected (known as the primary purpose), or for a secondary purpose if an exception applies. In such instances the contractor must secure the information in accordance with Chapter 11: APP 11—Security of personal information.
Hong Kong's Personal Data Privacy Amendment	The Data User (the data controller) needs to have a written agreement that includes the requirements for complying with the Personal Data Privacy Amendment, with commensurate indemnifications for breaches. Data Users should verify that the intended third-party use of the personal data is consistent with the consent.

Additional legal requirements for vendor oversight are often established within:

- Contracts enterprises have with other businesses and clients, and through standards such as PCI-DSS, HIPAA or ISO 27001
- Privacy notices posted on the enterprise's own website

1.8.2 Management Procedures

ISACA Privacy Principle 11: Third Party/Vendor Management provides guidance for how enterprises can manage vendor oversight.[36] Through the data controller, the enterprise should provide ongoing oversight of third-party access to any type of personal information or sensitive information. To ensure that necessary privacy issues and activities have been addressed and included, based on the vendor's service or product, a privacy practitioner role should actively participate in overall vendor oversight, and manage and evaluate vendor contracts. The privacy practitioner should provide guidance for service level agreements and other requirements that involve personal information or could affect privacy in some way.

The privacy practitioner should ensure that relationships with vendors include:[37]

- Implementation governance and risk management processes that apply contractual, administrative and audit measures to ensure that the appropriate protections governing use of personal information and sensitive information are transferred to and accessible to all associated third parties, and appropriately maintained, processed and controlled.
- Requirements for all third parties with any type of access to personal information and sensitive information to commit to a variety of actions, such as:
  - Reporting personal information breaches to the data controller in a timely manner without delay (as defined by the data controller to the third party and as required by any applicable data protection authorities)
  - Retaining data for a specified period of time or according to specific conditions
  - Ensuring that data transfers are secured
  - Documenting data transfers to other countries
  - Maintaining documentation of countries to which data transfers are not allowed

To determine if the enterprise has sufficient vendor oversight, privacy practitioners should answer the following questions:[38]

- Are procedures in place to ensure that contracted entities have privacy management programs that, at a minimum, meet the requirements and policies of the enterprise contracting them?
- Is there a process to establish and maintain an up-to-date inventory of all third parties, and the associated types of personal information to which they have access?
- Do contracts with third parties include privacy and security requirements? For example, asking third parties to provide documentation validating their most recent risk assessment, or outlining training they provided to their employees, etc.

If the answer to any of these questions is “no,” then the enterprise needs to create the related documents or implement the related practices.

Privacy practitioners can help the third-party or vendor management team implement the following procedure to provide the enterprise with comprehensive knowledge about its service providers:[39]

- **Step 1: Compile a list of all enterprise service providers.** If an enterprise works with dozens or hundreds of third-party providers, compiling a comprehensive list may be challenging. An enterprise should have thorough knowledge of all its third-party providers, in all areas of its operation, including smaller providers and those that provide services or goods of lesser monetary value or to a narrow business niche. This information should ideally be kept in a single database.
- **Step 2: Compile a list of services rendered by all third parties**. This list should include every service that the enterprise receives from third parties. Assign each service a significance rating to indicate the importance of the service to the enterprise business. Use of a finite numerical scale or a set of quality descriptors for this rating is recommended. Rating the business importance of services allows for more precise risk profiles. The rating of the services depends on the requirements defined in the enterprise and their significance for the enterprise.
- **Step 3: Link each service with its provider**. The links allow an enterprise to identify the providers that require special attention (e.g., those that process enterprise data, including personal data, or host enterprise IT systems). A single provider may provide multiple services. Sometimes, the linking process reveals that some vendors do not have assigned services, or some services do not have assigned vendors.

- **Step 4: Create a privacy risk profile for each provider**. The enterprise should assess two aspects of each third party. A privacy risk-profile questionnaire—which can be combined with an information security risk-profile questionnaire if an enterprise determines it would work more efficiently—can support this process:
  - Aspect 1—Privacy risk linked to the potential of the third party as a result of the way it runs its day-to-day business activities
  - Aspect 2—Privacy risk linked to the services rendered to the enterprise by the third party

1.9 Audit Process

Privacy audits, assessments, testing and compliance reviews are used to ensure that the enterprise's privacy policies, procedures, practices, personal information rules and standards comply with internal and external laws, regulations, directives, and other legal requirements and privacy standards. The privacy audit, assessments, etc., can also be used to identify failures of enterprise architecture and information architecture to support privacy based on design principles and considerations, creating business risks as a result.

Performing privacy audits demonstrates a standard of due care and also supports ISACA Privacy Principle 9: Monitoring, Measuring and Reporting,[40] which recommends the enterprise establish appropriate and consistent monitoring, measuring and reporting of the effectiveness of the privacy management program and tools. To support this, the enterprise should:

- Establish a framework for auditing, measuring/evaluating and monitoring the following:
  - Effectiveness of the privacy management program
  - Level of compliance with applicable policies, standards and legal requirements
  - Use and implementation of privacy tools
  - Advancements in privacy-enhancing technologies
  - Changes in privacy regulations and laws
  - Types and numbers of privacy breaches that occur
  - Privacy risk areas within the data controller's digital ecosystem
  - Third parties that have access to personal information, sensitive information and the associated risk levels
- Report compliance with privacy policies, applicable standards and laws to key stakeholders
- Integrate internationally accepted privacy practices into business practices and then check during privacy audits to ensure those practices have been implemented appropriately and are followed consistently
- Establish procedures that cover the use of personal data in investigating, monitoring, continuous auditing, analytics, etc., completed by internal or external auditors
- Anonymize data if the local/national law is not allowed to monitor pure personal data for fraud/crime prevention, etc.; perform audits to ensure the anonymization processes are effective and consistently applied throughout the enterprise

A privacy audit program addresses the breadth and depth of audit issues that need to be covered. An example of a privacy audit plan includes the following steps:[41]

1. **Determine the audit subject**—The first thing to establish is the audit subject. What does privacy mean in the enterprise? If there are distinct categories of data in use for different areas of the business, they should probably be recorded as separate audit universe items. Fundamentally, when considering privacy, the data can be broken down to data stored on customers and employees (individual rights). Besides databases, files and documents, it is important to consider where the data are stored and where they originated.
2. **Define the audit objective**—Once the scope of the audit is established, the audit objective should be determined. Why is the subject being audited? From an auditor's perspective, it is advisable to adopt a risk-based view and define the objectives.

3. **Set the audit scope**—After defining the objectives, the auditor should use a scoping process to identify the actual data that need to be audited. In other words, what are the limits of the audit? It could be limited to data in a specific application, process, location, or stored by certain devices. Setting the scope should be risk-based.
4. **Perform pre-audit planning**—After risk is identified, it should be evaluated to determine its significance. Conducting a risk assessment is critical in setting the final scope of a risk-based audit. The more significant the risk, the greater the need for assurance. Examples of privacy risk considerations based upon the privacy principles include those shown in **figure 1.8**.
5. **Determine audit procedures and steps for data gathering**—At this stage of the audit process, the audit team should have enough information to identify and select the audit approach or strategy, and start developing the audit program. With this information, the audit team should decide what documents need to be reviewed, determine which laws and regulations apply, set the criteria, and identify key stakeholders to interview. The team also should define the testing steps.

Figure 1.8—Examples of Privacy Risk

Privacy Category	Example Risk
Privacy of behavior and action	**Social media** contains information, images, video and audio that reveal personal activities, orientations and preferences, many of which are sensitive in nature and can impact the data subjects.
Privacy of thoughts and feelings	**Big data analytics** has the potential to take large amounts of data and reveal the thoughts and feelings of specific individuals based on data they provide or others provide about them. Such insights can result in negative impacts if actions are taken because of the analytics findings.
Privacy of location and space (territorial)	**Privately owned computing devices** that are used for business activities may be able to record images and audio. Such images and audio create privacy risks if the devices are also used to perform business activities within the workplace.

Source: Adapted from ISACA, *ISACA Privacy Principles and Program Management Guide*, USA, 2016

Applying the audit plan can help privacy engineers identify gaps in the engineering plans for enterprise services and products that involve personal information in a variety of forms and using various types of technology.

1.10 Privacy Incident Management

Many laws, regulations and industry standards require enterprises to comply with established privacy breach response rules following the discovery of a breach within the enterprise or within a third party. A few examples of breach notice legal requirements:

- At least 54 U.S. state and territory breach notice laws
- EU GDPR breach notice requirements
- HIPAA HITECH Act
- Canada Breach of Security Safeguards Regulations: SOR/2018-64
- US Securities and Exchange Commission (SEC) Commission Statement and Guidance on Public Company Cybersecurity Disclosures

- Australia Privacy Amendment (Notifiable Data Breaches) Act 2017
- South Africa Protection of Personal Information Act, 2013
- Colombia Breach Notification Law 1581
- Philippines Implementing Rules and Regulations of the Data Privacy Act of 2012
- Mexico Federal Law on Protection of Personal Data Held by Private Parties

A privacy incident management program is a necessary part of an enterprise's privacy management strategy to ensure that responses to all types of incidents, involving all forms of personal information and associated information, are consistent and comprehensive, and fulfill all the enterprise's legal obligations.

The privacy incident response team (PIRT) should have oversight of all organizational components that relate to privacy incident response. The PIRT should have oversight for any incident that involves personal information that is collected, processed, or maintained directly by the enterprise; or on its behalf by contractors, third parties, vendors and other types of contracted entities. An experienced privacy practitioner should serve as the PIRT lead, or a privacy officer should serve as a PIRT advisor to actively participate and contribute to privacy incident management when response activities are triggered.

The mission of a PIRT is to reduce the risk associated with the loss, unauthorized access to, or misuse of personal information and to oversee response efforts to mitigate privacy incidents as efficiently, effectively and quickly as possible.

An enterprise's PIRT plays an essential role in protecting the reputation and mission of the enterprise, and building and maintaining the trust between the enterprise and its customers, clients, patients, employees, and members of the public who have some invested interest in the enterprise.

All parts of the enterprise must comply with its privacy policies and procedures, including privacy incident response policies and procedures. The entire enterprise must comply with its obligations under all applicable legal requirements, including existing privacy breach notice laws, regulations and contractual provisions. Privacy practitioners should ensure enterprise awareness of privacy incident policies and procedures.

Loss of control over personal information can result from a variety of scenarios, including but not limited to loss or theft of enterprise devices in which personal information is stored, loss or theft of documents containing personal information, human error, or the exploitation of vulnerabilities within a technology. See section 1.12 Threats, Attacks, and Vulnerabilities Related to Privacy for more information.

Incident details come from various sources, including a specific employee, department, third party, system monitoring software, an individually reported loss, or a complaint, to name a few examples. Privacy incidents should be reported to the CPO or similar role. The CPO should then notify members of the PIRT.

Regardless of the source, the PIRT should oversee the privacy incident response to any incident that represents a potential failure by employees to properly protect and control the wide variety of personal information maintained throughout the enterprise. In consultation with the responsible department component, the PIRT should:

- Determine and advise of any privacy risks associated with the incident
- Direct and advise specific responses to the breach of personal information
- Identify and address potential legal and public relations issues
- Notify or manage notifications to internal and external entities as required, ensuring notices are provided in accordance with the applicable laws and regulations

For example, some breach notice laws require breach notification to be made "without undue delay." Some require notification to data protection authorities within 72 hours of discovering a breach, under the EU GDPR. Many US breach notice laws have 30- to 60-day notice requirements. Legal counsel should be consulted to determine all the breach notice time requirements for the enterprise.

The primary roles and responsibilities of the PIRT are to:

- Oversee privacy incident management activities for suspected or actual breaches of personal information
- Evaluate breaches or suspected breaches of PII and decide what actions should be taken
- Provide input to and approve incident response activities for incidents involving personal information
- Assess the responsible enterprise's proposed course of action, risk assessments, response plans, and proposed notification activities; provide feedback; and make recommendations for improvement
- Notify appropriate internal organizational leadership of a suspected or actual breach per PIRT-documented privacy incident response procedures
- Ensure proper reporting, notification and follow-up actions to stakeholders by the responsible enterprise components when an incident involving personal information occurs
- Ensure that all areas and levels of the enterprise manage privacy incidents according to established and applicable legal breach notification rules
- Work closely with the information security department and other organizational key stakeholders, such as legal, public relations and physical security, to coordinate privacy incident response activities and data collection
- Ensure that privacy incidents are coordinated with appropriate external entities, such as law enforcement, applicable federal agencies, and applicable data protection authorities
- Coordinate incident response capabilities with the enterprise's information security incident team to ensure effective and comprehensive management of incident identification, escalation, mitigation and closure data
- Conduct analysis of privacy incident data to identify trends and make recommendations on enhancements for protection of personal information
- Develop and maintain standard operating procedures to effectively manage potential or suspected privacy incidents

In addition to managing incident response efforts, the PIRT should regularly advise the CPO on ways to improve the protection of personal information by analyzing privacy incident data, developing recommendations to enhance protections, reviewing and approving incident response plans related to the mitigation of risks associated with the recurrence of an incident, and monitoring for environmental threats that could potentially impact the protection of personal information.

It is important to note that a privacy incident differs from a security incident. A security incident is an event that leads to a violation of an organization's security policies and puts sensitive data at risk of exposure. Security incident is a broad term that includes many kinds of events.

A privacy data breach incident is a type of security incident. All data breaches are security incidents, but not all security incidents are data breaches. A security incident can involve any type of data, including sensitive personal information or unregulated but sensitive data, such as intellectual property.

Part C: Risk Management

Addressing privacy risk is important for all types of enterprises worldwide. Privacy concerns can exist throughout the full data life cycle and throughout all levels and areas of an enterprise. The concerns and their significance may cross a wide spectrum. Some concerns may be unique to a specific device that involves personal data in some respect. Some may relate to the risks involved in collecting personal data, while some may involve the third parties with whom personal data is shared, to cite a few of the many possible scenarios.

Many privacy concerns do not involve the application of laws or regulations. Enterprises must understand the possible concerns that exist in house and those extending to their contracted third parties. They must understand the risks associated with those concerns and the best risk responses. This comprehensive understanding is necessary to enable the roles responsible for privacy and data protection to communicate the risks knowledgeably and effectively to key stakeholders, and to inform them of the enterprise's associated mitigation actions.

Enterprises must understand the full spectrum of adverse experiences that individuals (data subjects) may experience due to the use of their personal information within business activities. Privacy problem is a term commonly used to describe an adverse experience resulting from personal information processing. Other terms include privacy harm, privacy violation, privacy intrusion and privacy invasion.

1.11 Risk Management Process

A few fundamental components are critical for information security and privacy programs, including associated risk management. Professionals who know and understand these principles can perform risk management activities, assessments and projects; anticipate and respond to new threats; identify new vulnerabilities; and ensure that all legal requirements for data protection and privacy are addressed. These fundamental components include:[42]

- Defining, identifying and categorizing systems, applications and data according to the following needs:
  - Confidentiality
  - Integrity
  - Availability
- Identifying legal requirements for compliance with:
  - Laws and regulations
  - Contracts, including data processing agreements
  - Privacy and security notices and other legally binding statements
- Identifying and planning to address risk on an ongoing basis by:
  - Performing risk assessments and PIAs in collaboration with cybersecurity personnel, addressing privacy compliance and risk mitigation in coordination with the security risk assessment process
  - Assigning mitigation and remediation responsibilities, where opportunities for process improvement should be identified
- Determining how best to mitigate risk and enable mitigation effectiveness and continual improvement (CI), which also include:
  - Establishing a CAP for the risk findings
  - Establishing a plan of action and associated milestones (POA&M)

Implementing these actions requires proper consideration and design of a security, privacy and compliance governance structure for each of the enterprise's business environments, and a full data processing ecosystem.

It is helpful to use existing standardized frameworks when managing risk to ensure that all considerations are covered. Examples of frameworks include:

- COBIT 2019
- NIST Risk Management Framework
- NIST Privacy Framework
- ISO 31000—Risk Management

Security, privacy and compliance activities must be documented and implemented considering sustainability, role responsibilities and assignments for the associated business organizational structure. This approach helps ensure that ongoing continuous monitoring and improvement support not only immediate organizational needs, but also future organizational needs.

Following a feasible, applicable and proper governance structure aligned to the business environment is of critical importance. A POA&M should consider the following fundamental assessments:

- Describe the current disposition of discovered vulnerabilities and system findings and include the enterprise's intended corrective actions for those findings.
- Devise a well-organized, structured approach to track risk mitigation activities.
- Identify tasks that need to be accomplished to mitigate risk.
- Establish continuous monitoring activities to address all identified vulnerabilities and findings.

1.12 Problematic Data Actions Affecting Privacy

Before performing privacy risk management activities, it is important to understand two primary components of privacy risk:

1. Threats and vulnerabilities created by problematic data actions resulting in privacy risks
2. Resulting effects

When considering privacy, the resulting effects should be considered not only for the enterprise, but also for the associated individuals.

Problematic data action describes data actions that cause an adverse effect, or problem, for individuals associated with the data. Privacy risk has a similar meaning as threats and attacks, as those terms are used within information security risk assessments and management, but it applies uniquely to privacy.

1.12.1 Vulnerabilities

The number of privacy-related vulnerabilities is growing. **Figure 1.9** lists some of these common vulnerabilities.

Figure 1.9—Privacy-related Vulnerabilities

Vulnerability	Example
Mistakes made by those who handle personal data	An employee leaves patient records viewable by anyone in the vicinity on a health clinic reception desk.
Lack of separation of duties	The person who submits a surveillance request for an individual is the same person who gives approvals for surveillance requests.

Figure 1.9—Privacy-related Vulnerabilities (cont.)	
Vulnerability	Example
Lack of awareness and training	Privacy training is never, or rarely (less than once a year), provided.
Applications with insufficient built-in privacy controls	A web-based application does not use secure protocols to encrypt sensitive personal data input.
Systems with insufficient built-in privacy controls	No passwords are required for access to customer databases.
Networks with insufficient built-in privacy controls	Access to personal data files is allowed through a uniform resource locator with no authentication required.
Devices with insufficient built-in privacy controls	Smartphones do not require passwords.
Known vulnerabilities in devices	A bug in the software allows unauthorized access to memory where user IDs and passwords are found in clear text.
Unauthorized physical access to digital personal data	Hard copy loan customer files are left in unlocked file cabinets in rooms where employees and the general public gather.
Unauthorized physical access to hard copy personal data	Employee appraisal files are left on the top of managers' desks in unlocked offices.
Unsecure hard copy disposal methods	Hard copy patient files are thrown away into publicly accessible dumpsters
Unsecure digital data disposal methods	Universal serial bus (USB) drives containing business and customer data are thrown away into public trash receptacles without smashing them or degaussing the hardware first.
Unsecure hardware disposal methods	A credit union sells office desktop computers in an online auction and fails to remove data prior to the sale.

1.12.2 Problematic Data Actions

Some common threats where problematic data actions could occur:

- **Malicious intent from outsiders**—For example, a hacker exploits an enterprise's firewall vulnerabilities to gain access to personnel records.
- **Malicious intent from insiders**—For example, a healthcare provider staff member who has access to all patient information shares patient information with outsiders who then use it to commit identity fraud or other crimes, or take other actions harmful to the associated patients.
- **Mistakes and errors made by authorized users**—For example, an HR employee mistakenly sends the salary and benefits spreadsheet for all employees to an external television station email address instead of an authorized coworker who needed it to perform work activities, because both email addresses started with the same characters.
- **Advanced persistent threats (APTs)**—APTs are generally extended continuous attacks from an unauthorized source using a variety of tools to achieve a single and specific malicious objective. For example, cybercriminals use an APT to get access into the enterprise network through a website when an employee visits it, and then steal the personal data the employee accesses when carrying out work activities.

- **Malicious websites**—For example, a website can be created to look like a legitimate bank website, but it is actually a clone. It will collect the website visitors' ID, password, and other sensitive personal information to allow cybercriminals to then use those stolen credentials to access legitimate bank accounts.
- **Device theft**—For example, a criminal takes a person's computing device containing large amounts of personal data, which was left unattended on a seat in an airport terminal boarding area.
- **Privacy attacks**—A wide range of privacy attacks can be used. See Methods for Exploiting Vulnerabilities for more information.
- **Linkability**—A specific individual, or group of individuals, can be distinguished from applicable information items, even in the absence of specific names or unique identifiers.
- **Identifiability**—A subtype of linkability, it's the result of an unauthorized entity identifying a specific individual or group of individuals based on the context of a situation. For example, a message is sent to the parents of a school class describing an incident involving a student in the class, and because of the class demographics, the description of the incident makes the identity of the student apparent.
- **Nonrepudiation**—An unauthorized entity uses methods to gather evidence to counter the claims of the repudiating party, and to prove that the targeted party knows, has done, or has said something. Nonrepudiation is often considered a benefit for data security purposes. However, nonrepudiation can be used to invade privacy. For example, individuals having a meeting in a private home may want privacy, so others do not have knowledge of the meeting. However, an unauthorized entity may deploy a surveillance device, such as a drone, to record a video of the meeting on the private property and share with others to provide nonrepudiation, in order to prove that such a meeting occurred.
- **Detectability**—Without having access to the data, a threat actor knows it exists. Existence of data is sufficient to infer more sensitive information. For example, by detecting that a celebrity has a health record in a rehabilitation facility, one can infer the celebrity has an addiction, even without having access to the actual record.
- **Information disclosure**—Sensitive information is exposed to unauthorized individuals. For example, employees talk about a specific client's personal information while at a crowded public restaurant and others within earshot listen.
- **Content unawareness**—The entity providing the information is unaware of the information that is being disclosed. For example, an individual submits a message to a bank through an online form and provides more information than necessary on the form to support the message. Then, the information is received by a staff member supporting the messaging service who should not have seen that type of personal information.
- **Policy and consent noncompliance**—A process, system, application or network collects, shares, uses or safeguards personal information in violation of the enterprise's established privacy policies, posted privacy notice or applicable legal requirements. For example, an enterprise's posted privacy notice states that personal data will be encrypted in all storage locations, but servers behind the enterprise's firewall, or within a contracted entity's server storage, do not encrypt the personal data in storage.

Methods for Exploiting Vulnerabilities

Many types of methods are used to exploit vulnerabilities, leading to privacy breaches and other types of privacy harms. More methods to exploit vulnerabilities emerge as time goes on. Some commonly used methods are shown in **figure 1.10.**

Figure 1.10—Methods for Exploiting Vulnerabilities

Category	Subcategory	Description
Social engineering	Phishing	Phishing is a type of email attack that attempts to convince a user that the originator is genuine, but with the intention of obtaining information for use in social engineering.
	Vishing	Vishing are scams over traditional phones, voice email or Voice over Internet Protocol (VoIP) calls.
	Spear phishing	Spear phishing uses social engineering techniques that allow an attacker to masquerade as a trusted party to obtain important information, such as passwords, from the victim.
	Whaling	Whaling is a specific kind of phishing that targets high-ranking enterprise officials.
	Cat phishing	Cat phishers create fake identities on dating apps and social media to coax targets into fake online relationships. They often quickly move to personal channels such as phone or email, using the target's trust to acquire money or personal information that helps them hide their criminal activities.
Identity theft		Identity theft is wrongfully obtaining and using another person's identifying information in a way that involves fraud or deception.
Identity fraud		Identity theft and identity fraud are terms used to refer to crimes that involve someone wrongfully obtaining and using another person's personal data in a way that involves fraud or deception, typically for economic gain.
Keystroke monitoring		Keystroke monitoring is the process used to view or record both the keystrokes entered by a computer user and the computer's response during an interactive session. Keystroke monitoring is usually considered a special case of audit trails. It is also used to capture victim's user IDs, passwords, and other sensitive and personal information.
Identity spoofing	Digital spoofing	Digital messages appear to be from someone the recipient knows, or may know, but they are actually from cyber crooks.
	Phone spoofing	Local area codes make it appear as though someone in the same town or neighborhood is calling.
	Physical mail spoofing	Postal letters or packages are sent from what is represented to be a government agency or business enterprise, but the sender is really a criminal.

Figure 1.10—Methods for Exploiting Vulnerabilities *(cont.)*

Category	Subcategory	Description
Eavesdropping		An intruder gathers the information flowing through the network with the intent of acquiring and releasing the message contents either for personal analysis or for third parties that might have commissioned such eavesdropping. This is significant when considering that sensitive information traversing a network—including email, passwords and, in some cases, keystrokes—can be seen in real time by all other machines. Eavesdropping activities can enable the intruder to gain unauthorized access, to use information such as credit card accounts fraudulently, and to compromise the confidentiality of sensitive information that could jeopardize or harm an individual's or an enterprise's reputation.
Ransomware		Ransomware is a type of malicious software, or malware, designed to deny access to a computer system or data until a ransom is paid. Ransomware typically spreads when victims are duped by phishing emails, or when they unknowingly visit infected websites. Ransomware can be devastating to an individual or an enterprise. Anyone with important data stored on a computer or network is at risk, including government or law enforcement agencies, healthcare systems, and other critical infrastructure entities. Recovery can be a difficult process that may require the services of a reputable data recovery specialist. Some victims pay to recover their files, but there are no guarantees of recovery even if victims meet the ransom demands.
Digital identity spoofing		Identity spoofing refers to assuming the identity of some other entity (human or nonhuman) and then using that identity to accomplish a goal. An adversary may craft messages that appear to come from a different principal or use stolen/spoofed authentication credentials. Alternatively, adversaries may intercept messages from legitimate senders and attempt to make it look like the messages come from them, without changing the content. This form of attack can be used to hijack credentials from legitimate users. Identity spoofing attacks are not limited to transmitted messages; any resource associated with an identity (e.g., a file with a signature) can be the target of an adversary who attempts to change the apparent identity. This type of attack differs from content spoofing attacks in which the adversary does not wish to change the apparent identity of the message but instead wishes to change what the message says. In an identity spoofing attack, the adversary is attempting to change the identity of the content.
Exploiting known vulnerabilities in devices		Using descriptions of device vulnerabilities, adversaries access device software, data, firmware or other components.
Exploiting known vulnerabilities in applications		Using descriptions of applications vulnerabilities, such as cross-site scripting, structured query language (SQL) injection, command injection, path traversal and insecure server configuration, adversaries gain access into networks, databases and other digital assets.

Figure 1.10—Methods for Exploiting Vulnerabilities *(cont.)*		
Category	**Subcategory**	**Description**
Adversarial AI and machine learning attacks		Examples include: • Training phase attacks that attempt to acquire or influence the machine learning training data or model • Data access attacks that access some or all of the training data and use it to create a substitute model • Testing (inference) phase attacks that test the effectiveness of the data substitutions • Poisoning, also known as causative, attacks that involve altering the data or model indirectly or directly Logic corruption is accomplished by an adversary who can tamper with the machine learning algorithm to alter the machine learning process and model itself.
Source: Data from The MITRE Corporation, "Common Attack Pattern Enumeration and Classification," *https://capec.mitre.org/*; Federal Communications Commission, "Scam Glossary," *www.fcc.gov/scam-glossary*; National Institute of Standards and Technology, "Computer Security Resource Center," *https://csrc.nist.gov/glossary*; National Institute of Standards and Technology, "A Taxonomy and Terminology of Adversarial Machine Learning," USA, 2019; United States Cybersecurity and Infrastructure Security Agency, "Ransomware," *https://us-cert.cisa.gov/Ransomware*; and United States Government Accountability Office, "Cybercrime: Public and Private Entities Face Challenges in Addressing Cyber Threats," USA, 2007		

1.12.3 Privacy Harms and Problems

The NIST Privacy Risk Assessment Methodology[43] provides a useful catalog listing a non-exhaustive, illustrative set of problems, or harms, that individuals may experience as the result of personal data processing or their interactions with systems, products or services, along with harms caused by unauthorized use of personal data.

Examples of Common Privacy Harms

Figure 1.11 lists common privacy harms.

Figure 1.11—Common Privacy Harms Examples	
Privacy Harm	**Description**
Dignity loss	Embarrassment and emotional distress can result. For example, when explicit scenes showing the victims of a violent incident are published online and made publicly available, surviving family members could be deeply emotionally distressed.
Discrimination	Unfair or unethical differential treatment of individuals, whether singly or as a group, can arise from the processing of data. This includes the harms of stigmatization and power imbalance.
Economic loss	Direct financial losses or the inability to receive fair value in a transaction can result from identity theft.

Figure 1.11—Common Privacy Harms Examples	
Privacy Harm	Description
Loss of self-determination	An individual can lose personal sovereignty or the ability to freely make choices. This includes the harms of loss of autonomy, exclusion and loss of liberty. • **Loss of autonomy**—loss of control over information processing or interactions with systems/products/services, and needless changes in ordinary behavior, including self-imposed restrictions on expression or civic engagement • **Exclusion—**failure to provide individuals with notice and input about their associated personal data records, e.g., when an enterprise sells its customer call history to marketing agencieswithout the customer's knowledge or consent • **Loss of liberty—**improper exposure to arrest or detainment due to incomplete or inaccurate data; abuses of governmental power due to improper exposure or use of information
Physical harm	Physical harm or death can result, e.g., when a stalker social engineers the authentication information for the intended victim's location-tracking car capability and then uses that access to locate and assault the victim.
Loss of trust	The breach of implicit or explicit expectations or agreements about the processing of data can diminish morale or leave individuals reluctant to engage in further transactions, potentially creating larger economic or civic consequences.

Examples of Problematic Data Actions Related to Data Processing

The NIST Privacy Risk Assessment Methodology[44] provides a useful catalog listing a non-exhaustive, illustrative set of problematic data actions that individuals could experience as the result of data processing, or as a consequence of their interactions with systems, products or services.

Figure 1.12 lists some common problematic data actions.

Figure 1.12—Problematic Data Actions Related to Data Processing	
Problematic Data Action	Description
Appropriation	Data are used in ways that exceed an individual's expectation or authorization, either implicit or explicit. Appropriation includes scenarios in which the individual would have expected additional value for the use of the data, if given more complete information or negotiating power. Privacy problems that can result from appropriation include loss of trust, loss of autonomy, and economic loss.
Distortion	Inaccurate, misleading or incomplete data are used or disseminated. Distortion can present users in an inaccurate, unflattering or disparaging manner, opening the door to stigmatization, discrimination, or loss of liberty.
Induced disclosure	Induced disclosure can occur when individuals feel compelled to provide information disproportionate to the purpose or outcome of the transaction. Induced disclosure can include leveraging access or rights to an essential or perceived essential service. Induced disclosure can lead to problems such as discrimination, loss of trust, or loss of autonomy.
Insecurity	Lapses in data security can result in various problems, including loss of trust, loss of dignity, exposure to economic loss, and other identity theft-related harms.

Figure 1.12—Problematic Data Actions Related to Data Processing *(cont.)*	
Problematic Data Action	Description
Re-identification	De-identified data, or data otherwise disassociated from specific individuals, becomes identifiable or associated with specific individuals again. This can lead to problems such as discrimination, loss of trust, or loss of dignity.
Stigmatization	Data are linked to an actual identity in such a way as to create a stigma that can cause dignity losses or discrimination. For example, transactional or behavioral data, such as accessing certain services (e.g., food stamps or unemployment benefits) or locations (e.g., healthcare providers), may allow inferences about individuals that can cause dignity losses or discrimination.
Surveillance	Data, devices or individuals are tracked or monitored in a manner disproportionate to the purpose. The difference between benign action and problematic data action can be narrow. Tracking or monitoring may be conducted for operational purposes, such as cybersecurity or to provide better services, but it can become surveillance when it leads to problems such as discrimination; loss of trust, autonomy or liberty; or physical harm.
Unanticipated revelation	Data reveal or expose an individual or facets of an individual in unexpected ways. Unanticipated revelation can arise from aggregation and analysis of large or diverse data sets. Unanticipated revelation can give rise to dignity losses, discrimination, and loss of trust and autonomy.
Unwarranted restriction	Unwarranted restriction includes blocking access to data or services, and limiting awareness of the existence of data or their uses in ways that are disproportionate to operational purposes. Operational purposes include fraud detection or other compliance processes. When individuals do not know what data an entity has or can make use of, they do not have the opportunity to participate in decision-making. Unwarranted restriction diminishes accountability regarding the appropriateness of the entity possessing the data, or whether the data will be used in a fair and equitable manner. Lack of access to data or services can lead to problems including loss of self-determination, loss of trust, and economic harm.

1.13 Privacy Impact Assessment

A PIA is an analysis of how personal information is collected, used, shared and maintained for a specified scope of consideration. PIAs are structured processes for identifying and mitigating privacy risks, including risks to confidentiality. PIAs are used within a defined information system. The scope of these defined information systems may span physical processes, administrative processes, technical processes, or a combination of one or more of these three categories.

After identifying risks, the next step in the PIA is to provide analysis to support informed decision-making, identify requirements, and make recommendations for how to mitigate or otherwise respond to the risks.

At a high level a PIA has four general goals:

1. Ensuring conformance with applicable legal, regulatory, contractual and policy requirements for privacy
2. Determining the threats, vulnerabilities, effects (harms and problems), and resulting risks
3. Evaluating protections and alternative processes for mitigating identified privacy risks
4. Developing a prioritization process for implementing the mitigation processes and associated privacy practices

A PIA should be performed using a methodology that is often established through a government or industry standard or regulation. Using a methodology ensures the PIA process is repeatable and can be consistently performed from one PIA project to the next. Before choosing a specific PIA process, privacy engineers and privacy practitioners should check to see if regulators have published specific guidance applicable to the scope of the PIA. If an enterprise operates in multiple jurisdictions, it is usually most efficient for privacy engineers and other practitioners to combine PIA methodologies and use the strictest approaches to avoid duplication of reassessment. Other specifically defined types of PIAs include a privacy risk assessment[45] and DPIA.

Privacy practitioners typically lead PIA projects, but do not perform them on their own. A typical PIA team includes:

- Privacy practitioners
- Information security practitioners
- IT department contact
- Representative from the business unit where the PIA is being performed
- Third-party representatives, if their enterprises are within the PIA scope
- Legal department contact
- HR department contact, if appropriate for the PIA scope
- Physical security department practitioner, if part of the PIA scope
- Public relations department contact, if part of the PIA scope
- Marketing and sales department contact, if part of the PIA scope

A PIA should be carried out whenever there is a change that is likely to involve a new use or to significantly change the way personal data are handled, e.g., when a redesign of an existing process or service, or a new process or information asset is introduced.[46] The following are types of events should trigger a PIA:

- System conversions
- Significant system management changes
- Mergers
- New intercompany data flows or collection processes
- New technologies within the enterprise's digital ecosystem (e.g., IoT devices, surveillance systems)
- A privacy breach
- Preparation for a privacy certification audit
- Implementation of new types of data handling technologies, such as AI, blockchain, RPA, and IoT devices and related systems

1.13.1 Established PIA Methodologies

A variety of PIA methodologies have been published and used in the last 20 years. This section provides a few examples to demonstrate how a PIA can follow different methodologies but still meet similar goals.

US Government PIAs

Section 208 of the E-Government Act of 2002[47] requires each federal agency to:

- Conduct a PIA
- Ensure the review of the PIA by the chief information officer (CIO) or equivalent official, as determined by the head of the agency

- Make the PIA publicly available on the website of the agency, through publication in the *Federal Register*, or by other means, if practicable, following the CIO's review

Per the E-Government Act, each federal agency must ensure the PIA is commensurate with the size of the information system being assessed, the sensitivity of information in identifiable form in that system, and the risk of harm from unauthorized release of that information.

The E-Government Act[48] also requires each PIA to address and document:

- What information will be collected
- Why the information will be collected
- The agency's intended use of the information
- With whom the information will be shared
- What notice or opportunities for consent will be provided to individuals regarding the information being collected and how that information will be shared
- How the information will be secured
- Whether a system of records will be created under the Privacy Act

The Office of Management Budget (OMB) provides specific requirements for performing PIAs.[49] They include the following high-level requirements:

- Each federal agency must conduct a PIA before
  - Developing or procuring IT systems or projects that collect, maintain or disseminate information in identifiable form, from or about members of the public;
  - Initiating, consistent with the Paperwork Reduction Act, a new electronic information collection system in identifiable form for 10 or more persons (excluding agencies, instrumentalities or employees of the federal government).
- PIAs must be performed and updated as necessary when a system change creates new privacy risks.

In addition to the legally required activities, the E-Government Act authorizes the director of OMB to require agencies to conduct PIAs of existing electronic information systems or ongoing collections of information in identifiable form as the director deems appropriate.

The Office of Personnel Management (OPM) also provides a PIA methodology in the Privacy Impact Assessment Guide[50] to support the E-Government Act PIA requirements.

The NIST Privacy Framework[51] can be a useful tool to support PIAs.

Canadian Government PIAs

The Office of the Privacy Commissioner (OPC) of Canada provides an abundance of direction and tools for performing PIAs. "Expectations: OPC's Guide to the Privacy Impact Assessment Process" describes a PIA as "a risk management process that helps institutions ensure they meet legislative requirements and identify the impacts their programs and activities will have on an individuals' privacy."[52]

The OPC notes that programs should incorporate good practices to minimize negative impacts on individuals' privacy. It also notes that the PIA may not completely eliminate the risk but should be used to help identify and manage the risk.

According to the OPC, a PIA is not:

- A superficial legal checklist
- A one-time exercise
- A marketing tool that only shows the benefits of a project
- A justification for policies already decided, or practices already in place
- Necessarily long, complicated and resource-intensive

PIAs are required:

- When personal information may be used as part of a decision-making process that directly affects the individual
- When there are major changes to existing programs or activities that may use personal information for an administrative purpose (meaning as part of a decision-making process that directly affects the individual)
- When there are major changes to existing programs or activities as a result of contracting out or transferring programs or activities to another level of government or to the private sector

While the tools and materials provided on the Canadian Privacy Commissioner's site are meant to support Canada's legal requirements for performing PIAs, the tools and information can also be very helpful for enterprises in other countries to establish their own PIA methodologies.

Singapore Government DPIAs

The Personal Data Protection Commission Singapore (PDPC) provides a guide to performing DPIAs.[53]

The PDPC DPIA methodology can be conducted on systems (e.g., public-facing websites, cloud storage platforms, customer relationship management systems) and processes (e.g., going through a health screening and receiving the medical report, purchasing an item from an online portal and receiving the item from a courier). The key tasks for performing a DPIA include:

- Identifying the personal data handled by the system or process, and the reasons for collecting the personal data
- Identifying how the personal data flows through the system or process
- Identifying data protection risks by analyzing the personal data handled and its data flows against PDPA requirements or data protection best practices
- Addressing the identified risks by amending the system or process design, or introducing new enterprise policies
- Checking to ensure that identified risks are adequately addressed before the system or process is in effect or implemented

Specific examples of when to perform DPIAs include:

- Creating a new system that involves handling personal data (e.g., new website that collects personal data)
- Creating a new automated or manual process that involves the handling of personal data (e.g. receptionist collecting personal data from visitors)
- Changing the way existing systems or processes handle personal data (e.g., redesign of the customer registration process)
- Changing the enterprise structure that affects the department handling personal data (e.g., mergers and acquisitions, restructuring)

Philippines Government PIAs

The Philippines government provides a guide[54] to conducting PIAs. The guide emphasizes that a PIA is a process that begins at the earliest possible stages of an initiative, when there are still opportunities to influence its outcome and thereby ensure privacy by design. It is a process that continues until, and even after, the project has been deployed. The guide includes the following:

- Project/system description
- Threshold analysis
- Stakeholder engagement
- Personal data flows
- Privacy impact analysis
- Privacy risk management
- Recommended privacy solutions

United Kingdom Government DPIAs

The United Kingdom Information Commissioner's Office (ICO) published guidance for how to perform DPIAs.[55] In addition to providing a sample DPIA template, it provides a mechanism to contact the ICO with questions about performing DPIAs.

Some key UK DPIA compliance requirements include:

- Describing the nature, scope, context and purposes of the processing
- Assessing necessity, proportionality and compliance measures
- Identifying and assessing risks to individuals
- Identifying additional measures to mitigate those risks

The guidance stresses that to adequately assess the level of privacy risk, entities must consider both the likelihood and the severity of any impact on individuals. For example, the guidance indicates that high risk could result from either a high probability of some harm, or a lower possibility of serious harm.

1.13.2 NIST Privacy Risk Assessment Methodology

The NIST Privacy Risk Assessment Methodology (PRAM) is a tool that applies the risk model from NISTIR 8062[56] and helps enterprises analyze, assess and prioritize privacy risks to determine their responses and select appropriate solutions. The PRAM can help drive collaboration and communication between various components of an enterprise, including privacy, cybersecurity, business and IT personnel.

Unlike an information security risk assessment, the PRAM considers how processing personal information in authorized and unauthorized ways can create problems for the associated individuals (data subjects). Privacy risk factors considered in a PRAM include:

- **Likelihood**—a contextual analysis that a data action is likely to create a problem for a representative set of individuals
- **Problematic data actions**—See section 1.12.3 Privacy Harms and Problems for more information
- **Impacts**—An analysis of the costs should the problem occur

Conducting a PRAM helps an enterprise identify privacy risks created by the system, product or service of considered scope, and prioritize them to make informed decisions about how to respond to the identified risks. Once

it has determined which risks to mitigate, the enterprise can refine the privacy requirements and then select and implement controls, such as technical capabilities and policy and procedures safeguards, to meet the defined requirements.

An enterprise may use a variety of sources to select controls, such as *NIST SP 800-53: Security and Privacy Controls for Information Systems and Organizations.* After implementing controls, an enterprise should iteratively assess the controls for their effectiveness in meeting the privacy requirements and managing privacy risk. In this way, an enterprise creates traceability between the controls and the privacy requirements, and demonstrates accountability between the enterprise's systems, products and services, and its organizational privacy goals.

Privacy risk management is not a static process. An enterprise's privacy engineers, and other supporting privacy practitioners, need to monitor how changes in the business environment and corresponding changes to its systems, products, and services affect privacy risk and then repeat the practices, such as those described in the *NIST Privacy Framework*, to adjust accordingly.

Tools found within the PRAM to support performing a privacy risk assessment include:

- Worksheet 1: Framing Business Objectives and Organizational Privacy Governance
- Worksheet 2: Assessing System Design; Supporting Data Map
- Worksheet 3: Prioritizing Risk
- Worksheet 4: Selecting Controls
- Catalog of Problematic Data Actions and Problems

1.13.3 EU GDPR DPIA Methodology

The EU GDPR[57] requires DPIAs to be performed in 11 different situations:

1. When the personal data being processed could pose a high risk to the data subjects if an incident were to occur
2. When processing old data sets or personal data
3. Prior to the first time any new business process involving personal data is completed
4. Where a business process involving personal data has not undergone a DPIA in the past
5. When personal data, including IP addresses, are being used to make decisions regarding a data subject (profiling)
6. When public areas are being monitored on a large scale
7. When sensitive categories of data, criminal data, or national security data are being processed on a large scale (not personal data from patients or clients)
8. If a business process incorporates a new technology
9. If a business process involves automated decision making, i.e., "the ability to make decisions by technological means without human involvement"
10. When processing personal data involves the systematized processing of personal data
11. When there is a change of the risk represented by processing operations

For the GDPR, a DPIA is not mandatory when processing personal data involves personal data from patients or clients by an individual physician, other healthcare professionals, or lawyers. However, in some jurisdictions it is mandatory. Legal counsel should provide advice as to what is applicable to the enterprise.

The GDPR requires a DPIA to contain at least the following information:

- A systematic description of the envisaged processing operations and the purposes of the processing, including, where applicable, the legitimate interest pursued by the controller

- An assessment of the necessity and proportionality of the processing operations in relation to the purposes—an assessment of risks to the rights and freedoms of data subjects referred to, and the measures envisaged to address the risks, including safeguards, security measures and mechanisms to ensure the protection of personal data and to demonstrate compliance with this Regulation considering the rights and legitimate interests of data subjects and other persons concerned.

Article 36 of the GDPR describes the situations when the enterprise (data controller) must consult with the applicable supervisory authority.

---

1 ISACA, *ISACA Privacy Principles and Program Management Guide,* USA, 2016
2 CourtListener, *Roberson v. Rochester Folding Box Co.,* 64 N.E. 442 (N.Y. 1902), www.courtlistener.com/opinion/3641834/roberson-v-rochester-folding-box-co/
3 *Ibid.*
4 GDPRHub, "Rb. Gelderland - C/05/368427," 23 May 2020, https://gdprhub.eu/index.php?title=Rb._Gelderland_-_C/05/368427
5 The European Parliament and the Council of the European Union, *General Data Protection Regulation,* 27 April 2016, https://eur-lex.europa.eu/legal-content/EN/TXT/HTML/?uri=CELEX:32016R0679&qid=1499881815698&from=EN
6 United States Department of Health and Human Services, "Rite Aid Agrees to Pay $1 Million to Settle HIPAA Privacy Case," 7 June 2017, www.hhs.gov/hipaa/for-professionals/compliance-enforcement/examples/rite-aid/index.html
7 Digital Advertising Alliance (DAA), "DAA Self-Regulatory Principles," https://digitaladvertisingalliance.org/principles
8 *Op cit* ISACA 2016
9 North American Energy Standards Board (NAESB), "The NAESB Energy Provider Interface Model Business Practices Information Page," www.naesb.org/ESPI_Standards.asp
10 American Farm Bureau Federation, "Privacy and Security Principles for Farm Data," www.fb.org/issues/innovation/data-privacy/privacy-and-security-principles-for-farm-data
11 European Commission, "European Framework for Safer Mobile Use by Younger Teenagers and Children," https://ec.europa.eu/digital-single-market/en/european-framework-safer-mobile-use-younger-teenagers-and-children
12 Infocomm Media Development Authority, "APEC Privacy Recognition for Processors (PRP) Certification," www.imda.gov.sg/programme-listing/Privacy-Recognition-for-Processors-Certification
13 Bioethics Advisory Committee Singapore, *Ethics Guidelines for Biomedical Research,* Singapore, June 2015, www.bioethics-singapore.gov.sg/files/publications/reports/ethics-guidelines-for-human-biomedical-research-report-only.pdf
14 *Op cit* ISACA 2016
15 HHS.gov, "Informed Consent FAQs," www.hhs.gov/ohrp/regulations-and-policy/guidance/faq/informed-consent/index.html
16 *Op cit* ISACA 2016
17 Herold, Rebecca,.; *Managing an Information Security and Privacy Awareness and Training Program,* 2nd Edition, CDC Press, USA, 2010
18 *Op cit* European Parliament
19 HHS.gov, "Enforcement Highlights," www.hhs.gov/hipaa/for-professionals/compliance-enforcement/data/enforcement-highlights/index.html
20 *Op cit* European Parliament
21 US Department of Justice, "Privacy Act of 1974," www.justice.gov/opcl/privacy-act-1974
22 *Op cit* Herold
23 *Op cit* ISACA 2016
24 *Op cit* European Parliament
25 *Op cit* ISACA 2016
26 *Op cit* European Parliament
27 US Department of Health and Human Services, *HIPAA Administrative Simplification Regulation Text,* 26 March 2013, www.hhs.gov/sites/default/files/ocr/privacy/hipaa/administrative/combined/hipaa-simplification-201303.pdf
28 National Institute of Standards and Technology, *NIST Privacy Framework: A Tool for Improving Privacy Through Enterprise Risk Management,* USA, 2020, https://nvlpubs.nist.gov/nistpubs/CSWP/NIST.CSWP.01162020.pdf.
29 *Ibid.*
30 *Op Cit* ISACA 2016
31 *Ibid.*
32 *Op cit* Herold
33 *Ibid.*
34 *Ibid.*
35 ISACA, *Implementing a Privacy Protection Program: Using COBIT® 5 Enablers With the ISACA Privacy Principles,* USA, 2017
36 *Op cit* ISACA 2016
37 *Ibid.*
38 *Ibid.*
39 Anisimowicz, J.; "Ensuring Vendor Compliance and Third-Party Risk Mitigation." *ISACA Journal,* Vol. 5, 23 October 2019
40 *Op cit* ISACA 2016
41 Cooke, I.; "IS Audit Basics: Auditing Data Privacy," *ISACA Journal*, Vol. 3, 1 May 2018
42 ISACA, *Continuous Oversight in the Cloud: How to Improve Cloud Security, Privacy and Compliance*, USA, 2019.
43 National Institute of Standards and Technology, *NIST Privacy Risk Assessment Methodology,* USA, 2019, www.nist.gov/itl/applied-cybersecurity/privacy-engineering/resources
44 *Ibid.*

[45] National Institute of Standards and Technology, "Risk Assessment Tools," 28 October 2018, www.nist.gov/itl/applied-cybersecurity/privacy-engineering/collaboration-space/focus-areas/risk-assessment/tools

[46] *Op cit* ISACA 2016

[47] Govinfo, "Public Law 107 - 347 - E-Government Act of 2002," www.govinfo.gov/app/details/PLAW-107publ347

[48] Office of Management and Budget, *M-03-22, OMB Guidance for Implementing the Privacy Provisions of the E-Government Act of 2002,* USA, 2003, https://www.justice.gov/opcl/page/file/1131721/download

[49] *Ibid.*

[50] United States Office of Personnel Management, "Privacy Impact Assessment (PIA) Guide," 22 April 2010, www.opm.gov/information-management/privacy-policy/privacy-references/piaguide.pdf

[51] *Op cit* NIST Privacy Framework 2020

[52] Office of the Privacy Commissioner of Canada, "Expectations: OPC's Guide to the Privacy Impact Assessment Process," 3 March 2020, www.priv.gc.ca/en/privacy-topics/privacy-impact-assessments/gd_exp_202003/

[53] Personal Data Protection Commission Singapore, "Guide to Data Protection Impact Assessments," 1 November 2017, www.pdpc.gov.sg/-/media/Files/PDPC/PDF-Files/Other-Guides/guide-to-dpias—-011117.pdf

[54] National Privacy Commission, *NPC Privacy Toolkit: A Guide for Management & Data Protection Officers*, Singapore, 2018

[55] Information Commissioner's Office, "Data protection impact assessments," https://ico.org.uk/for-organisations/guide-to-data-protection/guide-to-the-general-data-protection-regulation-gdpr/accountability-and-governance/data-protection-impact-assessments/

[56] National Institute of Standards and Technology, *NISTIR 8062: An Introduction to Privacy Engineering and Risk Management in Federal Systems,* USA, 2017, https://nvlpubs.nist.gov/nistpubs/ir/2017/NIST.IR.8062.pdf

[57] *Op cit* European Parliament

Chapter 2:

Privacy Architecture

Overview

Part A: Infrastructure

Part B: Applications and Software

Part C: Technical Privacy Controls

Overview

With the arrival of data privacy as a critical legislative focus globally, the architects of systems are now evolving from a data protection-centric architecture to a broader infrastructure architecture that includes:

- Data protection
- Data management
- Data privacy

It is now crucial that the systems that provide the data are protected, but also that the data are classified, protected and used as stated in policies and procedures or as required by law.

The objective of this domain is to ensure that the privacy engineer understands how systems, technologies, protocols and data protection methodologies pertain to a data privacy architecture holistically, and understands the considerations needed when making technology, infrastructure, data protection, risk management and information security decisions.

Domain 2 represents 36 percent (approximately 43 questions) of the exam.

Domain 2: Exam Content Outline

Part A: Infrastructure

1. Technology Stacks
2. Cloud-Based Services
3. Endpoints
4. Remote Access
5. System Hardening

Part B: Applications and Software

1. Secure Development Life Cycle
2. Applications and Software Hardening
3. APIs and Services
4. Tracking Technologies

Part C: Technical Privacy Controls

1. Communication and Transport Protocols
2. Encryption, Hashing and De-identification
3. Key Management
4. Monitoring and Logging
5. Identity and Access Management

Learning Objectives/Task Statements

Within this domain, the data privacy practitioner should be able to:

- Identify the internal and external requirements for the organization's privacy programs and practices
- Coordinate and perform privacy impact assessment (PIA) and other privacy-focused assessments

- Participate in the development of procedures that align with privacy policies and business needs
- Implement procedures that align with privacy policies
- Participate in the management and evaluation of contracts, service level agreements, and practices of vendors and other external parties
- Collaborate with other practitioners to ensure that privacy programs and practices are followed during the design, development and implementation of systems, applications and infrastructure
- Evaluate the enterprise architecture and information architecture to ensure it supports privacy by design principles and considerations
- Evaluate advancements in privacy-enhancing technologies and changes in the regulatory landscape
- Identify, validate and implement appropriate privacy and security controls according to data classification procedures
- Design, implement and monitor processes and procedures to keep the inventory and dataflow records current

Suggested Resources for Further Study

Breaux, Travis; *An Introduction to Privacy for Technology Professionals,* International Association of Privacy Professionals, USA, 2014

Cloud Security Alliance, *CSA Security Guidance for Critical Areas of Focus in Cloud Computing, v4.0*, USA, 2017

Cloud Security Alliance, "Guideline on Effectively Managing Security Service in the Cloud," 2018, www.csaapac.org/cssm.html

International Organization for Standardization, *ISO/IEC/IEEE 15288:2015: Systems and Software Engineering – System Life Cycle Processes*, Switzerland, 2015

ISACA, *Cybersecurity Fundamentals Study Guide,* 2nd Edition, USA, 2017

ISACA, *ISACA Privacy Principles and Program Management Guide,* USA, 2016

National Institute of Standards and Technology, *NIST Special Publication SP 800-145: The NIST Definition of Cloud Computing*, USA, 2011

National Institute of Standards and Technology, *NISTIR 8062: An Introduction to Privacy Engineering and Risk Management in Federal Systems,* USA, 2017

Shaw, Thomas J; *DPO Handbook: Data Protection Officers Under the GDPR,* Second Edition, USA, 2018

Page intentionally left blank

Self-assessment Questions

CDPSE self-assessment questions support the content in this manual and provide an understanding of the type and structure of questions that typically appear on the exam. Often a question will require the candidate to choose the **MOST** likely or **BEST** answer among the options provided. Note that these questions are not actual or retired exam items. See the "About This Manual" section for more guidance regarding practice questions.

1. Which of the following **BEST** describes an advantage of using cloud computing over on-premises infrastructure?

   A. More control over the system
   B. Low downtime
   C. Increased scalability
   D. Increased security

2. An organization is proposing to establish a wireless local area network (WLAN). Which of the following would be the **MOST** appropriate recommendation for security control for the WLAN?

   A. Physically secure wireless access points to prevent tampering.
   B. Use service set identifiers that clearly identify the organization.
   C. Encrypt traffic using the Wired Equivalent Privacy mechanism.
   D. Implement the Simple Network Management Protocol to allow active monitoring.

3. Which of the following **BEST** provides message integrity, authentication of sender's identity, and nonrepudiation?

   A. Symmetric cryptography
   B. Message hashing
   C. Message authentication code
   D. Public key infrastructure

Answers on page 80

Chapter 2 Answer Key

Self-Assessment Questions

1. A. Self-managed, or on-premises, infrastructures allow enterprises more control over their systems as they do not need to rely on third parties for management.
   B. Self-managed infrastructures provide lower latency than cloud computing infrastructures.
   C. Cloud computing infrastructures typically offer a pay-as-you-go model for services as opposed to self-managed systems that require significant upfront costs.
   D. In general, self-managed infrastructure is considered more secure than cloud-based infrastructure because of the control provided to the IT and DevOps teams when designing and creating the infrastructure.

2. **A. Physically securing access points, such as wireless routers, prevents theft and addresses the risk of malicious parties tampering with device settings. If access points can be physically reached, it is often a simple matter to restore weak default passwords and encryption keys or to totally remove authentication and encryption from the network.**
   B. Service set identifiers should not be used to identify the organization because hackers can associate the wireless local area network with a known organization, which can increase both their motivation to attack and, potentially, make the information available to do so.
   C. The original Wired Equivalent Privacy security mechanism has been demonstrated to have a number of exploitable weaknesses. The more recently developed Wi-Fi Protected Access and Wi-Fi Protected Access 2 standards represent considerably more secure means of authentication and encryption.
   D. Installing Simple Network Management Protocol (SNMP) on wireless access points can actually open up security vulnerabilities. If SNMP is required at all, then SNMP v3, which has stronger authentication mechanisms than earlier versions, should be deployed.

3. A. Symmetric cryptography provides confidentiality.
   B. Hashing can provide integrity and confidentiality
   C. Message authentication codes provide integrity.
   D. Public key infrastructure (PKI) combines public key encryption with a trusted third party to publish and revoke digital certificates that contain the public key of the sender. Senders can digitally sign a message with their private key and attach their digital certificate (provided by the trusted third party). Senders cannot deny that they are authors of the message, thus PKI ensures nonrepudiation. These capabilities simultaneously provide authentication, integrity validation and nonrepudiation.

Part A: Infrastructure

Information and computing systems infrastructures are essential technical components, both physical and virtual, used for collecting, processing, storing, communicating about and distributing data. The size and complexity of any systems infrastructure is relative to its function, the data it processes, and how it processes that data. Infrastructures can be centralized or decentralized (e.g., data centers, colocations, cloud or virtualized instances).

Core components of a computing infrastructure are outlined in **figure 2.1**.

Figure 2.1—Core Components of a Computing Infrastructure

Core Component	Description
Hardware	The physical machines or appliances in an IT Infrastructure that comprise all the elements necessary to support the basic functioning of the infrastructure itself, including: • Computers • Servers • Storage • Switches • Hubs • Routers • Power conditioning • Cooling • Cabling
Software	Software refers to the applications used by the enterprise both for internal business operations and external-facing applications and services, including: • Operating systems • Web servers • Enterprise resource planning • Customer relationship management • Database systems • Office productivity applications • Finance applications • Human resources applications • Business applications or services operated on the hardware

Figure 2.1—Core Components of a Computing Infrastructure (cont.)

Core Component	Description
Network	Network infrastructure refers to the hardware and software necessary to allow internal and external communications with all devices on the network, including: • Internet connectivity • Load balancers • Firewalls (hardware appliance or software-based) • Network management system
People	IT and DevOps engineers are critical to the design, building and maintenance of a computing infrastructure. Additionally, compliance, legal, governance, system administration and end users are part of the infrastructure, as they provide the requirements and guidance on how the infrastructure should support enterprise needs, and the department or use case needs.

Source: Adapted from Techopedia, "IT Infrastructure," *www.techopedia.com/definition/29199/it-infrastructure*

The different types of IT infrastructures are dependent on the size and complexity of the enterprise, the products and services the enterprise offers, and the tools or systems necessary to support the enterprise.

The design and development of an IT infrastructure varies based on the business type and the specific needs of the enterprise. After the specific needs of the enterprise are determined, architectural and system design decisions can be made.

Traditional infrastructure design and implementation requires a mastery of skills ranging from networking, databases and storage to security, monitoring and system health. In the past, these considerations were discussed almost exclusively by business owners and engineers. With the new global focus on data privacy and personally identifiable information (PII), legal and compliance are included in these discussions throughout the infrastructure life cycle.

Because legal and compliance contribute to the infrastructure design and development process, new process steps are now requirements for the system—including data assessment, data classification, data inventory, policies and procedures as they relate to the data within the system. The components of privacy architecture are shown in **figure 2.2**. When properly implemented, a systems infrastructure and privacy architecture will allow the system to adhere to the principles of processing personal information.

Figure 2.2—Components of Privacy Architecture

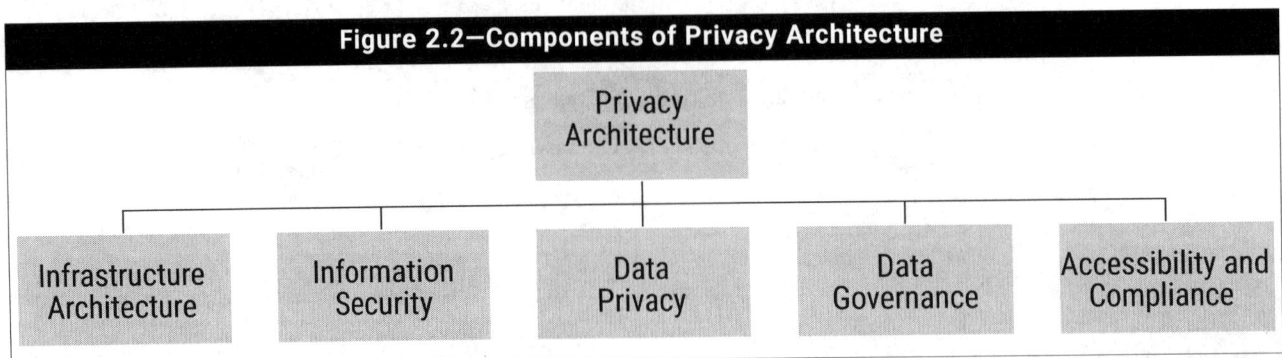

In privacy architecture, the disciplines of information security and data privacy are distinct, but they work together to create a comprehensive solution:

- **Information security** is the protection of information (personal or other) from unauthorized access, use and disclosure.
- **Data privacy** includes rules that govern the collection and processing of personal information within a system, and the data subjects' rights to control their individual personal information, notice and consent.

Understanding global data privacy regulations is essential, because the implementation of technology, policies and procedures that govern the use of data within a system or across the enterprise must follow and comply with these laws. See Chapter 1 Privacy Governance for more information.

2.1 Self-managed Infrastructure, Including Technology Stacks

There are many types of computing infrastructures. The two primary categories are self-managed and cloud-based (**figure 2.3**). Within each, there are different models and a variety of ways infrastructure can be deployed and supported.

Figure 2.3—Data Center Comparison

	Self-Managed Data Center	Cloud-Based Data Center
Location	On-premises/physically accessible	Off-premises/virtualized
Management	Enterprise	Third-party provider
Administration	Internal IT team	Service provider
Reliability	Internal service level agreement with IT department	Service level agreement with provider
Cost	High	Pay-as-you-go
Scalability	Requires procurement, installation and configuration	Instantaneous

A self-managed infrastructure is an infrastructure that is provided on-premises and managed internally by either IT, DevOps or both, depending on the enterprise's services needs and support requirements. This infrastructure type can range from a simple office network or a technology stack that is application- or service-specific, to an enterprise infrastructure providing:

- Networking
- Storage
- Compute and application hosting
- Security
- Centralized logging
- Internet access
- Back-up/disaster recovery
- Power
- Heating, ventilation and air conditioning (HVAC) services
- Redundant services (e.g., circuits, power, cooling)

Every aspect of the design, development and support of these infrastructure types is dependent on the company's IT team.

2.1.1 Non-Cloud Alternatives to On-premises Centers

Some common alternatives to self-managed infrastructures are described in the following sections.

Managed Service Data Centers

A managed data center is a data center model that is deployed, managed and monitored at or from a third-party data center service provider (off-premises). It provides features and functionality similar to that of a standard data center, but through a managed service platform (MSP).

Managed data centers can be partially or entirely managed. A partially managed data center enables enterprises to have some level of shared administrative control over the data center infrastructure or service. In an entirely managed data center, the bulk or all of the back-end data center administration and management is done by the data center provider.[1]

Colocation Data Centers

Colocation (colo) data centers, independently owned off-premises facilities, rent space to other enterprises. The colocation data center is responsible for the building, cooling, redundant power, building security, segregation within the data center, and networking. The enterprise that rents space and core infrastructure from the colo provides and manages its own components (e.g., servers, firewalls, storage) within the colo facility. Colos are considered self-managed facilities with service level agreements (SLAs) covering power, cooling, Internet circuits and physical security of the data center.

2.1.2 The Advantages of a Self-Managed Infrastructure

One of the critical decisions in the design, development and implementation of an IT infrastructure is whether to host the infrastructure on-premises or in a self-managed data center, or to leverage the cloud infrastructure provided by a cloud service provider (CSP).

Understanding the enterprise's needs and requirements, and the market the enterprise is addressing, gives insight into which type of infrastructure is best. Additional considerations include:

- Cost
- Maintenance
- Security
- Availability
- Scale and jurisdiction in light of the infrastructure location
- Applications running within it and the data it processes

Enterprises should compare the advantages and limitations of each infrastructure type.

Control

From the purchase of the hardware systems to the installation, configuration, deployment of software, ongoing maintenance and security of the systems, an on-premises infrastructure is completely managed and internally supported by the enterprise. Control over every aspect of the system is the most significant benefit of a self-managed infrastructure.

Deployment

When leveraging a self-managed infrastructure solution, the enterprise is responsible for maintaining the system, and all related processes and aspects of the system. All deployments in support of the overall infrastructure are handled by internal staff and carried out on the local infrastructure.

Security

In general, a self-managed infrastructure is considered more secure than a cloud-based infrastructure because of the control provided to the IT and DevOps teams when designing and creating the infrastructure. With self-managed systems, enterprises can determine or define the roles, access permissions, and all internal and external connectivity of the infrastructure at every level.

These decisions are made with business objectives, risk tolerance, and specific system security needs in mind. While listed as an advantage, it should not be assumed that security is higher because the environment is self-managed. Proper due diligence in reviewing the business needs, the design of the system, information security, privacy, governance, monitoring, logging and adequate system hardening needs to be completed for this to be true.

Governance

Internal organizational policies and procedures govern self-managed systems built with the collaboration of IT, DevOps, engineering, legal, compliance, and many other internal teams, and the data within those systems. This collaboration prevents the random creation of environments and systems, and the misuse of corporate data or PII—issues that can go unnoticed when leveraging an extensive cloud-based infrastructure.

2.1.3 The Limitations of a Self-Managed Infrastructure

The limitations of a self-managed infrastructure are discussed below.

Cost

The initial funding required to procure the hardware and software necessary to build a complete self-managed infrastructure is usually high compared to the initial costs of leveraging a cloud-based infrastructure. The cost of the self-managed system is a function of the size and desired capabilities of the infrastructure, as defined by the business requirements and the users/enterprise the system supports.

While the initial cost of infrastructure acquisition is one data point for comparing infrastructure options, to accurately calculate the cost of any system, the total cost of ownership (TCO) for the proposed system should also be calculated. The TCO calculation accounts for not only the initial cost of the hardware and software but also the costs associated with research, design, sourcing, purchase, installation, development, training and deployment. Additionally, TCO includes the costs of system management, maintenance, support, downtime, depreciation and system retirement.[2]

System Management

With self-managed systems, system upgrades, patching, monitoring, logging, security, etc., are all functions provided by the IT, DevOps and network operation center (NOC) teams. While having to perform these duties is not a limitation, system management is an operational overhead that can be transferred, like risk, to a service provider.

Doing so decreases the overall cost and provides methods of remediation should the environments not be appropriately maintained or otherwise not adhere to the SLA with the service provider.

Note: The transference of system management to a service provider, while decreasing overall cost and operational overhead, does mean that control over the environment and its data is potentially at risk.

Scalability

Unlike a cloud-based infrastructure, when scaling a self-managed system, the supporting teams need to procure, cable, power, configure and secure the hardware to allow for additional capacity. Unless reserve capacity is already standing by, undertaking the procurement steps to deployment in a production capacity takes time.

System Availability

System availability is a metric that refers to the percentage of time a system is operational, reliable and stable. System uptime, like system management, is guaranteed by internal enterprise resources (IT, DevOps) based on system operational requirements. The higher the system availability needed, the greater the critical infrastructure redundancy required (**figure 2.4**).

Figure 2.4—System Availability

Availability, %	Downtime/Year	Downtime/Month	Downtime/Week
99	3.65 days	7.31 hours	1.68 hours
99.9	8.77 hours	43.83 minutes	10.08 minutes
99.99	52.6 minutes	4.38 minutes	1.01 minutes
99.999	5.26 minutes	26.30 seconds	6.05 seconds
99.9999	31.56 seconds	2.63 seconds	604.8 milliseconds

The factors in calculating availability are mean time between failures (MTBF), the average time that passes between system or component failures, and mean time to repair (MTTR), which is the time needed to recover from a failure.

This necessary redundancy of high-availability infrastructure elements results in a higher overall cost to the system—for physical hardware, for software, and for the people required to maintain, monitor, secure and support it. The additional component costs and operational overhead for system availability are limitations of on-premises systems.

In a cloud-based system, all the needed infrastructure, people, processes, and tools exist so that uptime and availability are more easily facilitated.

2.1.4 Key Privacy Concerns

The understanding or assumption that a self-managed infrastructure is more secure than a cloud-based infrastructure is based on the direct control that engineers have over the infrastructure. This also includes the capabilities of the team building and supporting the infrastructure, and the policies and procedures that govern the use of the infrastructure and the data processed within it. This assumption may not be accurate and should be reviewed during the requirements and design phase of infrastructure planning and development. Proper due diligence must be conducted in reviewing the infrastructure designs and implementation plans for privacy.

Permissions and Access to Systems

Enterprise systems present privacy concerns because data are housed within these systems. Permissions and access control are essential to ensure the right people have access to the right data at the right time. Physical security is also a key issue. Some steps to address privacy considerations include:

- Determine who in the organization has access to the data center
- Log physical access, noting entry and exit, including date/time/duration
- Establish a procedure for regularly auditing access and permissions
- Ensure system/application permissions are role-based
  - What are the roles and the permissions that go with them?
  - Who has access to the system and in what role?
  - Is there a procedure for regularly auditing access and permissions?
  - Is least privilege maintained for all roles?

Logging

Logs present another privacy concern. When considering application or system logging, error logs should include:

- Application errors
- System errors
- Network errors

System access logs to all systems within the stack should include:

- Failed/successful access attempts
- System/date/timestamp/IP address/count/session duration
- Log access—who has it, when logs are accessed, and how often

Change logs should include:

- System changes
- System environment or application parameter adjustments or changes
- Data changes or element changes (integrity)
  - Data edits
    - Changes to data elements from an administrative or privileged account
    - Direct database access
      - System/date/timestamp/IP address/count/session duration

When evaluating log data retention, consider the following:

- Review and establish the duration of log persistence
  - How long do you need the data for analysis?
- Establish an aggregate or view for historical review
  - Reporting
  - Historical system operations and trends analysis
- Review the process of deleting log data
  - Frequency

- Review logs for PII or information that should not be present in the logs
  - Systems should not write PII to the logs.
  - Data changes or element changes (integrity)
- Monitor data edits
  - Changes to data elements from an administrative or privileged account
  - Direct database access
    - System/date/timestamp/IP address/count/session duration

Monitoring and Alerting

In the application, system, logs and environment, systems need to be in place that aggregate, quantify, alert and report on logs and critical events within the system. Escalation paths for immediate attention need to be established and periodically reviewed.

The enterprise also needs to establish parameters and monitor the physical environment of the data center and set alerts if the parameters exceed design thresholds.

Privacy Law Review

Privacy laws impact the handling of data within enterprise systems, so it is essential to review applicable privacy laws.

A gap analysis should be performed to identify overlapping and distinct requirements. This review should guide the creation of policies and procedures for systems and the data they process. Legal, compliance and risk professionals should help determine an operational baseline for privacy compliance. It's important to establish an appropriate interval for the review and adjustment of all applicable privacy laws.

2.2 Cloud Computing

The US National Institute of Standards and Technology (NIST) and the Cloud Security Alliance (CSA) define cloud computing as "a model for enabling ubiquitous, convenient, on-demand network access to a shared pool of configurable computing resources (e.g., networks, servers, storage, applications and services) that can be rapidly provisioned and released with minimal management effort or service provider interaction."[3]

The primary purpose of cloud computing is to outsource the management and delivery of hardware and software resources to third-party companies that specialize in offering a particular service or service options at a much lower price, and with better quality than those operated internally or within a self-managed infrastructure.

By leveraging the cloud, teams of DevOps engineers or the IT department can purchase access to hardware resources based on demand, without the costs and time delays of procuring the hardware independently and maintaining it.

The model for cloud computing, as defined by NIST, is composed of five essential characteristics, three service models and four deployment models. Because of the differences in each of the cloud models, it is imperative that when considering the cloud from a security and data protection perspective, the privacy engineer must understand where the cloud provider's responsibilities end and where the enterprise's begin. These responsibilities will depend on the service model provided by the CSP but are critical when making policy, security, governance and privacy decisions in a cloud environment.

2.2.1 Cloud Data Centers

Cloud data centers provide the same infrastructure elements that traditional on-premises data centers offer and serve the same general purpose. These facilities are physically located off-premises and usually in multiple locations. Access to these data centers is provided over the Internet to many enterprises by the CSP. Depending on the customer's needs, infrastructure is deployed in the following four primary models: private, community, public and hybrid (**figure 2.5**). **Figure 2.6** provides a comparison of the four models.

Figure 2.5—Cloud Computing Deployment Models

Deployment Model	Description of Cloud Infrastructure	To Be Considered
Private cloud	• Operated solely for an organization • May be managed by the organization or a third party • May exist on-premises or off-premises	• Cloud services with minimum risk • May lack scalability and agility of public cloud services
Community cloud	• Shared by several organizations • Supports a specific community that shares a mission or interest • May be managed by the organizations or a third party • May reside on-premises or off-premises	• Same as private cloud, plus: ▪ Possibility that data may be stored with the data of competitors
Public cloud	• Made available to the general public or a large industry group • Owned by an organization selling cloud services	• Same as community cloud, plus: ▪ Possibility that data may be stored in unknown locations and not be easily retrievable
Hybrid cloud	• A composition of two or more clouds (private, community or public) that remain unique entities but are bound together by standardized or proprietary technology that enables data and application portability (e.g., cloud bursting for load balancing between clouds)	• Aggregate risk of merging different deployment models • Benefit of classification and labeling to ensure that data are assigned to the correct cloud type

Figure 2.6—Cloud Deployment Model Comparison

	Private	Community	Public	Hybrid
Scalability	Limited	Limited	Very High	Very High
Security	Most Secure	Very Secure	Moderately Secure	Very Secure
Performance	Very Good	Very Good	Low to Medium	Good
Reliability	Very High	Very High	Medium	Medium to High
Cost	High	Medium	Low	Medium

Source: Pal, D.; S. Chakraborty; A. Nag; "Cloud Computing: A Paradigm Shift in IT Infrastructure," *CSI Communications*, Vol. 38, January 2015

2.2.2 Essential Characteristics of Cloud Computing

There are five essential characteristics of cloud computing:[4]

- **On-demand self-service**—Consumers can automatically provision cloud services (e.g., compute or storage) as needed, without interaction from the service provider.
- **Broad network access**—Cloud resources can be accessed and provisioned through basic network connections supporting multiple devices (e.g., tablets, laptops, phones).
- **Resource pooling**—Through multi-tenancy or virtualization, computing resources are pooled so multiple users can leverage the same hardware more effectively and efficiently.
- **Rapid elasticity**—Cloud systems are elastic in that they can be provisioned, released, sized and resized as needed in real time (by the user or automatically).
- **Measured service**—The term measured service refers to the automatic monitoring or measuring of provisioned cloud services (e.g., storage, processing, bandwidth) by a cloud provider. This measurement is to provide transparency in billing, provide system reporting, and aid in resource allocation and system planning.

2.2.3 Cloud Service Models

Cloud services are diverse, ranging from hardware infrastructure, software services and data storage to operating systems and applications. Depending on the CSP, there are three different cloud delivery models: Infrastructure as a Service (IaaS), Platform as a Service (PaaS) and Software as a Service (SaaS) (**figure 2.7**).

Figure 2.7—Cloud Computing Service Models

Service Model	Definition	To Be Considered
Infrastructure as a Service (IaaS)	IaaS is the capability to provision processing, storage, networks and other fundamental computing resources, offering the customer the ability to deploy and run arbitrary software that may include operating systems and applications. IaaS puts these IT operations into the hands of a third party.	Options to minimize the impact if the cloud provider has a service interruption

Figure 2.7—Cloud Computing Service Models		
Service Model	**Definition**	**To Be Considered**
Platform as a Service (PaaS)	PaaS is the capability to deploy onto the cloud infrastructure customer-created or acquired applications using programming languages and tools supported by the provider.	• Availability • Confidentiality • Privacy and legal liability in the event of a security breach, as databases housing sensitive information will be hosted offsite • Data ownership • Concerns around e-discovery
Software as a Service (SaaS)	Capability to use the provider's applications running on cloud infrastructure. The applications are accessible from various client devices through a thin client interface such as a web browser (e.g., web-based email).	• Who owns the applications? • Where do the applications reside?

Source: ISACA, *Cloud Computing: Business Benefits With Security, Governance and Assurance Perspectives*, USA, 2009, *www.isaca.org/Knowledge-Center/Research/ResearchDeliverables/Pages/Cloud-Computing-Business-Benefits-With-Security-Governance-and-Assurance-Perspective.aspx*

2.2.4 Shared Responsibility Model

The shared responsibility model (SRM) is defined as "a cloud security framework that dictates the security obligations of a CSP and its users to ensure accountability." When an enterprise moves to a public cloud-based infrastructure, it abdicates some, but not all, of the IT security responsibilities to the CSP. The CSP and the enterprise are responsible for different aspects of security within the environment to provide comprehensive coverage (**figure 2.8**).

Figure 2.8—Shared Responsibility Model for Security in the Cloud

On-Premises	IaaS	PaaS	SaaS
User access	User access	User access	User access
Data	Data	Data	Data
Applications	Applications	Applications	Applications (provider-managed)
Operating systems	Operating systems	Operating systems (provider-managed)	Operating systems (provider-managed)
Network traffic	Network traffic	Network traffic (provider-managed)	Network traffic (provider-managed)
Virtualization	Virtualization (provider-managed)	Virtualization (provider-managed)	Virtualization (provider-managed)
Infrastructure	Infrastructure (provider-managed)	Infrastructure (provider-managed)	Infrastructure (provider-managed)
Physical security	Physical security (provider-managed)	Physical security (provider-managed)	Physical security (provider-managed)

[ ] Enterprise-managed [shaded] Provider-managed

Source: TechTarget, "Infrastructure as a Service (IaaS)," *https://searchcloudcomputing.techtarget.com/definition/Infrastructure-as-a-Service-IaaS*

As shown in **figure 2.8**, when an enterprise operates an on-premises or self-managed data center, the company is responsible for the security of the facility, infrastructure and data, and for the applications that run within the data center.

General CSP responsibilities include:

- Provisioning of the physical data center, hardware and networking infrastructure
- Establishing and maintaining the power and redundant power, cooling, fire suppression, flood protection and surveillance of the physical facility and the infrastructure hardware
- Basic network security including firewalls and anti-distributed denial of service (anti-DDoS)
- Security of cloud infrastructure, networking, storage and virtualization (tenant resource isolation and virtualization resource management)
- Multi-tenant identity management and access control
- Secure tenant access to cloud resources
- Security management, operations and infrastructure monitoring
- Service continuity planning and testing

Cloud consumer responsibilities include:

- Identity management and access control of applications within the environment
- Data security
- Security management of systems, devices, applications, hardware and software tools that access the cloud environment

While this model of security is dependent on both the CSP and the customer, any applications or services the customer deploys or operates, and any data they collect are the customer's responsibility. The measures provided by the CSP alone are not sufficient to provide an adequate or compliant level of security for the customer's applications and data. Failure of the customer to implement the proper protection within its public cloud environment exposes the enterprise to risk and vulnerabilities.

The SRM provides a good foundation for assessing a public-cloud environment. Understanding where the handoffs are, the IT and DevOps teams can begin to review the environment at each level and formulate a security plan. Assessment steps include:

1. Conduct a security gap analysis of the application, host, storage and network layers where security is crucial. Understand what the CSP provides and what is required for an application or system to operate in a public cloud.
   a. This is accomplished by reviewing the SRM, business requirements, information security requirements, compliance requirements and legal requirements.
2. Formulate a plan to remediate all identified gaps that fall within these areas.
   a. Implement access management, such as the policy of least access.
   b. Logical segmentation—Segment accounts according to data sensitivity.
   c. Monitoring—Leverage tools to provide early detection of system exposures, insecure configurations and vulnerabilities.
3. Leverage privacy-by-design through training that will enable development teams to plan for and build in security at every stage of the development and implementation life cycle.
4. Build a culture that supports the proactive use, review and practice of both system and data security.
   a. Develop policies and procedures that are easy to read and understand. Make it easy for the team to identify and report issues and concerns.
   b. Train everyone in security best practices and the laws the enterprise must adhere to.
   c. Support and reward those who help raise the bar for system security and data handling.

2.2.5 Advantages of Cloud Computing

Advantages of cloud computing are listed below.

Cost

One of the main differences between the on-premises and cloud infrastructure models is the upfront cost. Because of the significant investment in procuring the hardware, software, staff, facilities and tools necessary to support an on-premises infrastructure implementation, moving to a cloud-based solution is often the more economical approach. Most cloud providers offer their services on a pay-as-you-go basis. Unlike self-managed systems with high upfront costs, the pay-as-you-go model allows enterprises to control their usage of cloud systems and features, and be billed only for the functionality used.

Engineers should properly compare the capital expenses (capex) versus operational expenditures (opex) of on-premises and cloud-based systems. The actual cost of these environment types is directly related to the systems and the scale at which they will be leveraged. Typically, the capex associated with an on-premises system is significantly higher than with a cloud-based system. Cloud-based systems work differently in that the upfront capex is not present, but the opex can be high over the lifecycle of the environment with the pay-as-you-go model (i.e., ingress and egress of data).

Because many factors can affect the size, scale and movement of data within a cloud-based system, the opex is variable and directly proportional to the scale, use and management of the system and cloud accounts. Before choosing an infrastructure type, the key is to use proper due diligence and compare estimated capex versus opex for each model. If moving to the cloud is the desired option, proper policies and procedures for creating cloud environments, costs, scaling, etc., should be in place prior to making the investment.

Security

The security of systems and data within the infrastructure is always a primary concern. CSPs provide baseline protections for their platforms, and consumers supplement that protection with additional security measures specific to their application or infrastructure needs. Because the CSP provides platform security and data protection services as part of its product offering, consumers benefit from the resources and specialization of the CSP in the area of security for those baseline infrastructure elements.

Scalability

The IT needs of every enterprise are different, and they change over time. Traditionally, in an on-premises system, IT or the enterprise estimates capacity requirements, and then all the hardware is purchased to facilitate that anticipated need.

A cloud-based infrastructure allows an enterprise to scale the environment both vertically (up/down) and horizontally (out/in) based on its individual business needs in a pay-as-you-go manner.

Scale Up/Down (Vertical Scaling)

Scaling up is accomplished by adding more resources to an existing system (e.g., central processing unit, memory, disk, network) to reach the desired level of performance from that system. When scaling in a cloud-environment, applications may be moved to different (or more powerful) virtualized instances or hosts. Software can be scaled up by increasing threads for the application's operation or increasing connections.

Scale Out/In (Horizontal Scaling)

Scaling out is a type of capacity expansion that leverages the addition of new hardware as opposed to increasing the capacity of existing equipment (scaling up). Scaling out is typically used in storage systems, which can increase capacity in blocks, thereby maintaining a pay-as-you-go model while increasing both the storage and data traffic capacity in parallel (load balancing).

There are three methods of scaling systems or infrastructure in the cloud.[5]

Scaling Methods

There are three methods of scaling systems or infrastructure in the cloud (**figure 2.9**).

Figure 2.9—Scaling Methods

Scaling Method	Description
Manual scaling	Manual scaling is deployed when IT or DevOps watches and decides when to scale the infrastructure. Manual scaling: • Involves watching the infrastructure and its performance and then initiating the change when needed. • Introduces risk into the operation of the system. ▪ If capacity is required and not added in the proper time frame, the system's performance can degrade to unacceptable levels. ▪ When using manual scaling, if the system is not appropriately scaled, the company can pay for resources it is not using, resulting in higher costs.
Scheduled scaling	Scaling based on a schedule accommodates predictable load changes. Scheduled scaling leverages a demand curve to trigger environment changes. The system automatically scales out at predictable times of need and then scales in when the demand decreases.
Automatic scaling	Automatic scaling increases compute, storage and database resources automatically based on the operational thresholds or rules. Automatic scaling ensures that the system is always available and leverages the needed resources to provide optimal service. With automatic scaling, a system can scale out/in and up/down based on usage rules.

Data Accessibility

When enterprise systems and their data reside in the cloud, the data are accessible from anywhere in the world with an Internet-connected device. While this is an advantage for cloud computing, this benefit comes with risk. Leveraging a public cloud for applications and data persistence means that the data is commingled in a multi-tenant environment operated by the CSP. While the CSP is responsible for the security of the infrastructure, the company is responsible for protecting its data in the cloud. Per the SRM, the responsibility of securing the data also applies to IaaS and SaaS environments.

2.2.6 Limitations of Cloud Computing

The limitations of cloud computing are listed below.

Loss of Control

When leveraging a cloud environment, securing the core infrastructure and data center is the CSP's responsibility. This means that enterprises do not have the same control over the back-end infrastructure (e.g., server shell access, updates, firmware management) as they would have with an on-premises system.

Cost

When comparing the cost of a cloud environment versus an on-premises data center, the cloud, regardless of deployment model, is considered an advantage. However, cost can become problematic in cloud environments when cloud resources are mismanaged. Mismanaging resources can lead to paying for unused resources or overpaying for resources that are inappropriately leveraged, thus leading to increased costs. (See Scalability for more information.)

Internet Dependency/Downtime

When using a cloud environment, an Internet connection is necessary. Should the Internet connection go down or its performance degrade, the management of the cloud environment and the data is compromised. Managing the risk involves understanding the enterprise requirements for Internet access, the need for persistent access to the cloud environment, the service providers in the associated area/country, and the likelihood of an outage occurring.

With regard to the Internet (circuit) or CSP downtime, it's important to understand the SLA offered by the providers. If the vendor provides 99.9 percent uptime, an enterprise could experience 44.38 minutes of downtime per month. It is critical to understand the impact of downtime on the enterprise and its customers. Depending on the business requirements and the services provided to the enterprise and its customers, a more fault-tolerant or highly available cloud environment may be required. Incorporating fault tolerance or high availability into any infrastructure design results in higher costs, whether in the cloud or on-premises.

Security and Privacy

Although CSPs provide good security at the core hardware and network infrastructure level of their deployment models, some data security and data privacy requirements still fall to the enterprise leveraging the service. CSPs state in their shared responsibility terms that they are responsible for the facilities and hardware that constitute the global infrastructure and any software that defines infrastructure as computer, storage, networking or database resources. The enterprise leveraging the cloud must fully understand where the responsibilities of the CSP begin and end, and what's needed to secure the enterprise's applications and data within those systems.

Understanding what is needed to secure systems and software operating in a cloud environment depends on several things. The enterprise is required to secure its systems and data to meet the specific needs and requirements. In addition, proper due diligence needs to be applied when reviewing both international and domestic laws that require the protection of data. See Chapter 1 Privacy Governance for more information.

2.3 Endpoints

An endpoint is any computing device (e.g., tablet, phone, laptop) that is connected to a local area or wide area network and accepts communications back and forth over the network. In networking security terms, an endpoint typically refers to any device outside the firewall.

Endpoints are more prevalent in the workforce, both inside and outside the office. The mobility of today's workforce drives adopting devices to satisfy the need for instant access to all things—work and personal—at all times from any location. With this mobile access come unique security concerns for the IT and privacy professional.

Endpoint security involves the comprehensive protection of customer and enterprise data, critical business systems and intellectual property. In addition, it involves protection from viruses, malware and phishing attacks. Tools that address the security concerns associated with endpoints range from endpoint protection platforms (EPP) and mobile device management (MDM) solutions to virtual private networks (VPN) that allow access to the controlled network environment. Comprehensive solutions are policy-based and enable access to corporate resources based on the role's requirements.

2.3.1 Approaches to Endpoint Security

Endpoints include corporate, personal, and contractor or visitor devices. Because of this diversity, the IT team is not always in control of the configuration of these devices. Supporting these devices on corporate infrastructure requires a bring-your-own-device (BYOD) policy enforced through a security practice or collection of security controls (approaches) that allow for the protection of data and applications, and the network itself.

Endpoint security considerations include:

- **Enterprise devices**—The enterprise can require employees to use computers, phones, tablets, etc., that it issues. IT can configure those devices for access to the enterprise network while ensuring that the proper software and applications installed protect both the device and the network.
- **Device controls**—With the installation of an MDM or other solution, IT can control the device from the central application, enabling authentication, data encryption, remote tracking and remote wipe.
- **Access policies**—Devices accessing the corporate network can be restricted to specific systems, data repositories or applications. Access policies can specify days of the week and times of day that access is allowed. Policies should be role-based and applied to all devices of the individual accessing the enterprise systems.
- **Data transfer limits**—Depending on the individual's role within the enterprise and the enterprise's policies for data access, limitations as to how much data can be downloaded or uploaded can be applied.
- **BYOD/enterprise device policies**—Regardless of the device type, each team member should be informed of the enterprise policies on BYOD and enterprise devices. These policies should provide details as to acceptable use, permitted functions and allowed applications; details concerning monitoring, provisioning, and deprovisioning of devices; and device access to the network.
- **Endpoint detection and response (EDR)**—EDR is an integrated endpoint security solution that combines continuous real-time monitoring and the collection of endpoint data with rules-based automated response and analytics capabilities. The primary functions of an EDR system are to monitor and collect activity data from endpoints, analyze the data to identify threats or patterns, automatically respond to identified threats (remove, contain, notify), and provide forensic and analysis tools.

Components of endpoint security include:

- Antimalware and antivirus protection
- Insider threat protection
- Web security and monitoring
- Data classification and data loss prevention
- Centralized MDM
- Endpoint data encryption
- Application control (i.e., prevention of unauthorized application execution)
- Network access control

- Two-factor authentication (2FA) or single sign-on
- Policies that require endpoint devices to meet enterprise security standards before gaining access

2.4 Remote Access

Remote access is the ability to access a computer or an office network from a remote location. Remote access allows people to work offsite from home or any other location while still having office network connectivity.

2.4.1 Virtual Private Networks

Internet Protocol security (IPsec) is a network layer security control used to protect communications over public networks, encrypt IP traffic between hosts, and create virtual private networks (VPNs). A VPN provides a secure communication mechanism for data and control information between computers or networks, and the Internet key exchange (IKE) protocol is most commonly used to establish IPsec-based VPNs.

Issues

VPNs offer a good solution for remote access but present some security challenges or risks. Credential management and protection are essential with VPNs. Anyone with stolen VPN client software and credentials can access the enterprise network. VPNs can create an issue for vendor access. Depending on the enterprise's policies for vendor access over the VPN, and the VPN software itself, it can be challenging to manage third-party vendors. Depending on the laws and regulations an enterprise must comply with, VPNs can add compliance risk. This risk is associated with policies and procedures, and with the VPN itself. Depending on the sophistication of the VPN software, the needed logs and usage details may not be present. As a result, compliance issues can arise.

While VPN connections offer secure connectivity between the client PC and the enterprise network, a VPN does not provide personal security features to the client, or protect it from Internet-based attacks, malware or viruses. The VPN connection provides data confidentiality and authentication services. Should a remote computer become compromised, the attacker can use the compromised system as a means of accessing the corporate network.

Risks

Some common risks of concern to the privacy professional are discussed in the following sections.

User Credential Risks

VPN security is only as strong as the methods used to authenticate the users and devices leveraging the VPN. Simple authentication methods based on passwords can be circumvented or socially engineered. 2FA (something you know and something you have) is a minimum requirement for providing secure VPN access to the corporate network. Depending on the needs of the company, three-factor authentication (something you know, something you have, and something you are) may be necessary.

Malware and Viruses

Every remote computer that does not meet the security requirements for network access represents a threat to the enterprise. Malware and viruses can migrate from a remote machine to the enterprise network. Up-to-date antivirus software and EDR software are required to mitigate this type of risk.

Split Tunneling

A VPN routes Internet traffic through an encrypted tunnel to protect data. Split tunneling occurs when a computer on the remote end of a VPN tunnel simultaneously shares network traffic with both the public network and the internal private network without first placing all traffic inside the VPN tunnel. If improperly configured, split tunneling provides a means for attackers on the shared network to compromise the remote computer and use it as an entry point to the internal (private) network.

2.4.2 Desktop Sharing

Desktop-sharing software allows users to connect via a client to their remote system. Once a user is authenticated, the files and data on the remote computer are available to the local computer. Sharing can range from access to online presentation and conference software to complete remote control of the enterprise system.

Issues and Risks

Credential management is a significant risk with desktop-sharing applications. If stolen, anyone can access the remote machine and begin exfiltrating information or installing malware, etc. All desktop-sharing tools are not created equal. In general, many lack the necessary enterprise controls (logging and monitoring) to be safely accessed by all users within an enterprise.

2.4.3 Privileged Access Management

Privileged access management (PAM) provides a scalable set of tools used to secure, authorize and monitor all privileged accounts, processes and systems across the enterprise. Privileged accounts include:

- Local administrative accounts
- Domain administrative accounts
- Service accounts
- Active directory or domain service accounts
- Application accounts

PAM systems consist of three primary components:

- **Access manager**—The access manager gives administrators visibility into who is using the systems, and data within those systems, so vulnerabilities and threats can be detected.
- **Session manager**—The session manager helps control system access in real time. This manager integrates with security information and event management systems, automatic security orchestration solutions, and intrusion detection systems to identify and stop attacks as they occur. With this integration comes an unalterable audit trail for compliance and regulator obligations.
- **Password manager**—The password manager stores and protects passwords and provides rules for the creation and administration of passwords. Administrators can use the password manager to automate the management, issuing and cycling of passwords. Passwords creation can be accomplished manually by an administrator or through an automated function. Each time a user requests access, the system can create a new password automatically to avoid password reuse or a credential leak, while ensuring that the target system and the new credential are aligned, guaranteeing secure access.

- **2FA**—Because of the functionality associated with a PAM, multifactor authentication is a fundamental part of a successful PAM deployment.

Privilege-related risks solved by PAM include:

- Lack of visibility and awareness of privileged users, accounts, assets and credentials
- Over-provisioning privileges
- Shared accounts and passwords
- Hard-coded/embedded passwords
- Manual or decentralized credential management
- Visibility into service and application account privileges
- Siloed identity management tools and processes
- Cloud and virtualization administration
- DevOps environments

Benefits of PAM include:

- A smaller attack surface that protects against internal and external threats—By limiting the privileges of people, processes and applications, the points of entry for exploits are significantly reduced.
- Reduction in malware infection and propagation—Malware typically depends on elevated credentials in order to install and execute itself. Removal of excessive privileges through the principle of least privilege, enforced across the enterprise, prevents the propagation of malware.
- An audit-friendly environment—Limiting privileged activities across the enterprise, while providing monitoring and logging of all sessions and activities, facilitates audits.

2.5 System Hardening

System hardening is the practice of securing a computer by reducing its attack surface through configuration, tools and best practices. The approach to hardening a system is based on the system itself, the operating system used, networking, data persistence, and the applications or software running on the system.

The attack surface of a system is the combination of all the potential flaws and backdoors in technology that can be exploited by hackers. The attack surface can include:

- Default passwords
- Hard-coded passwords
- Unpatched software and firmware
- Unpatched operating systems
- Improperly configured BIOS, firewalls, ports, servers, switches, routers, etc.
- Unencrypted network traffic
- Passwords or credentials stored in plain text
- Lack of privileged access

System hardening can be achieved by removing unused software (tools or applications), removing unnecessary services, changing default settings and passwords, and closing unnecessary network ports. A comprehensive approach that includes multiple layers of the infrastructure is needed to properly harden systems. The system hardening approach should be based on the enterprise requirements for the infrastructure, regulatory or compliance requirements, information security requirements and risk.

System hardening best practices are shown in **figure 2.10**.

Figure 2.10—System Hardening Best Practices

Component	Best Practice
Operating system hardening	• Apply OS updates, patching and service packs routinely after testing on a non-production machine. • Remove unnecessary files, drivers, file sharing, software, services and functionality. • Encrypt local hard disks. • Manage system permissions, ensuring adherence to the InfoSec policy. • Enable comprehensive logging of all activities, errors and warnings.
Accounts	• Remove all unnecessary or default accounts. ■ If accounts cannot be removed, then update the credentials associated with unnecessary or default accounts throughout the infrastructure at every level.
Database hardening	• Create/implement administrative restrictions or role-based permissions on database systems to control what can be done either to the system or within the database itself. • Encrypt data in transit and at rest. Use encryption methods or standards based on the enterprise information security policy. • Audit database accounts regularly and remove all unused accounts regularly.
Application/software hardening	• Manage application passwords centrally (e.g., PAM). This management should enforce password generation in alignment with the information security policy, and handle password rotation and deprecation. • Audit or review dependent systems of all applications to identify areas of potential risk. • Remove all unnecessary components, integration components or privileges.
Server hardening	• All servers should be in a secure facility with proper access control and surveillance.
	• All servers should be hardened and tested prior to being placed on the Internet or external networks. • Avoid installing software that is not necessary for normal system operation. • Configure administrative and SA shares appropriately and limit access in line with the principle of least privilege.
Network hardening	• Conduct regular audits of firewall rules and configuration settings. • Conduct regular audits of routers and layer 3 switches • Block any unused or unnecessary ports. • Disable any unused or unnecessary protocols and services. • Encrypt network traffic (TLS v1.2/1.3, wherever possible)
Patch security vulnerabilities	• Patch all security vulnerabilities at all levels of the infrastructure. • If possible, test patches outside the production environment before applying to the production infrastructure.

Figure 2.10—System Hardening Best Practices (cont.)

Component	Best Practice
Conduct regular system audits	• Plan for regular, comprehensive system audits: ■ Penetration testing ■ Configuration management ■ Vulnerability scanning • Create a process for reviewing the audit results and prioritizing the mitigation or repair of discovered issues.
Desktop or laptop computer	• Password-protect the BIOS. • Boot only from hard drive. • Allow only non-storage universal serial bus (USB) ports for keyboard, mouse and headsets.

Part B: Applications and Software

The applications and software used or created by an enterprise as part of its infrastructure come with unique privacy considerations. This section reviews common areas related to enterprise use and creation of applications and software and points out what the privacy engineer should consider in these areas.

2.6 Secure Development Life Cycle

The secure development life cycle (SDL) expands on the traditional software development life cycle (SDLC), defining processes and standards for developing software and applications in a secure environment.[6] The SDL was developed by Microsoft in response to a challenge by Bill Gates in the early 2000s to build security into all of its products.[7] Since then, it has been adopted on a broader basis.

The SDL follows the same phases:

- Requirements gathering
- Design and coding
- Test and release
- Maintenance

Security standards ensure that the product protects the users' information since security is built in from beginning to delivery. An enterprise-wide SDL ensures that all products created by a company are secure for its customers.

2.6.1 Privacy and the Phases of the Secure Development Life Cycle

As shown in **figure 2.11,** the SDL aims to ensure that security is incorporated into all software development phases.

Figure 2.11—Embedding Security in Software Development

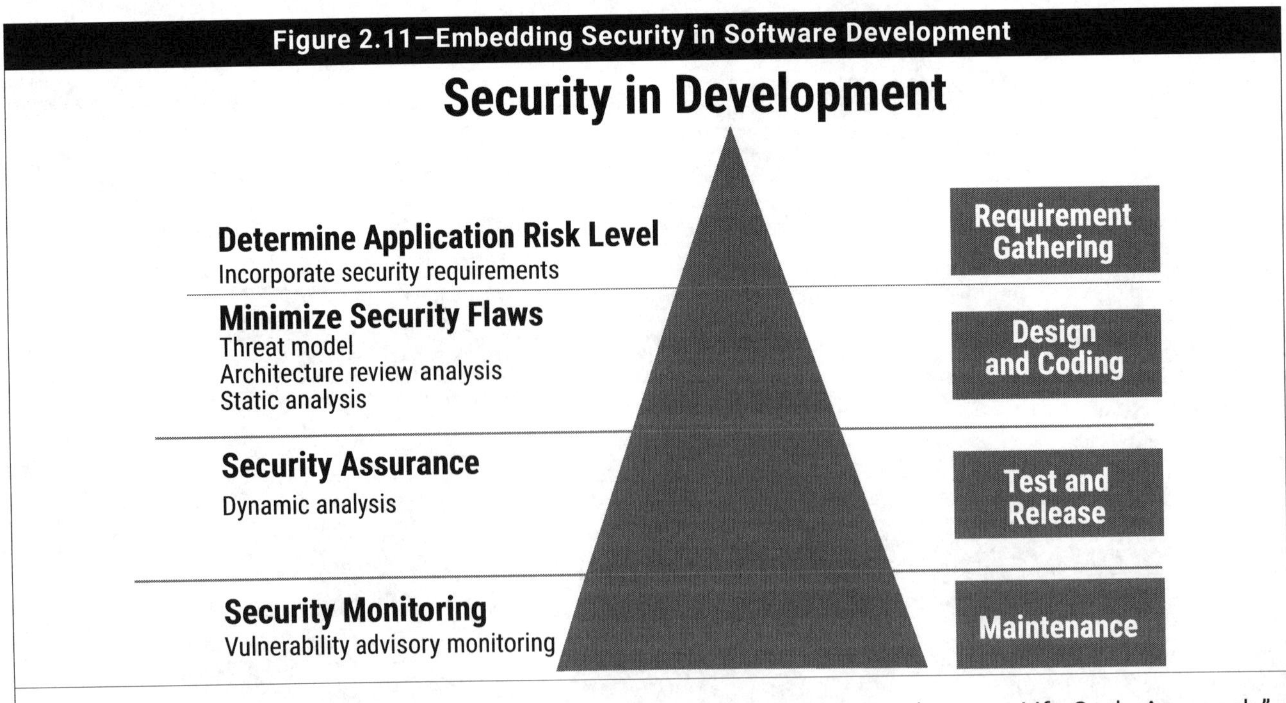

Source: Rajendran, S.; "Safeguarding Mobile Applications With Secure Development Life Cycle Approach," *ISACA Journal*, Vol. 3, 1 May 2017

Requirements Gathering

As noted in section 1.7 Privacy Training and Awareness, a key first step in establishing an SDL is ensuring that employees know privacy is the responsibility of everyone in the enterprise. This keeps privacy and security considerations at the forefront of all procedures and processes.

The enterprise should document the enterprise privacy philosophy that informs its business activities, including:[8]

- Establishing a documented enterprise privacy policy that describes the privacy philosophy for the data controller, expressing clear executive support. This would ensure evaluation of the potential effect new initiatives and changes to enterprise structure could have on the security and privacy of personal information and sensitive information.
- Ensuring executive support for the identification of personal and sensitive information security and privacy risk connected to enterprise events.
- Communicating executive support for enterprise-wide privacy roles and responsibilities during the implementation of IT systems, the adoption of new or updated manual or computerized business processes, and the launch of enterprise programs and operations involving personal information.

In addition to a privacy awareness program, security requirements should be defined for all development products, regardless of the development methodology in use. Best practices for security and privacy can be derived from industry standards, previous lessons learned and many other sources.[9] Users' perspectives are especially useful during requirements gathering to help to ensure that their privacy and security concerns are addressed.

Design and Coding

The design phase typically occurs prior to actually writing code. During the design phase, the requirements become the architecture of the product. According to Rajendran, "Constructing a secure design minimizes the majority of security issues, because code-level issues can be identified with static analysis or manual code review."[10]

It is also critical that the information security and compliance teams collaborate during the design phase. This will ensure that both the design and all stakeholders in the chain of compliance and data protection are actively engaged. Periodic code reviews involving both teams should be held during the development phase to validate that what is being built is in line with security and compliance requirements.

Threat modeling greatly helps to assess the likelihood that the software or application will be attacked and gauge the impact of potential attacks. Threat modeling can be described as "the process of thinking through how a feature or system will be attacked, and then mitigating those future attacks in the design before writing the code."[11]

After the design is determined, the code can be written, and requirements are translated into software or an application. An SDL should define a secure coding guide that includes expectations and guidance for when issues arise.[12]

Testing and Release

After a product is designed and coded, testing can begin. This includes vulnerability scanning, penetration testing and dynamic security testing (DAST). Testing may uncover any remaining security issues. Penetration testing, especially, aims to exploit an application's security protections. However, it may not be feasible to perform a penetration test for every product.

Static code analysis and code review (also known as static code review or static application security testing) are methods of security testing that check the code for flaws, security issues and overall quality issues. When these

methods are combined, they help developers ensure that their code is free from potential exploits and meets company security standards and requirements. Using static code analysis allows developers to identify and mitigate vulnerabilities in the early stages of development. The final secure code review process ensures that the application or service has undergone a comprehensive security test before reaching production. This approach to code analysis, review, and testing works very well with privacy by design principles as a process of validation. When testing is complete and security is confirmed, the product can be released to customers. A release should include a mechanism for end-users to report security problems.[13]

Maintenance

The SDL does not end at release. Security is ongoing as the threat environment continues to evolve. Monitoring and identifying new vulnerabilities can help an enterprise be proactive in protecting its products. Resources like the NIST National Vulnerability Database (NVD) and the MITRE Corporation Common Vulnerabilities and Exposures (CVE) can be useful. Updates and patches can be developed to address vulnerability concerns.

2.6.2 Privacy By Design

Privacy by design was originally a philosophy that was promoted to enterprises to consider embedding privacy controls into the design of technology from the very beginning of a project.[14] The focus later broadened to include business practices, physical design and infrastructures in addition to technologies.

The seven elements of privacy by design are:[15]

1. Recognizing that privacy interests and concerns must be addressed proactively
2. Applying core principles expressing universal spheres of privacy protection
3. Mitigating privacy concerns early when developing information technologies and systems, throughout the entire information life cycle—end to end
4. Needing qualified privacy leadership and/or professional input
5. Adopting and integrating privacy-enhancing technologies
6. Embedding privacy in a positive-sum, not zero-sum, manner to enhance privacy and system functionality
7. Respecting user privacy

The privacy-by-design concept has evolved into a more mature methodology that has been recognized as a global privacy standard. The UK Information Commissioner's Office (ICO)[16] created a privacy model consisting of the following eight privacy-by-design principles:

- Principle 1—Processing personal data fairly and lawfully
- Principle 2—Processing personal data for specified purposes
- Principle 3—The amount of personal data that enterprises may hold
- Principle 4—Keeping personal data accurate and up to date
- Principle 5—Retaining personal data
- Principle 6—The rights of individuals (including subject access request, damage or distress recourse, preventing direct marketing, allowing for automated decision making, rights for correcting inaccurate personal data, compensation for privacy harms)
- Principle 7—Information security
- Principle 8—Sending personal data outside the European economic area

Privacy-by-design is not a legal requirement, but the ICO encourages enterprises to use the approach to help ensure that privacy and data protection are appropriately addressed throughout the entire life cycle of all projects.

The privacy-by-design concept can be used by any enterprise in any location throughout the world to help ensure that privacy is appropriately addressed from the time that a new process, service or product is created, through its entire life cycle.

2.7 Application and Software Hardening

Hardening is the process of taking a finished application or software program and making it more difficult to reverse engineer and tamper with.[17] Essentially, software hardening reduces the attack surface. Combined with secure coding practices, application hardening is a best practice for enterprises to protect their applications' Internet protocol (IP) addresses and prevent misuse, cheating and repackaging.

Hardening adds to existing software and applications, and injects new code that protects the application against static and dynamic attacks. Hardening protects the software/application from basic issues, e.g., issues that can result from not verifying a sender, destination or message format. Some system hardening examples are listed in **figure 2.12**.

Figure 2.12—Types of System Hardening

Types of Hardening	Description
Data obfuscation	This is a method for hiding information by scrambling data using encryption or tokenization. This results in attackers obtaining only unintelligible data.
Native code obfuscation	Similar to data obfuscation, this makes it difficult to analyze the source code of an application.
Anti-debug/Anti-tamper	This uses specific functions to check for the presence of debuggers or attempts to tamper with the program.
Emulator detection	An emulator is designed to mimic the original operating system of an application to analyze or modify the application. A virtual machine may also be used. Anti-emulators look for artifacts left by these programs.
Root/jailbreak detection	This technique involves looking for write access in the application to parts of the system that are usually protected, i.e., areas that are normally not accessible to an application, or looking for known values typically used by rooted or jailbroken devices.

Source: Rupp, M.; "General Concepts of Application Hardening for Mobile Banking Apps," Cryptomathic, 18 December 2019, *www.cryptomathic.com/news-events/blog/general-concepts-of-application-hardening-for-mobile-banking-apps*

Prior to system hardening, the DevOps or engineering team should engage with compliance, IT and information security (depending on the enterprise's organizational matrix), to review the application, the data it is processing, and the anticipated hardening techniques. Compliance and information security can participate by making suggestions or providing additional guidance for ensuring the application is properly hardened.

Internal systems that are hardened should be reviewed on a regular basis. Since code and systems evolve over time, periodic audits of the application or system should be conducted to validate that the system is still secure.

2.7.1 Best Practices for Hardening

The *BeyondTrust Resources Glossary* provides a list of best practices for choosing and implementing application and software hardening (**figure 2.13**).

Figure 2.13—Application and Software Hardening Best Practices

Hardening Best Practices	Description
Patch vulnerabilities immediately.	Create an automated and comprehensive vulnerability identification and patching system.
Apply application hardening.	• Remove any components or functions you do not need. • Restrict access to applications based on user roles and context, such as with application control. • Remove all sample files and default passwords. Then, manage application passwords via an application password management/privileged password management solution, that enforces password best practices, such as password rotation, length, etc. • Application hardening should also entail inspecting integrations with other applications and systems, and removing, or reducing, unnecessary integration components and privileges.
Apply database hardening.	Create admin restrictions, such as: • Controlling privileged access, on what users can do in a database. • Turn on node checking to verify applications and users. • Encrypt database information—both in transit and at rest. • Enforce secure passwords. • Introduce role-based access control (RBAC) privileges. • Remove unused accounts.
Apply operating system hardening.	• Apply OS updates, service packs, and patches automatically. • Remove unnecessary drivers, file sharing, libraries, software, services, and functionality. • Encrypt local storage. • Tighten registry and other systems permissions. • Log all activity, errors, and warnings. • Implement privileged user controls.
Eliminate unnecessary accounts and privileges.	Enforce least privilege by removing unnecessary accounts (such as orphaned accounts and unused accounts) and privileges throughout the IT infrastructure.
Deploy web application firewalls (WAF).	WAFs, when deployed, can be used to filter the traffic coming into application servers and validate the requests and responses.

Source: BeyondTrust, "Glossary," *www.beyondtrust.com/resources/glossary*

2.8 APIs and Services

As the use of Internet-connected and mobile devices has increased over the decades, the use of application programming interfaces (APIs) and other services has also grown. Many applications and websites use APIs to exchange data, resulting in the emergence of many privacy considerations concerning the use of consumer data.

2.8.1 APIs

An API is an interface used to program software that interacts with an existing application. Specifically, an API is a set of functions and procedures that allow individuals to access and build upon the data and functionality of an existing application.

An API often uses private end user data. If compromised, it can open a site or enterprise's system to misuse and invade the privacy of the end user. A security breach could mean leaking sensitive customer data or even personally identifying information in healthcare or finance, which is regulated by law.

Often, API calls are necessary for enterprises when interacting with third-party service providers. For example, a customer can register for a course or exam through a company's website. The website then uses an API to provide the customer information to the learning management system or testing provider that hosts the course or exam. This results in a streamlined process for the end user.

APIs are typically internally developed or externally developed and used by the enterprise (e.g.; used for marketing purposes).

Four different types of APIs are typically used by developers:

- Content-focused APIs—These provide access to content/data published by the original service, such as articles on a news service website.
- Feature APIs—These APIs integrate other sites or applications into the application or site of another service, such as opening YouTube videos in an application.
- Unofficial APIs—These APIs are typically created for internal use by an enterprise but may be useful for third parties.
- Analytics APIs—These APIs are used to gather information about visitors or users of a website or application. This information is then used by the enterprise to make a variety of decisions or to target content and advertisements to specific users.

Advertisers use APIs to help target specific advertisements or content to users to ensure the best value for their investment in the application or website. For example, advertisers can use information from users' Facebook profiles to determine their interests and show them content related to those interests. The amount of data an advertiser can obtain depends on the platform's API. This can be determined by how much information the original site obtains from a user and company policies.[18]

API security generally includes logs that show access activity. If an API's velocity of interactions increases and/or the number of failed attempts increases, those may be symptoms of privacy compromise. For example, if the normal activity on an API is 100 times per hour, but a notable increase in velocity occurs, say to 10,000 times per hour, that could indicate a compromised API.

A secure API is one that can guarantee the confidentiality of the information it processes by making it available only to the applications, systems and users authorized to use it. Additionally, from a data privacy perspective, these APIs must guarantee the integrity of the data received from other systems or third parties.

Understanding who, or what system, is making an API call is important when determining what the response should be. As with role-based permissions within infrastructure, APIs can provide returns with varying degrees of information based on how their identity is determined. A response—based on role, level of access, or the API call itself—should be mapped out with permissions and returns predetermined, based on the level of access provided.

For example, internal API calls should have full access to the data within the system, i.e., the applications or services within the system that are talking to each other. To provide this access, the application needs a distinct identifier, so the system knows an authorized application or service is making requests. This is where application hardening and APIs overlap. If properly designed and hardened, the system or service will know it is talking to itself by an internal ID that rotates or changes on an interval or with every internal API call made (e.g., tokenization) and that it can return the data requested securely, and per the data classification and protection requirements determined by the enterprise, compliance and information security team.

External users of API calls can be assigned IDs (a GUID or hash value that identifies a distinct developer or requestor). This value is then compared against a roles or permissions matrix to determine if the requestor has permissions or access to the API call being made. If permission is granted, the API returns the requested information. If permission is not granted, the API can return an error message or a NULL.

APIs should be reviewed on a regular basis to ensure they are still secure.

2.8.2 Web Service

A web service is a resource that is made available over the Internet to support interoperable machine-to-machine interactions over a network. Often, web services use Simple Object Access Protocol (SOAP), a messaging protocol that shares XML data via HTTP requests.

2.9 Tracking Technologies

Tracking and surveillance technologies are becoming ubiquitous and they are often unnoticeable.[19] Drones, RFID tags, CCTV, GPS trackers and other types of surveillance-specific technologies are becoming widely used by enterprises and the general public. In addition, a wide range of tracking software and firmware is being built into the smartphones, tablets and technologies that are used by individuals for business and personal activities. Such tracking and surveillance capabilities create a wide range of new and emerging privacy risks. As a result, tracking and surveillance technologies create risk, which can be categorized into the privacy types shown in **figure 2.14** and must be considered and appropriately addressed by the enterprise that is adopting tracking and surveillance policies.[20]

Website tracking is a means of collecting data about individuals as they use the Internet. The purpose of tracking is to create rich profiles of individual users. The collecting enterprise can either market and sell more effectively to specific users, or it can share or sell the data it collects with data aggregators who create more comprehensive user profiles. The aggregated data are usually sold to companies looking for specific customers to target, based on their profiles. Most online cookies serve this purpose.

While the purpose of most tracking technologies is to provide targeted sales leads to companies, there are more nefarious uses of consumer profiles. Depending on the depth of the data collected on an individual, many political, religious, gender and financial inferences can be made. Such inferences can be used to message directly to consumers on topics they will likely consume or be drawn to. This leads to misinformation campaigns and selective manipulation of people *en masse*.[21]

Web-tracking technologies get more sophisticated each year. Also, the methods used to combine gathered data have changed, allowing creation of very detailed profiles. Cookies, being the most understood of these technologies can track many things:

- The user's queries in search engines
- The sites the user visits
- The frequency of a user's return visits to a site
- What the user clicks on
- How long the user lingers on a site
- The user's scrolling speed
- Where the user stops
- The movements of the mouse around a web page
- The comments and reactions the user might add on a site or on social media

Common uses of web tracking include:

- **Statistics and usability**—Many trackers can measure a website's use and help developers and marketing teams optimize the design of the site and its content to aid in making impressions and driving interactions with the site.
- **eCommerce**—Tracking technologies are used to track items purchased, abandoned carts, sales campaigns, the response to advertisements (A-B testing) and pricing.
- **Profiling and targeted marketing**—Some websites allow third-party advertisers to track their users and display advertisements to them based on their online profiles (ad networks, news and social media).

Figure 2.14 describes privacy risks associated with tracking technologies.

Figure 2.14—Privacy Risks Associated With Tracking and Surveillance Technologies

Privacy Category	Risk
Privacy of person	A wide range of tracking and surveillance devices are being created to be worn on or placed within an individual's body to use for a variety of security authorization activities.
Privacy of behavior and action	The very nature of tracking and surveillance technologies creates the ability, in most cases, to determine the data subject's behaviors and actions.
Privacy of thoughts and feelings	Many types of tracking and surveillance technologies are capable of capturing the thoughts and feelings of those in the vicinity of the technology's use, e.g., webcams that secretly record the conversations and images of the individuals using laptops.
Privacy of communication	Tracking and surveillance have been used many times throughout the world in recent years to scrutinize online communications. Voice communications and eavesdropping on conversations are also pervasive.
Privacy of data and image (information)	The information accessible through the use of tracking and surveillance methods is unlimited.
Privacy of location and space (territorial)	Surveillance technologies have been used for decades to record the activities, and those doing them, within the reach of their lenses and microphones. Surveillance technologies continue to evolve. For example, drones are now being used for surveillance.
Privacy of association	Tracking and surveillance technologies are increasingly capable of revealing the associations between individuals.

Source: ISACA, *ISACA Privacy Principles and Program Management Guide*, USA, 2016

Tracking technologies have implications for people's privacy online and offline and are often the targets of misuse and abuse. With the invention of location-capable smart devices, tracking users and their movements has become

affordable, easier and more pervasive. Governments, employers and retailers now have a broad range of embedded tools and tracking capabilities they can use to monitor people's actions.

2.9.1 Types of Tracking Technologies

Types of tracking technologies are discussed below.

Cookies

A cookie is a string of text that is downloaded by a user when visiting a website. Cookies are used to enable the website to recognize its returning users, preferences and settings from the site. Cookies can also monitor and provide data on a user's interactions with a website. Global privacy laws classify cookies into three different categories.[22] **Figure 2.15** describes these cookie categories.

Figure 2.15—Cookie Categories

Category	Type	Description
Duration	Session cookies	These cookies are temporary and exist only during the active browsing session.
	Persistent cookies	These are cookies that are stored on your machine until erased. While persistent cookies have expiry dates, their duration can vary from hours to years. According to the ePrivacy Directive, persistent cookies should not last more than 12 months.
Provenance	First-party cookies	These are cookies placed on a machine while the user is visiting a website.
	Third-party cookies	These are cookies placed on a user's computer or device by a third party. These cookies are usually advertising, tracking or analytical cookies.
Purpose	Necessary cookies	These cookies are those that are essential for the proper operation of the website a user is currently visiting. These cookies are generally first-party cookies and provide functionality to the end-user that makes the browsing experience optimal (i.e., remembering items in a shopping cart). While consent for necessary cookies is not required, the use of these cookies and why they are necessary should be explained in the site's cookie policy.
	Preference cookies	These are cookies that allow a website to remember the user's choices, options and preferences for the visited website. These cookies are not required for using the website but offer convenience and an enhanced web experience.
	Statistics cookies	These cookies collect information about how the user interacts with a website (i.e., pages visited, mouse clicks). The data gathered by statistical cookies is aggregated for detailed analysis. These data do not identify a distinct user but provide the host of the website the necessary statistics and operational insight to optimize the web experience.
	Marketing cookies	These cookies track a user's online activity and help advertisers deliver more specific and targeted ads to the individual web user. Often these cookies share their data among marketing or data aggregation services (data brokers). These are third-party cookies and are persistent until erased.

Tracking Pixels

A tracking pixel is a 1×1 transparent image consisting of one pixel and embedded (invisibly) on a website. When a user accesses a website with tracking pixels enabled, a tracking pixel is downloaded to the user's local machine. That enables the sender of the tracking pixel to know that a web page has been loaded, an advertisement has been seen, or an email has been opened. Typical information retrieved by a tracking pixel includes:

- The operating system of the machine
- The browser or mail program in use
- The time the website was visited
- When an email was read
- User behavior on the website visited
- IP address and location of the user

Digital Fingerprinting/Browser Fingerprinting

Digital fingerprinting is the use of an application or website to obtain information about the user's machine and system settings. When leveraged, the website or application can obtain the following information:

- Location, time zone and language settings for the local machine
- Browser plug-ins loaded or used
- System configuration (e.g., motherboard, video card, networking card or Wi-Fi)
- Screen size, resolution and bit-depth
- Fonts used
- Microprocessor serial number or processor type
- Hard disk type and serial numbers

This information, when used in combination, creates a digital fingerprint for a specific user. This technology is very accurate in identifying users and their systems when online. Using a digital fingerprint circumvents VPNs, proxies, and the disabling of cookies.

GPS Tracking

Most mobile devices include GPS (global positioning system), a feature that lets the device pinpoint its location using GPS coordinates. GPS can help travelers find their way through such applications as Google Maps and Apple Maps. GPS in company-supplied phones makes it easy to track where the device is, and by extension, the location of the employee holding it.

Radio Frequency Identification

Radio frequency identification (RFID) uses radio waves to identify tagged objects within a limited radius. A tag consists of a microchip and an antenna. The microchip stores information, along with an ID, to identify a product. The antenna transmits the information to an RFID reader.

Tags can be used to identify an item based either on direct product identification or carrier identification. With carrier identification, an article's ID is manually fed into the system (e.g., using a bar code) and is used along with strategically placed radio frequency readers to track and locate the item.

Personal privacy rights or expectations may be compromised if an RFID system uses what is considered personally identifiable information for a purpose other than originally intended or understood. The personal possession of functioning tags also is a privacy risk because possession can enable tracking of those tagged items.

Part C: Technical Privacy Controls

Technical privacy controls are the information technology components used to process personal data. Privacy controls can include:

- Communication and transport protocols
- Encryption, hashing and de-identification
- Key management
- Monitoring and logging
- Identity and access management

Technical controls are implemented in the technical infrastructure during project development and when there are major changes to the technological base.

2.10 Communication and Transport Protocols

A **communication protocol** refers to the set of rules that computers use to communicate with each other. The protocol defines the signals the computers give each other, and details such as how communication begins and ends.

A **transport protocol** is a communication protocol responsible for establishing a connection and ensuring that all data has arrived safely. It is defined in layer 4 of the Open Systems Interconnection (OSI) model. Often, the term transport protocol implies transport services, including the lower-level data link protocol that moves packets from one node to another.

The way networks allow systems and applications to communicate is complicated. The OSI model defines a networking framework for implementing protocols in seven layers. Each of the layers within the model performs a specific job and then passes data on to the next layer. The first four layers in this model (1-4) are considered lower layers, and are those that involve the transportation of data. Layers 5-7 are the upper layers, which contain application data. The layers are defined as follows:[23]

- **Layer 7-Application**—Everything at this layer is application-specific. It provides application services for file transfers, email and other network services. Layer 7 includes browsers, NSF, Telnet, HTTP and FTP protocols. In this layer, communication partners are identified, user authentication and privacy are considered, and any constraints on data syntax are identified.
- **Layer 6-Presentation**—Sometimes called the "syntax layer," this layer works to transform data into a form the application layer (7) can accept. This layer formats and encrypts data to be sent across the network.
- **Layer 5-Session**—This layer establishes and manages session/connections between applications. All connections are initiated, managed and terminated from this layer.
- **Layer 4-Transport**—This layer enables the transfer of data between systems or hosts. This layer is responsible for end-to-end error recovery and flow control, and it ensures compete data transfer between systems.
- **Layer 3-Network**—This layer provides virtual circuits for the transmission from node to node (switching and routing). Routing, forwarding, addressing, internetworking, congestion control and error handling are functions of this layer.
- **Layer 2-Data Link**—The data link layer encodes and decodes data packets into bits. It provides transmission protocol knowledge and management and handles flow control and frame synchronization. This layer is divided into two sub-layers: the media access control (MAC) layer and the logical link control (LLC) layer. The MAC layer controls how a device on the network gains access to the data and permission to transmit it. The LLC layer controls frame synchronization, flow control and error checking.

- **Layer 1-Physical**—The physical layer provides the hardware necessary to send and receive data on a carrier. This layer enables networking hardware to receive signals (radio, light or electrical impulse) and transmit them over the network. This layer includes cables, cards, and other physical media or hardware required for data transmission.

2.10.1 Types of Communication Protocols

Common communication protocols:

- Hypertext Transfer Protocol (HTTP) is used for accessing and receiving Hypertext Markup Language (HTML) files on the Internet.
- Simple Mail Transfer Protocol (SMTP) is used for transferring email between computers.
  - Post Office Protocol version 3 (POP3) is the most common account type for personal email. Messages are typically deleted from the server when email is read.
  - Internet Message Access Protocol (IMAP) is a protocol for email retrieval and storage; it is an alternative to POP.
- File Transfer Protocol (FTP) is used for showing files to be copied between devices.
- Transmission Control Protocol (TCP) ensures the delivery of information packets across networks.
- IP is responsible for logical addressing called "IP address" to route information between networks.
- Point-to-Point Protocol (PPP) is a data link (layer 2) protocol used to establish a direct connection between two nodes.

2.10.2 Local Area Network

A local area network (LAN) covers a small, local area—from a few devices in a single room to a network across a few buildings. The increase in reasonably priced bandwidth has reduced the design effort required to provide cost-effective LAN solutions for enterprises of any size.

New LANs are almost always implemented using switched Ethernet (802.3). Twisted-pair cabling—100-Base-T or better, and wireless LANs (WLANs)—connect floor switches to the workstations and printers in the immediate area. Floor switches can be connected to each other with 1000-Base-T or fiberoptic cabling. In larger enterprises, the floor switches may be connected to larger, faster switches designed to properly route the switch-to-switch data.

As LANs get larger and traffic grows, it is increasingly important to carefully plan the logical configuration of the network. Network planners need to be highly skilled and very knowledgeable. Their tools include traffic monitors that allow them to observe volumes on critical links. Tracking traffic volumes, error rates and response times is every bit as important on larger LANs as it is on distributed servers and mainframes.

LAN Topologies and Protocols

LAN topologies define how networks are organized from a physical standpoint, while protocols define how information transmitted over the network is interpreted by systems. LAN physical topology was previously tied fairly tightly to the protocols that were used to transfer information across the wire. This is no longer true. For current technology, the physical topology is driven by ease of construction, reliability and practicality. Of the physical topologies that once were commonly used—bus, ring and star—only the star is used to any great extent in new construction. **Figure 2.16** illustrates commonly used physical topologies.

Figure 2.16—Commonly Used Physical Topologies

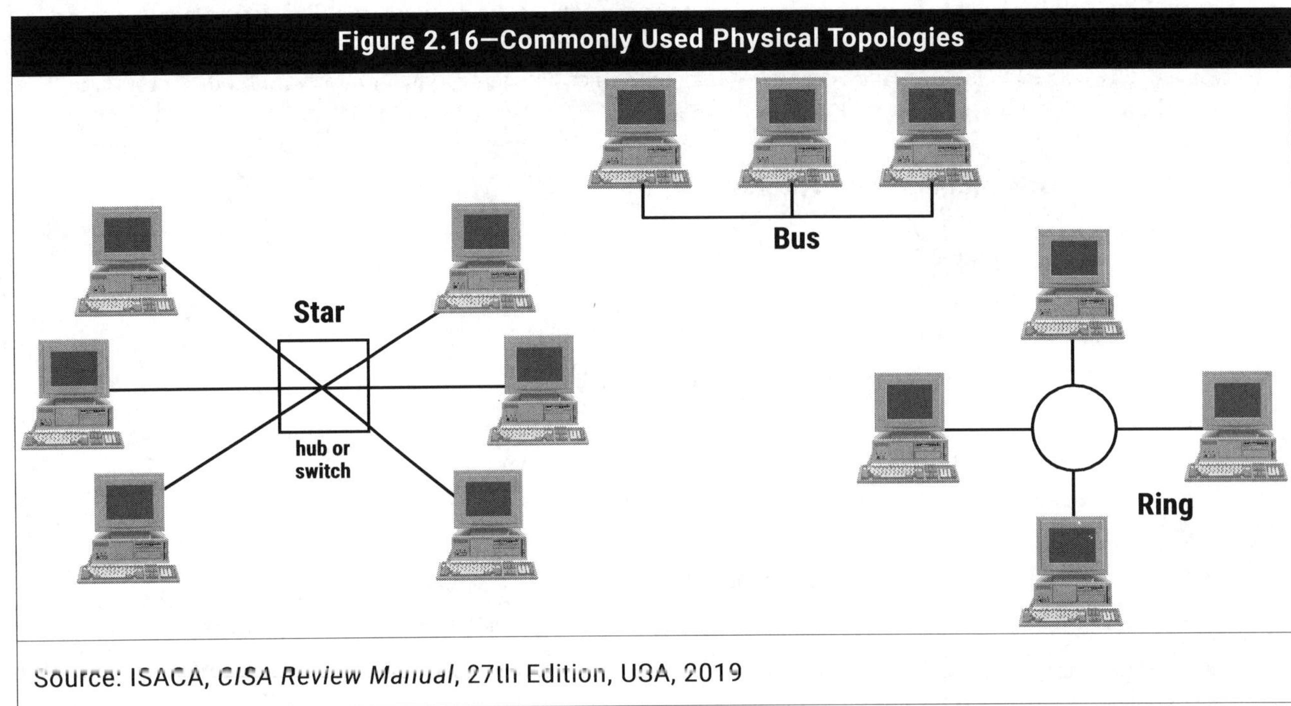

Source: ISACA, *CISA Review Manual*, 27th Edition, USA, 2019

LAN Components

Components commonly associated with LANs are repeaters, hubs, bridges, switches and routers.

Repeaters are physical layer devices that extend the range of a network or connect two separate network segments together. Repeaters amplify (regenerate) signals from one network segment to compensate for signals (analog or digital) that are distorted due to a reduction of signal strength during transmission (i.e., attenuation).

Hubs are physical layer devices that serve as the center of a star-topology network or a network concentrator. Hubs can be active (if they repeat signals sent through them) or passive (if they merely split signals).

Bridges are data link layer devices that were developed to connect LANs or create two separate LAN or WAN network segments from a single segment to reduce collision domains. The two segments work as different LANs below the data link level of the OSI reference model, but from that level and above, they behave as a single logical network. Bridges act as store-and-forward devices in moving frames toward their destination. This is achieved by analyzing the MAC header of a data packet, which represents the hardware address of an NIC. Bridges can also filter frames based on Layer 2 information. For example, they can prevent frames sent from predefined MAC addresses from entering a particular network. Bridges are software-based, and they are less efficient than similar hardware-based devices, such as switches. Therefore, bridges are not major components in today's enterprise network designs.

Layer 2 switches are data link level devices that can divide and interconnect segments and help to reduce collision domains in Ethernet-based networks. Furthermore, switches store and forward frames, filtering and forwarding packets among network segments, based on Layer 2 MAC source and destination addresses, as bridges and hubs do at the data link layer. Switches provide more robust functionality than bridges through use of more sophisticated data link layer protocols that are implemented via specialized hardware called application-specific integrated circuits (ASICs). The benefits of this technology are performance efficiencies gained through reduced costs, low latency or idle time, and a greater number of ports on a switch with dedicated high-speed bandwidth capabilities (e.g., many ports on a switch are available with 10/100 Ethernet and/or Gigabit Ethernet speeds).

Switches are also applicable in WAN technology specifications.

Routers are similar to bridges and switches in that they link two or more physically separate network segments. However, the network segments linked by a router remain logically separate and can function as independent networks. Routers operate at the OSI network layer by examining network addresses (i.e., routing information encoded in an IP packet). By examining the IP address, the router can make intelligent decisions to direct the packet to its destination. Unlike switches operating at the data link layer, routers use logically based network addresses, use different network addresses/segments off all ports, block broadcast information, block traffic to unknown addresses, and filter traffic based on network or host information.

Routers are often not as efficient as switches because they are generally software-based devices, and they examine every packet coming through, which can create significant bottlenecks within a network. Therefore, careful consideration should be given to where routers are placed within a network. This should include leveraging switches in network design as well as applying load balancing principles with other routers for performance efficiency considerations.

Advances in switch technology have provided switches with operating capabilities at Layer 3 and Layer 4 of the OSI model. A **Layer 3 switch** goes beyond the Layer 2-MAC addressing, acting at the network layer of the OSI model like a router. The Layer 3 switch looks at the incoming packet's networking protocol (e.g., IP). The switch compares the destination IP address to the list of addresses in its tables to actively calculate the best way to send a packet to its destination. This creates a virtual circuit (i.e., the switch has the ability to segment the LAN within itself and will create a pathway between the receiving and the transmitting device to send the data). The switch then forwards the packet to the recipient's address. This provides the added benefit of reducing the size of network broadcast domains. A broadcast domain is the domain segment or segments where all connected devices may be simultaneously addressed by a message using a special common network address range, referred to as a broadcast address. This is needed for specific network management functions.

As the broadcast domain grows larger, there may be resulting performance inefficiencies and major security concerns in terms of information leakage within a network (e.g., enumerating network domains and specific computers within a domain). Broadcast domains should be limited or aligned with business functional areas/workgroups within an enterprise to reduce the risk of information leakage to those without a need to know where systems can be targeted to exploit vulnerabilities. The major difference between a router and a Layer 3 switch is that a router performs packet switching using a microprocessor, whereas a Layer 3 switch performs the switching using application ASIC hardware.

In creating separate broadcast domains, Layer 3 switches enable the establishment of a virtual LAN (VLAN). A VLAN is a group of devices on one or more logically segmented LANs. A VLAN is set up by configuring ports on a switch, so devices attached to those ports may communicate as if they were attached to the same physical network segment, although the devices are located on different LAN segments. A VLAN is based on logical rather than physical connections and thus allows great flexibility. That flexibility enables administrators to restrict access to network resources to specific users, and segment network resources for optimal performance.

2.10.3 TCP/IP and Its Relation to the OSI Reference Model

The protocol suite used as the de facto standard for the Internet is known as the TCP/IP. The TCP/IP suite includes both network-oriented protocols and application support protocols. **Figure 2.17** shows where some of the standards associated with the TCP/IP suite fit within the OSI model. It is interesting to note that the TCP/IP set of protocols was developed before the ISO/OSI framework; therefore, there is no direct match between the TCP/IP standards and the layers of the framework.

TCP/IP Internet World Wide Web Services

The most common way a user accesses a resource on the Internet is through the TCP/IP Internet World Wide Web (WWW) application service.

To access a website, a user enters the site's location into a browser's URL space, or clicks on a hypertext link that will connect with the site. The uniform resource locator (URL) identifies the address on the WWW where a specific resource is located.

The web browser looks up the IP address of the site and sends a request for the URL via the HTTP. This protocol defines how the web browser and web server communicate with one another. Refer to **figure 2.17** for an explanation of the components of a URL.

Figure 2.17—Components of a URL

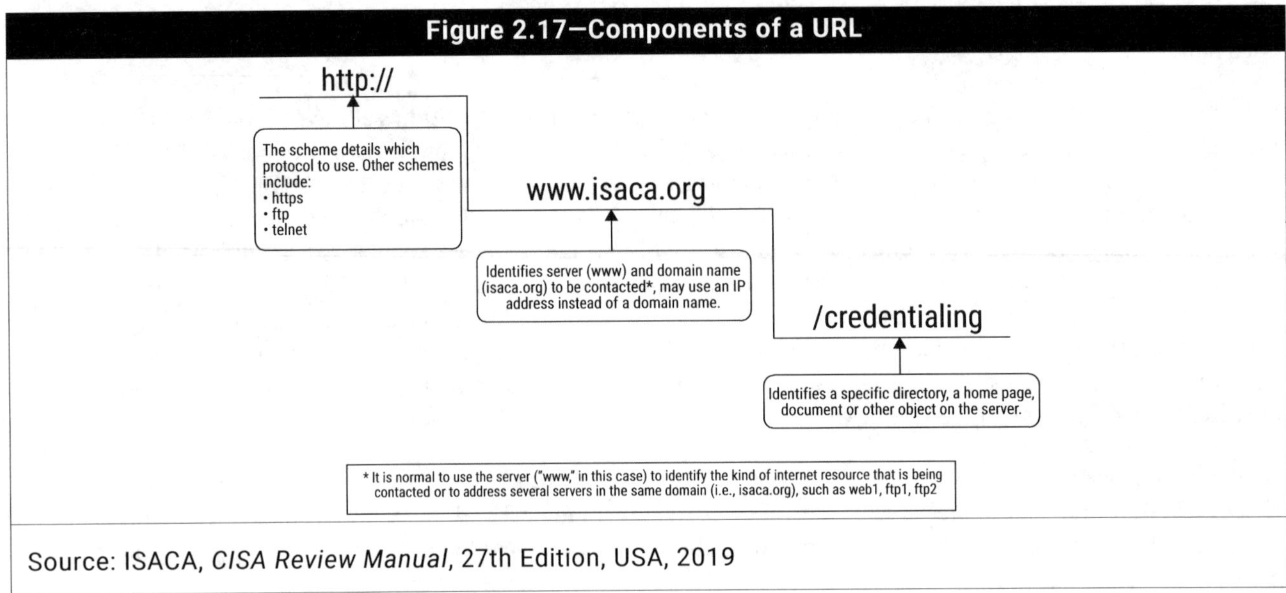

Source: ISACA, *CISA Review Manual*, 27th Edition, USA, 2019

A URL can be used to access other TCP/IP Internet services—for example:

- *ftp://isaca.org*
- *telnet://isaca.org*

A URL is the location of specific resources (e.g., pages, data) or services on the Internet.

In the example shown, the resource is a web page called "credentials," which is found on ISACA's web server.

The URL is the location of specific resources (e.g., pages, data) or services on the Internet. In the example, the resource is a web page called "credentials" and is found on the web server of ISACA. This request is sent over the Internet and the routers transfer the request to the addressed web server, which activates the HTTP protocol and processes the request. When the server finds among its resources the requested home page, document or object, it sends the request back to the web browser. In the case of an HTML page, the information sent back contains data and formatting specifications. These are in the form of a program that is executed by the client web browser and produces the screen displayed for the user. After the page is sent by the server, the HTTP connection is closed and can be reopened. **Figure 2.18** displays the path.

Figure 2.18—Internet Pathway Example

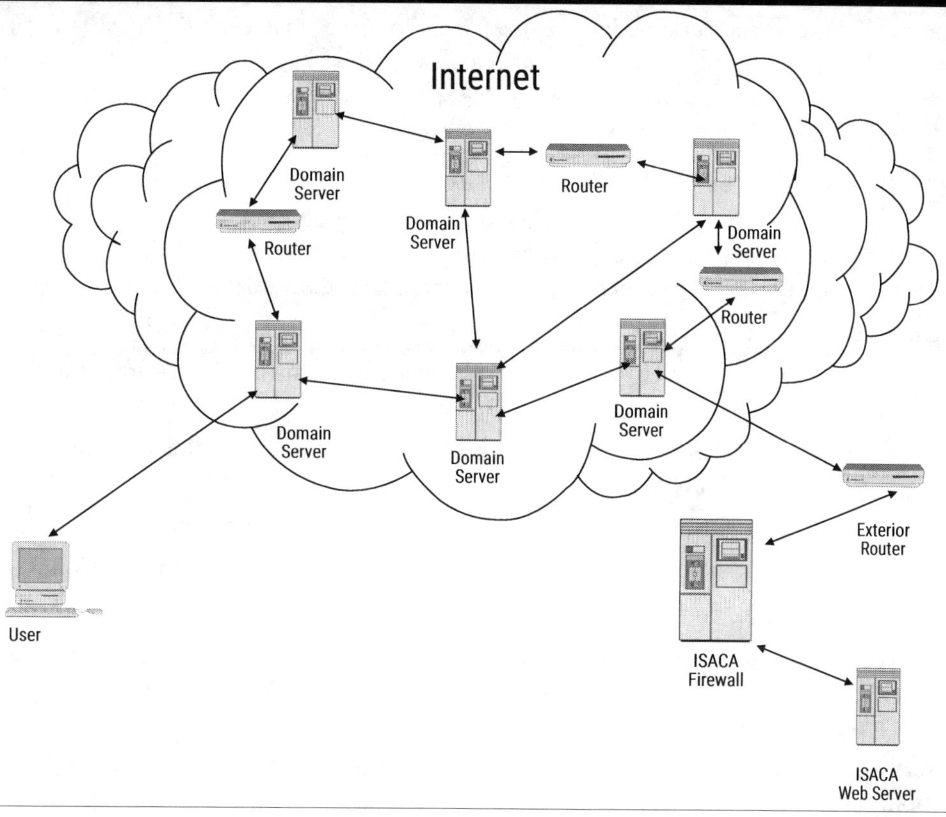

Source: ISACA, *CISA Review Manual*, 27th Edition, USA, 2019

A **cookie** is a message stored by the web browser for the purpose of identifying users and possibly preparing customized web pages for them. Depending on the browser, the implementation may vary, but the process is as follows: The first time a user enters a website that uses cookies, the user may be asked to go through a registration process, such as filling out a form that provides information, including name and interests. The web server will send back a cookie with information (text message in HTTP header), which will be kept as a text message by the browser. Afterward, whenever the user's browser requests a page from that particular server, the cookie's message will be sent back to the server so that the customized view, based on that user's particular interests and preferences, can be produced. Cookies are a very important functionality, because the HTTP protocol does not natively support the concept of a session. Cookies allow the web server to discern whether a known or new user is connected and to keep track of information previously sent to that user. However, the browser's implementation of cookies has allowed breaches of security and the theft of personal information (e.g., user passwords that validate the user's identity and enable restricted web services), prompting concerns over privacy and security.

Applets are programs written in a portable, platform-independent computer language, such as Java, JavaScript or Visual Basic. Applets expose the user's machine to risk if the applets are not properly controlled by the browser. For example, the user's browser should be configured to not allow an applet to access a machine's information without prior authorization of the user.

Servlets are Java applets or small programs that run within a web server environment. A Java servlet is similar to a CGI program. Unlike a CGI program, once it is started, it stays in memory and can fulfill multiple requests, thereby saving server execution time and speeding up the services.

A **bookmark** is a marker or address that identifies a document or a specific place in a document.

Wireless Local Area Networks

A WLAN is a group of wireless networking devices that use radio waves to exchange data wirelessly within a limited area of operation, such as an office building. The security of a WLAN is based on how well each of its components—client devices, access points (APs) and wireless switches—is configured. NIST recommends that enterprises implement its guidelines to improve WLAN security.[24]

- Use standardized security configurations for common WLAN components (client devices and APs).
  - A standard configuration based on an organization's security requirements and industry best practices reduces vulnerabilities and minimizes the impact of successful attacks. Having a standardized configuration decreases the time necessary to secure WLAN components as they are added to the system.
- When designing WLAN security, consider the entire network and not just the security of the WLAN.
  - WLANs are an element of an enterprise network that usually consists of both wired and wireless communications.
  - WLANs that need wired network access should be allowed access to only the necessary hosts on the wired network using the required protocols.
  - WLANs should be segregated based on security profile (guests and employees).
  - Devices on one WLAN should not be able to access devices on a logically separated WLAN.
- Establish policies and security controls for dual connections.
  - Dual connections refer to client devices that access a network from both a wired and WLAN connection at the same time. An attacker that gains access to a dual-connected wireless device can use that device to attack systems or resources on the wired network.
  - Enterprises should consider the risks when permitting devices to access the network over multiple connection types (wireless, wired, cell, WiMAX, and Bluetooth).
  - Policies on acceptable use and connection types permitted within the enterprise network need to be established and communicated to users. Security controls should be implemented for connection policy enforcement, reports and alerts. Training on risk and proper use should be provided to all users of the network.
  - Dual connection risks that cannot be mitigated may need to be prohibited.
- Review and verify that WLAN client devices and APs have configurations that are compliant with the enterprise's WLAN policies.
  - Perform periodic configuration and policy reviews.
  - Implement change control, so that configuration changes are reviewed prior to implementation.
- Implement monitoring, logging and alerting to support WLAN security.
  - Continuous monitoring of the WLAN—its use, connections and activity—should be implemented, along with alerting and reporting.
  - Conduct the same level of vulnerability monitoring and testing that is used on the wired network.
- Conduct security assessments of the WLAN.
  - Comprehensive security assessments should be conducted yearly, at a minimum, to evaluate the overall security of the WLAN.
- Periodic assessments should be conducted quarterly unless continuous monitoring is in place.

2.10.4 Transport Layer Security

Transport layer security (TLS) is a cryptographic protocol that provides secure communications on the Internet. TLS is a session- or connection-layered protocol widely used for communication between browsers and web servers.

Besides communication privacy, it provides endpoint authentication. The protocols allow client-server applications to communicate in a way designed to prevent eavesdropping, tampering and message forgery. **Figure 2.19** provides an overview of TLS.

Figure 2.19—Overview of Transport Layer Security Protocol

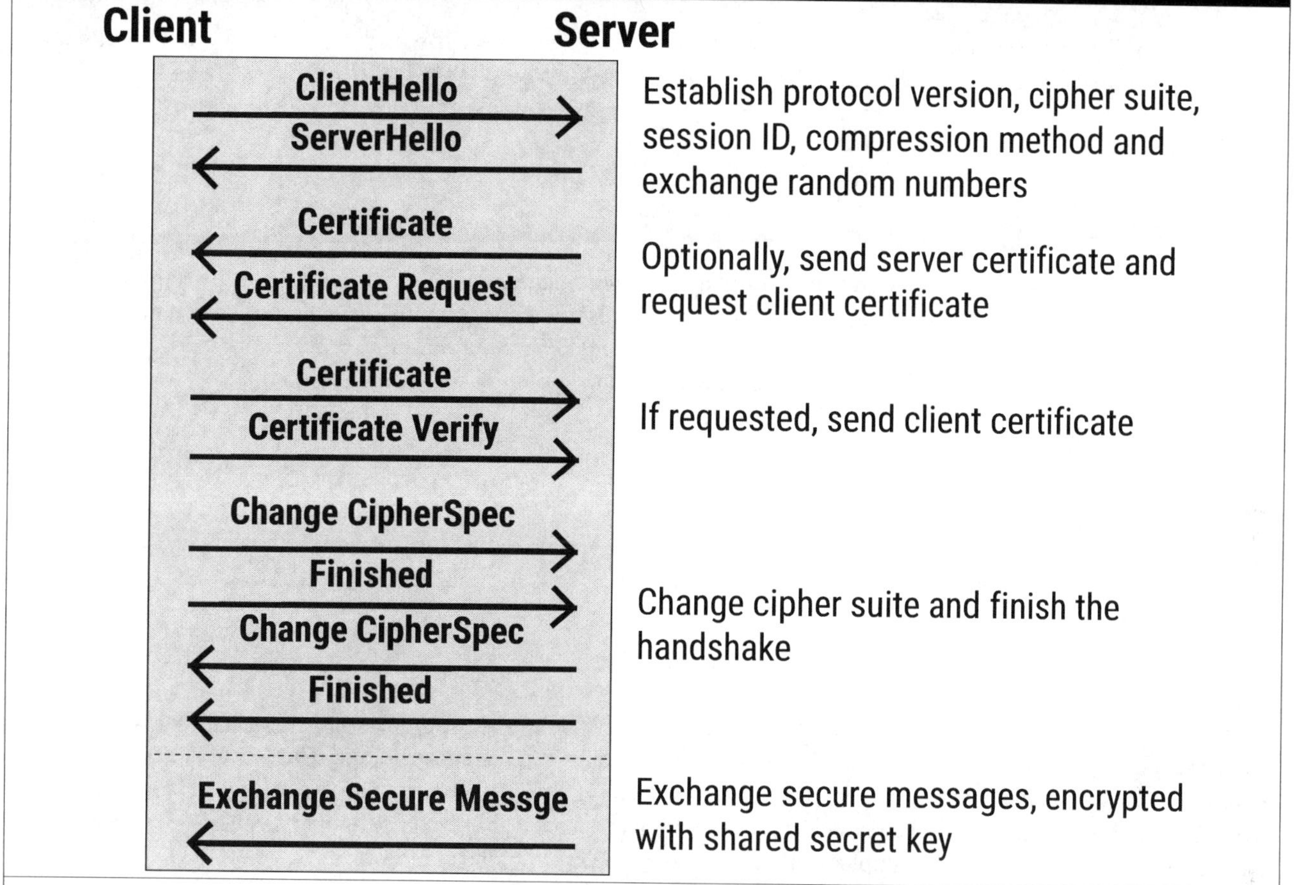

Source: Ben Hamida, S.; E. Ben Hamida; B. Ahmed; "A New mHealth Communication Framework for Use in Wearable WBANs and Mobile Technologies," *Sensors*, Switzerland, 3 February 2015, DOI: 10.3390/s150203379

TLS involves a few basic phases:

- Peer negotiation for algorithm support
- Public-key, encryption-based key exchange and certificate-based authentication
- Symmetric cipher-based traffic encryption

During the first phase, the client and server negotiate the cryptographic algorithms that will be used. Current implementations support the following choices:

- For public-key cryptography: RSA, Diffie-Hellman, DSA or Fortezza
- For symmetric ciphers: RC4, IDEA, Triple DES or AES
- For one-way hash functions: SHA-1 or SHA-2 (SHA-256)

TLS runs on layers above the TCP transport protocol and provides security to application protocols, even if it is most commonly used with HTTP to form Secure Hypertext Transmission Protocol (HTTPS). HTTPS serves to secure WWW pages for applications. In electronic commerce, authentication may be used in business-to-business (B2B) activities, in which the client and the server are authenticated, and business-to-consumer (B2C) interactions, in which only the server is authenticated.

In addition to TLS, Secure Socket Layer (SSL) protocol is widely used in real-world applications, even though its use was deprecated following discovery of a significant vulnerability in 2014.

TLS and SSL are not interchangeable.

2.10.5 Secure Shell

Secure shell (SSH) is a commonly used application layer protocol suite. While it is often used as a secure remote login application and a secure file transfer application, it can also be used to tunnel specific ports via an SSH connection to allow either a local connection to access a remote resource or a remote connection to access a local resource. SSH is often used on intermediary hosts (also called bastion hosts) to jump to other hosts, but that jump does not need to be to the remote login (SSH) host itself.

For instance, port 25 on localhost (127.0.0.1) could be made available to locally running mail clients. The SSH protocol allows for the secure transport of this traffic using the SSH VPN to the bastion host, where the SSH client will forward the decrypted traffic to a remote mail server's port 25. Because a single SSH tunnel can provide protection for several applications at once, it is technically a transport layer VPN protocol, not an application layer protocol.

2.11 Encryption, Hashing and De-identification

Encryption is a vital part of secure communications and is used widely in many products and systems throughout an enterprise, ranging from email to VPNs, access control, backup tapes and hard disk storage. The secure use of encryption requires the correct choice of algorithm, the protection of the encryption keys, the randomness of key generation, and limits on the length of time a key is used before being changed. In many cases, the breach of an implementation of encryption is due to user misuse or an error in the implementation, not to a problem with the algorithm.

2.11.1 Encryption

Encryption is the conversion of information into secret code to hide the information's true meaning. The science of encrypting and decrypting information is called cryptography. In computing, unencrypted data is also known as plaintext, and encrypted data is called ciphertext. Encryption is a two-way function; what is encrypted can be decrypted with the proper key.

Cryptography refers to the science behind encryption, a mathematical means of altering data from a plaintext (or cleartext) form that is easily readable into an unreadable format (ciphertext) in a manner that can be reversed by someone who has access to the appropriate key. Encryption may be used to protect the confidentiality of data by making data unreadable to anyone who is unauthorized. It protects the integrity of data by proving that the content has not been changed and confirming the identity of the sender, or both.

Data encryption provides several risk management benefits, including:

- Confidentiality
- Integrity
- Proof of origin (nonrepudiation)
- Access control
- Authentication

Encryption comes in two basic forms—symmetric and asymmetric—each of which has its own strengths and weaknesses. Each can be used in a variety of ways.

Symmetric Algorithms

An example of symmetric key cryptography is shown in **figure 2.20.**

Figure 2.20—Symmetric Cryptography

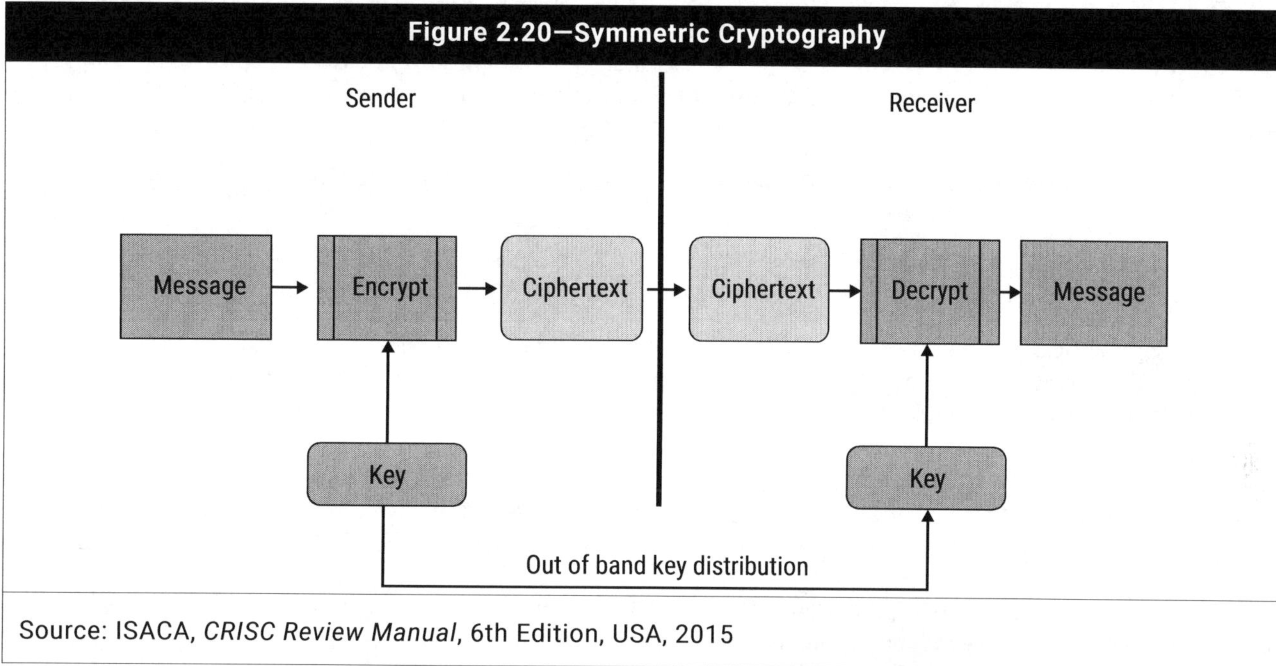

Source: ISACA, *CRISC Review Manual*, 6th Edition, USA, 2015

Symmetric key cryptography occurs when an encryption algorithm uses the same secret key to encrypt the plaintext into ciphertext and to decrypt the ciphertext back into plaintext. Symmetric key cryptosystems are generally less complicated than those that use asymmetric techniques and use less processing power, which makes symmetric key cryptosystems ideally suited for bulk data encryption.

The most common symmetric key cryptographic system currently in use is the Advanced Encryption Standard (AES), a public algorithm known as a block cipher because it operates on plaintext in blocks (strings or groups). AES supports keys from 128 bits to 256 bits in size. It replaced both the earlier Data Encryption Standard (DES), which was a public algorithm that used 56-bit keys, and an augmented variant of DES called Triple DES (3DES) that offered somewhat stronger security.

Because the length of a key determines the number of possible mathematical combinations, shorter keys pose an inherent security problem as processing power increases. DES is no longer considered a strong cryptographic solution because its entire key space can be tested against ciphertext by large computer systems within a relatively short period of time, a technique aptly known as brute force. AES includes a number of advanced mathematical techniques that allow it to generate stronger ciphertext than 3DES could generate. Nonetheless, ongoing advances in computing power virtually guarantee that any algorithm in use will eventually be rendered obsolete. Even the strongest algorithm with the most robust keys is only as secure as its key management system.

Symmetric key cryptography has two major disadvantages. One is that there is no easy way for one party to deliver keys to another with whom it would like to exchange data (particularly in e-commerce environments where customers are unknown and untrusted entities). Also, because a symmetric key is based on a mutually shared secret, there is no way to be sure which participant in a given key network originated a particular message.

Asymmetric Algorithms

Asymmetric key cryptographic systems are a relatively recent development that evolved to address the issues with symmetric key cryptosystems.

In 1976, Whitfield Diffie and Martin Hellman published the first public example of encryption based on two different keys, a technique known as the Diffie-Hellman model. In a Diffie-Hellman setup, two mathematically related keys are created—a private key and a public key. It is computationally infeasible to determine the value of one key from the other, but each has the effect, when used in an appropriate asymmetric algorithm, of creating ciphertext that only the other has the ability to return to plaintext. As a result of this relationship, two things become possible:

1. The public key may be freely distributed and used as the means of encrypting any message that should be readable only by its creator, who has sole access to the private key that allows the message to be decrypted.
2. Because the only messages that the public key can decrypt are those that were encrypted by the private key, to which its creator has sole access, any recipient can be certain that the key creator was the true author.

Because asymmetric algorithms use a public and private key pair, they are commonly referred to as public key algorithms. Each party using public key cryptography only needs one pair of keys (the private and the corresponding public key), and because the public key can be freely distributed, public key cryptography overcomes the weakness of scalability of symmetric key cryptography.

One disadvantage of using asymmetric algorithms is they are computationally intensive and slow relative to symmetric algorithms. For that reason, asymmetric cryptography is typically used only to encrypt short messages.

In fact, the most common use of asymmetric algorithms is to distribute symmetric keys that can then be used by the participants for fast, secure communication, as seen in **figure 2.21.**

Figure 2.21—Using Asymmetric Algorithms to Support Symmetric Cryptography

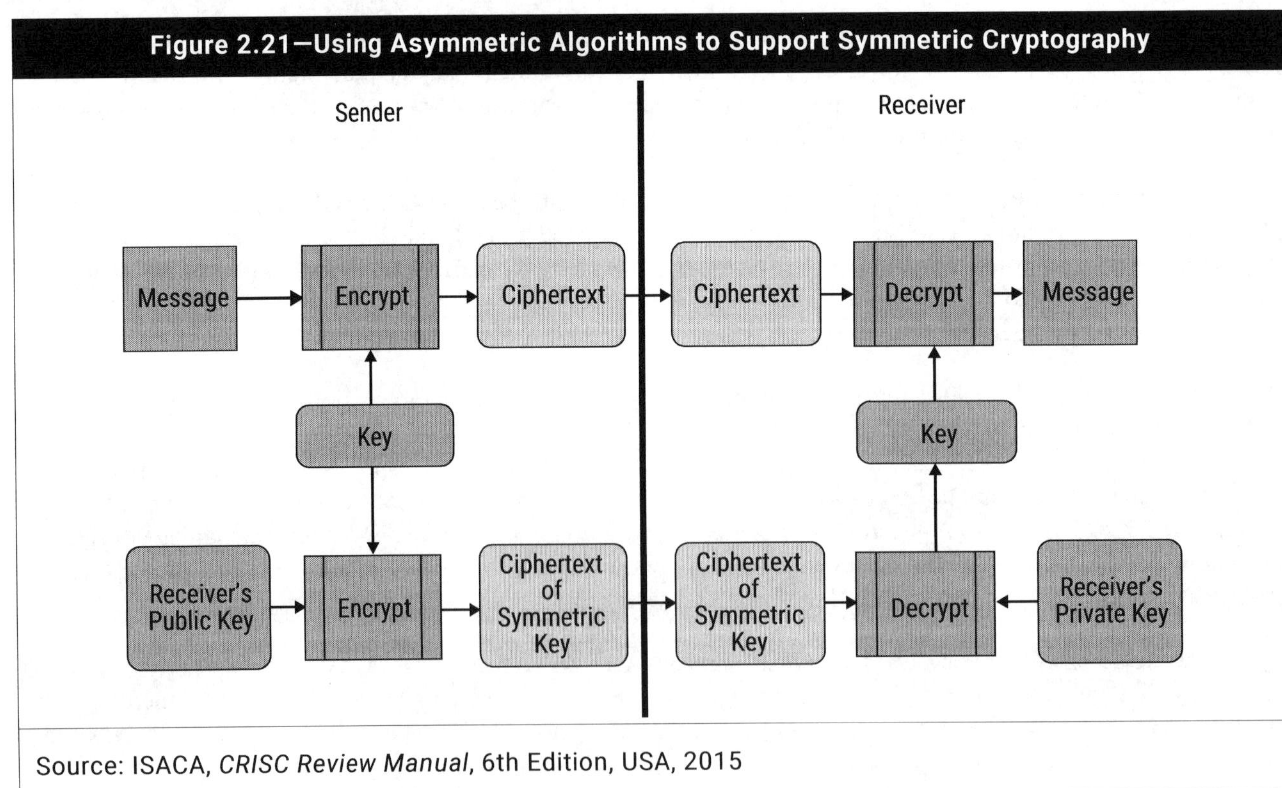

Source: ISACA, *CRISC Review Manual*, 6th Edition, USA, 2015

Quantum Cryptography

Quantum cryptography refers to the possibility of using properties of quantum computing (computer technology based on quantum theory) for cryptographic purposes, quantum key distribution (QKD) being the most important application. QKD schemes allow the distribution of a shared encryption key between two parties who can detect when another unauthorized party is eavesdropping on the key exchange channel. When this happens, the channel is inevitably disturbed, and the exchanged key is tagged as compromised.

Quantum computing is known to easily break the security of schemes like RSA. To overcome this drawback, postquantum encryption algorithms that are resistant to a quantum attack have been developed.

2.11.2 De-identification

Data de-identification refers to a technique of data protection that involves the removal of all PII. De-identification allows for the retention of data for statistical or analytical purposes without the need to bind that data to a distinct individual. Proper data de-identification requires that combining additional external data sources or data elements with the de-identified data will not create a pointer or reference to a distinct individual.

Strategies of de-identification include masking of personal identifiers, generalizing (quasi-identifiers), pseudonymization and *k*-anonymization.

Pseudonymization is the replacement of real names with a temporary ID. True identifiers for the data subject are masked or deleted to make individuals unidentifiable. Through pseudonymization, the life cycle of the data subject can be tracked and data can be used for analytical or statistical purposes without being attributable to a specific individual. This approach does allow the data records to be updated over time, however. Pseudonymization does not prevent re-identification of the individual when additional data sets are added to the pseudonymized record. It is possible to re-identify an individual whose data were pseudonymized by adding additional data elements to create one comprehensive record, which then re-identifies the individual data subject.

k-anonymization defines attributes that point indirectly to the individual's identity. These are called quasi-identifiers (QIs). This process ensures that at least *k* individuals have some combination of QI values.QI values are handled following specific standards. For example, the *k*-anonymization replaces some original data in the records with new range values and keeps some values unchanged. A new combination of QI values prevents the individual from being identified and avoids the need to destroy data records.[25]

2.11.3 Hashing

Hashing is a one-way function that scrambles plaintext to produce a unique message digest. Hashing is used with passwords. There is no way to reverse the hashing process to reveal the original password.

Message Integrity and Hashing Algorithms

Early computer networks used voice-grade telephone cable with limited bandwidth. The combination of slow speed and interference meant that error-correcting was needed to ensure that what was received matched what was sent.

Parity bits, checksums, and cyclic redundancy checks (CRC) proved effective in detecting accidental errors, but those mechanisms added data to each transmission.

Hashing refers to the mathematical transformation of data using an algorithm with a result that is predictable, repeatable, and entirely dependent upon the content of the message, and of a fixed length (regardless of the length of

the original message). A hash algorithm calculates a value known as a digest, fingerprint or thumbprint from an input message whose length depends on the hash algorithm used. For example, SHA1 generates a digest of 160 bits, while SHA512 generates a digest of 512 bits. A sender who wants to ensure that a message is not affected by noise or network problems can hash the message and send the digest along with the message to the receiver. The receiver can then hash the received message and verify that the resulting digest matches the digest sent with the message, as shown in **figure 2.22**.

Figure 2.22—Verifying Message Integrity Using a Hash Function

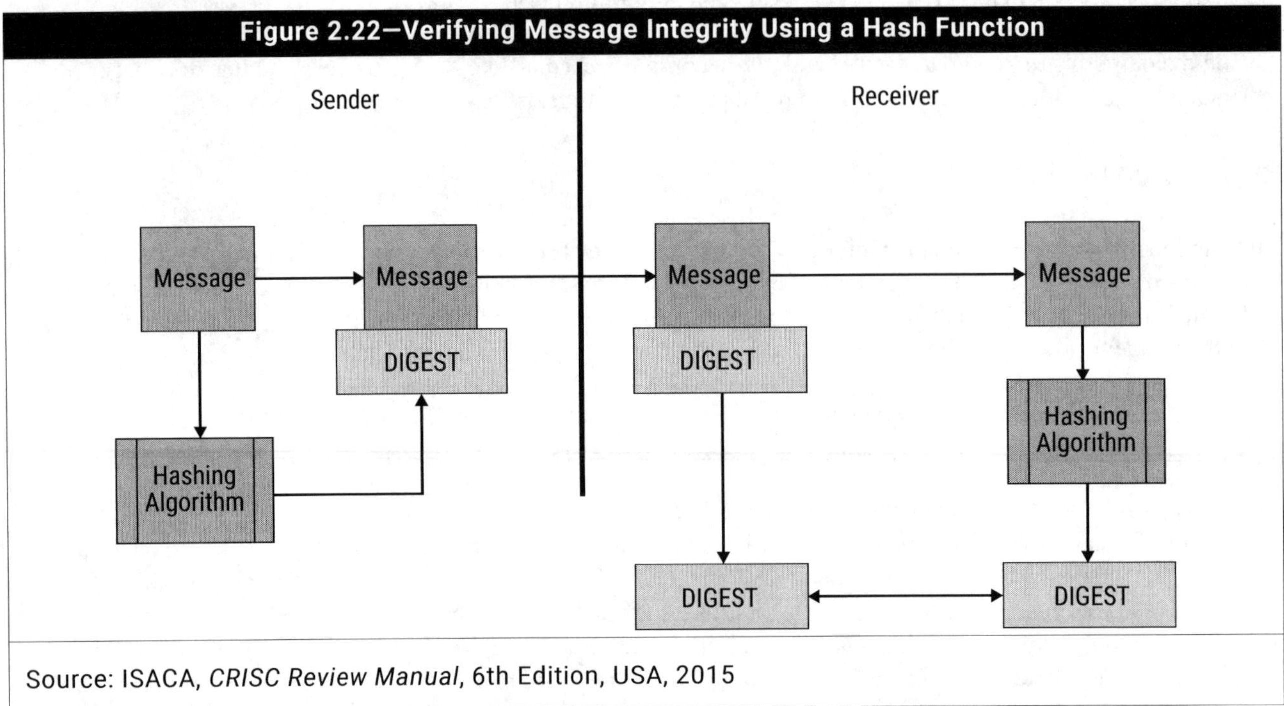

Source: ISACA, *CRISC Review Manual*, 6th Edition, USA, 2015

Hashing by itself provides effective protection against accidental changes in a message, such as those caused by interference. However, a malicious user who intercepts a transmission that includes a hash and changes the message likely would not be deterred by hashing but would simply create a new digest to send with the replacement message.

Digital Signatures

A digital signature combines a hash function with the asymmetric encryption ability to verify the author's identity. The receiver knows that the message was not changed, because the hash of the received message is the same as the hash (digest) that was signed by the sender. The receiver also knows the identity of the sender, because being able to decrypt the digital signature with the sender's public key means that it must have been encrypted with the sender's private key—and the sender cannot plausibly deny it, a characteristic known as "nonrepudiation," which makes digital signatures particularly valuable. **Figure 2.23** illustrates the use of digital signatures to verify integrity and proof of origin.

Figure 2.23—Verifying Message Integrity and Proof of Origin Using Digital Signatures

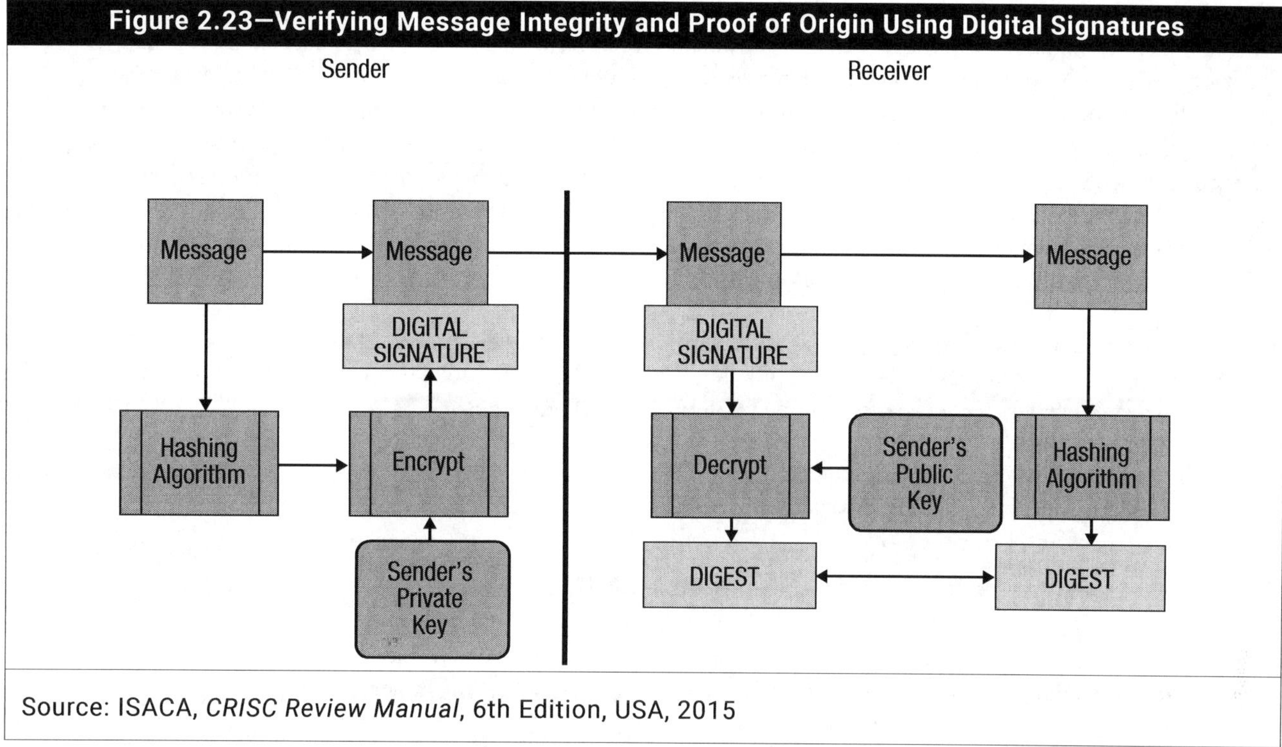

Source: ISACA, *CRISC Review Manual*, 6th Edition, USA, 2015

Digitally signing a message does not make the message itself confidential. A message may be encrypted and not signed, signed and not encrypted, or both signed and encrypted. Only a message that is both signed and encrypted is simultaneously afforded confidentiality, integrity and nonrepudiation.

Digital Envelope

Similar to a digital signature, a digital envelope is an electronic "container" that can be used to protect data or a message through the use of encryption and data authentication. The message is first encoded using symmetric encryption. Then the code to decrypt the message is secured using public key encryption. This provides a more convenient option for encryption.

2.11.4 Applications of Cryptographic Systems

Asymmetric and symmetric systems can be combined to leverage each system's peculiarities. A common scheme is to encrypt data using a symmetric algorithm with a randomly generated secret key. The secret key is then encrypted using an asymmetric encryption algorithm to allow secure distribution among those parties who need access to the encrypted data. Secure communications can thus enjoy both the speed of symmetric systems and the ease of key-distribution of asymmetric systems. In addition, because creating the secret key is an effortless operation, it can be employed for just a limited amount of data, after which a new secret key can be chosen. This method limits the opportunities for malicious third parties to decrypt the whole set of data because they would be required to attack multiple secret keys. This combined scheme is used in protocols such as TLS 1.3 (TLS 1.2 at a minimum) to protect web traffic, and S/MIME for email encryption. In the latter case, the resulting document—the combination of the encrypted message and the encrypted secret key—is called a digital envelope.

IP Security

IPSec is used for securing the communications at IP-level among two or more hosts, subnets, or hosts and subnets.

The IP network layer packet security protocol establishes VPNs via transport and tunnel mode encryption methods. For the transport method, the data portion of each packet, referred to as the encapsulation security payload (ESP), is encrypted to achieve confidentiality over the process. In the tunnel mode, the ESP payload and its header are encrypted. To achieve nonrepudiation, an additional authentication header (AH) is applied. In establishing IPSec sessions in either mode, security associations (SAs) are established. SAs define the security parameters that should be applied between the communicating parties as encryption algorithms, keys, initialization vectors, life span of keys, etc. Within either the ESP or AH header, respectively, an SA is established when a 32-bit security parameter index (SPI) field is defined within the sending host. The SPI is a unique identifier that enables the sending host to reference the security parameters to apply, as specified, to the receiving host.

IPSec can be made more secure by using asymmetric encryption through the use of Internet Security Association and Key Management Protocol/Oakley (ISAKMP/Oakley), which allows key management, use of public keys, negotiation, establishment, modification and deletion of SAs and attributes.

For authentication, the sender uses digital certificates. The connection is made secure by supporting the generation, authentication and distribution of the SAs and those of the cryptographic keys.

Secure Multipurpose Internet Mail Extensions (S/MIME)

S/MIME is a standard secure email protocol that authenticates the identities of the sender and receiver, verifies message integrity, and ensures the privacy of a message's contents, including attachments.

2.12 Key Management

In cryptography, a key is a string of characters used within an encryption algorithm for altering data so that it appears random. Like a physical key, it locks (encrypts) data so that only someone with the right key can unlock (decrypt) it. In computing, encryption is used to protect data stored on computers and storage devices and data in transit over networks.[26]

Combined with an encryption algorithm, a cryptographic key will scramble a text beyond human recognition.

Encryption key management is administration of the full life cycle of cryptographic keys, which includes generating, using, storing, archiving and deleting keys. Production of encryption keys includes limiting access to keys logically and through user guide access.[27]

2.12.1 Certificates

Public key encryption ensures that only the holder of a private key can decrypt what is encrypted with the corresponding public key, but it does not confirm the identity of the person who owns the public key being distributed. The purpose of a certificate is to link a public key with a specific owner by relying on the verification of a trusted third party known as a certificate authority (CA). The CA generates certificates that owners of public keys can use to prove their ownership. A recipient of a certificate created and signed by a CA can be confident that the public key in the certificate belongs to whomever is specified by the certificate. A recipient who opens a digital signature with that public key knows that the message was signed and sent by the sender.

The format of a certificate is based on a standard called X.509, which ensures that certificates can be accessed by most browsers and systems even if they are issued by different CAs. Each certificate is valid for a defined period of time, typically one year from the date of issue. However, the owner of a certificate may cancel it at any time during that period by notifying the CA, which will put the certificate on a certificate revocation list (CRL). Requests to validate a certificate that is on a CRL result in notification that the certificate has been revoked, warning that the certificate should not be trusted as a means of verifying identity.

2.12.2 Public Key Infrastructure

Public key infrastructure (PKI) is an encryption and cybersecurity framework that includes a set of roles, policies and procedures needed to create, manage, distribute, use, store, revoke digital certificates and manage public key encryption. PKI protects communications between the server (a website) and the client (the users). PKI works by using two different cryptographic keys: a public key and a private key. Public keys are generally available to any user who connects to the website. A private key (secret) is a unique key that is generated when a connection is made. When communicating, the client uses the public key to encrypt and decrypt, and the server uses the private key.

There are several elements required for PKI to function correctly:

- **Certificate authority (CA)**—CA is used to authenticate the digital identities of the users (i.e., servers, individuals, computer systems). Certificate Authorities prevent falsified entities and manage the life cycle of any number of digital certificates within the system.
- **Registration authority (RA)**—RA is authorized by the CA to provide digital certificates to users on a case-by-case basis. All certificates requested, received, and revoked by the CA and the RA are stored in an encrypted certificate database.
- **Certificate store**—Certificate store is a specific computer that functions as storage space for all relevant certificate history (i.e., certificate history, private encryption keys).

When hosting these elements on a secure framework, a PKI can protect both the identities and private information used in situations that necessitate digital security (i.e., digital signatures, encrypted documents, smart card logins).

Services or functions of a PKI include:

- **Authentication**—This is defined as a means of identification and is provided by using digital certificates.
- **Nonrepudiation**—The sender of information cannot deny sending or disown information sent at a later time. Nonrepudiation ensures that there is ownership of an electronic document. PKI facilitates this by using digital signatures.

PKI Encryption

A PKI uses both asymmetric and symmetric encryption. Symmetric encryption protects the private key generated with the initial exchange between parties. This secret key must be passed from one party to another so that all involved can decrypt the exchanged information.

2.13 Monitoring and Logging

Monitoring and logging work together to provide a range of information that tracks the health and performance of the IT infrastructure:[28]

- **Monitoring tools** show how applications are behaving.
- **Log data** from applications, network infrastructure and web servers provide greater insight as to why applications are performing the way they are.

From a privacy perspective, monitoring and logging provide the necessary information for the identification of issues, abuses and misuses of information or systems. While data privacy is not the first consideration when leveraging monitoring and system/application logs, thresholds should be set up to trigger privacy alerts. Events generating such alerts could include:

- Failed access requests
- Access to data repositories (frequency, duration, level of access)

- Data exfiltration (mass movement of data that exceeds normal operational parameters)
- Administrative access logs—who is accessing privacy systems and for what purpose (what is done while in those systems)
- System anomalies of events in log files

Many of these fall into logging and monitoring typically associated with incident response. When using these tools for data privacy, alerts and warnings need to be provided so that early detection of abuse or misuse of systems and the data they process can be investigated from a privacy perspective.

2.13.1 Monitoring

Monitoring uses application metrics to measure network availability and manage performance. Monitoring systems rely on metrics to alert IT (i.e., NOC), information security and compliance, security operation center (SOC) or DevOps teams to operating anomalies across applications and cloud services. Ideally, teams would implement instrumentation and monitoring on all systems and critical data stores across the entire operational infrastructure.

2.13.2 Logging

Logging is commonly provided by systems, devices and applications, and it remains the most consistently popular way to capture and store data for analysis. Analysis of log data can identify security violations and be instrumental in forensics investigations. Log analysis can also alert the enterprise to malicious activity, such as a developing attack or multiple attempts to break in, and it may be used to identify the source of an attack and assist in strengthening controls where necessary. Logs should have visibility, and by extension accountability, by more than one entity in the enterprise to reduce the insider threat of accessibility and motive to sabotage. Logs should be the first line of defense and an indicator to multiple lines of enterprise management of a security issue.

Logging has traditionally presented a trade-off between speed, detail and utility. If a log contains too many data from too many disparate sources, it may be difficult to notice significant individual events. Time synchronization of log entries can assist with correlation of events from multiple sources and improve the usefulness of review. Logging also takes time, potentially decreasing throughput for each transaction monitored.

Analysis of log data and control activity should answer the following questions:

- Are the controls operating efficiently?
- Is the level of risk acceptable?
- Are the risk strategy and controls aligned with business strategy and priorities?
- Are the controls flexible enough to meet changing threats?
- Is the correct risk data being provided in a timely manner?
- Is the risk management effort aiding in reaching corporate objectives?
- Is the awareness of risk and compliance embedded into user behaviors?

As network and client security systems continue to mature, logging for specific purposes is becoming more granular and offering a greater degree of detail for analysis. For instance, client-resident data leakage protection (DLP) software can integrate with antivirus and anti-malware modules to distinguish between interactive (human) and process-driven attempts to migrate data in ways that are forbidden. Such information might reveal the difference between inadequate user training (or a malicious insider) and a remotely compromised system. Logging by intrusion detection or prevention systems (IDS/IPS) placed within the network can also be useful in detecting suspicious traffic patterns, particularly when combined with advanced behavior-based (heuristic) analysis.

Logs may contain information that is sensitive or may be needed for forensic purposes, so they should be configured in ways that prevent alteration or deletion, while preventing access by unauthorized personnel. In particular, administrators with responsibility for systems or applications should generally not have the ability to alter or delete logs made against their own scopes of responsibility. Log access permissions should be considered as part of evaluating the potential insider threat.

2.13.3 Privacy and Security Logging

Figure 2.24 lists common privacy considerations for security logging.

Figure 2.24—Privacy and Security Logging

Consideration	Description
Application logging or system logging	Error logs include: ■ Application errors ■ System errors ■ Network errors • System access logs (to all systems within the stack) ■ Failed/successful attempts ■ System/date/timestamp/IP address/count/session duration ■ Log access (who has it, when are they accessed and how often) • Change logs ■ System changes ■ System environment or application parameter adjustments or changes ■ Data changes or element changes ■ Data edits - Changes to data elements from an administrative or privileged account - Direct database access o System/date/timestamp/IP address/count/session duration • Log data retention ■ Duration of log persistence - How long the data is needed for analysis - Aggregate or view for historical review o Reporting o Historical system operations and trends analysis o Process of log data deletion o Frequency o PII or information that should not be present in the logs o Systems writing PII to the logs o Data changes or element changes (Integrity) o Data edits o Changes to data elements from an administrative or privileged account o Direct database access o System/date/timestamp/IP address/count/session duration

2.14 Identity and Access Management

Identity and access management (IAM) is a framework of business processes, policies and technologies an enterprise uses to manage electronic or digital identities. Using an IAM framework, IT managers can control user access to

critical information within the enterprise. IAM products offer role-based access control, which lets the system administrator restrict user access to parts of the enterprise based on need.

Identification and authentication (I&A) is a critical building block of computer security because it is needed for most types of access control and is necessary for establishing user accountability. For most systems, I&A is the first line of defense because it prevents unauthorized access to a computer system or an information asset, and guards them from the use of unauthorized processes. Logical access can be implemented in various ways.

Logical access controls are used to manage and protect information assets. Logical security is often determined based on the job function of users. The success of logical access controls is tied to the strength of the authentication method. All user access to systems and data should be appropriately authorized and commensurate with the role of the individual. Authorization generally takes the form of signatures (physical or electronic) of relevant management. The strength of the authentication is proportional to the quality of the method used.

2.14.1 System Access Permission

System access permission is the prerogative to act on a computer resource. This usually refers to a technical privilege, such as the ability to read, create, modify or delete a file or data; execute a program; or open or use an external connection (i.e., API). See section 2.8.1 APIs for more information.

System access to computerized information resources is established, managed and controlled at the physical and/or logical level. Physical access controls restrict the entry and exit of personnel to an area such as an office building, suite, data center or room containing information-processing equipment such as a LAN server. There are many types of physical access controls, including badges, memory cards, guard keys, true floor-to-ceiling wall construction fences, locks and biometrics. Logical system access controls restrict the logical resources of the system (transactions, data, programs, applications) and are applied when the subject resource is needed. On the basis of identification and authentication of the user who requires a given resource and by analyzing the security profiles of the user and the resource, it is possible to make determinations about the requested access (i.e., the information that users can access, the programs or transactions they can run, and the modifications they can make). Such controls may be built into the operating system (OS) or invoked through separate access control software and incorporated into application programs, database, network control devices and utilities (e.g., real-time performance monitors).

Physical or logical system access to any computerized information should be on a documented need-to-know basis (often referred to as role-based) to meet a legitimate business requirement based on least privilege. Other considerations for granting access are accountability (e.g., unique user ID) and traceability (e.g., logs). These principles should be used when evaluating the appropriateness of criteria for defining permissions and granting security privileges. Enterprises should establish basic criteria for assigning technical access to specific data, programs, devices and resources, including who will have access and what level of access they will be allowed. For instance, it may be desirable for everyone in the enterprise to have access to specific information on the system, such as the data displayed on an enterprise's daily calendar of meetings. The program that formats and displays the calendar might be modifiable by only a few system administrators, while the OS controlling that program might be directly accessible by still fewer.

The IT assets under logical security can be grouped in four layers—networks, platforms, databases and applications. This concept of layered security for system access provides greater scope and granularity of control to information resources. For example, network and platform layers provide pervasive general systems control over users authenticating into systems, system software and application configurations, data sets, load libraries, and any production data set libraries. For best results, the granularity needs to match the logging enacted for easier alerting and quicker remediation. Database and application controls generally provide a greater degree of control over user activity within a particular business process by controlling access to records, specific data fields and transactions.

The information owner or manager who is responsible for the accurate use and reporting of information should provide written authorization for users or defined roles to gain access to information resources under their control. The manager should hand over this documentation directly to the security administrator to ensure that mishandling or alteration of the authorization does not occur.

Logical access capabilities are implemented by security administration in a set of access rules that stipulate which users (or groups of users) are authorized to access a resource at a particular level (e.g., read-, update- or execute-only) and under which conditions (e.g., time of day or a subset of computer terminals). The security administrator invokes the appropriate system access control mechanism upon receipt of a proper authorization request from the information owner or manager to grant a specified user the rights for access to, or use of, a protected resource. Access should be granted to the enterprise's information systems using the principles of need-to-know, least privilege and SoD.

Reviews of access authorization should be evaluated regularly to ensure that they are still valid. Personnel and departmental changes, malicious efforts, and just plain carelessness result in authorization creep and can impact the effectiveness of access controls. Many times, access is not removed when personnel leave an enterprise, thus increasing the risk of unauthorized access. For this reason, the information asset owner should review access controls periodically with a predetermined authorization matrix that defines the least-privileged access level and authority for an individual with reference to job roles and responsibilities. Any access exceeding the access philosophy in the authorized matrix or in actual access levels granted on a system should be updated and changed accordingly. One good practice is to integrate the review of access rights with human resource processes. When an employee transfers to a different function (e.g., promotion, lateral transfer or demotion), access rights should be adjusted at the same time. Development of a security-conscious culture increases the effectiveness of access controls.

Nonemployees with access to corporate IS resources should be held responsible for security compliance and be accountable for security breaches. Nonemployees include contract employees, vendor programmers/analysts, maintenance personnel, clients, auditors, visitors and consultants. It should be understood that nonemployees are accountable to the enterprise's security requirements. Nonemployees should be included in the organization's code of conduct and provide signed documentation affirming that they understand their responsibilities and the enterprise's expectations with respect to security and privacy requirements.

2.14.2 Mandatory and Discretionary Access Controls

Mandatory access controls (MACs) are logical access control filters used to validate access credentials that cannot be controlled or modified by normal users or data owners; they act by default.

Controls that may be configured or modified by the users or data owners are called discretionary access controls (DACs). MACs are a good choice to enforce a ground level of critical security without possible exception, if required by corporate security policies or other security rules. A MAC could be carried out by comparing the sensitivity of the information resources (such as files, data or storage devices) kept on a user-unmodifiable tag attached to the security object, with the security clearance of the accessing entity, such as a user or an application.

With MACs, only administrators may make decisions that are derived from policy. Only an administrator may change the category of a resource, and no one may grant a right of access that is explicitly forbidden in the access control policy. MACs are prohibitive; anything that is not expressly permitted is forbidden. DACs are a protection that may be activated or modified at the discretion of the data owner. This would be the case with data owner-defined sharing of information resources. In such cases, data owners may select who will be enabled to access their resources and designate the security level of the access. DACs cannot override MACs; DACs act as an additional filter, prohibiting still more access with the same exclusionary principle.

When information systems enforce MAC policies, the systems must distinguish between MAC and the discretionary policies that offer more flexibility. This distinction must be ensured during object creation, classification downgrading and labeling.

2.14.3 Information Security and External Parties

The security of the enterprise's information and information-processing facilities that are accessed, processed, communicated to or managed by external parties should be maintained, and should not be reduced by the introduction of external party products or services. Any access to the enterprise's information-processing facilities and processing and communication of information by external parties should be controlled. Controls should be agreed to and defined in an agreement with the external party. Enterprises shall gain the right to audit the implementation and operation of the resulting security controls. Such agreements can help reduce the risk associated with external parties.

Identification of Risk Related to External Parties

The risk to the enterprise's information and information-processing facilities from business processes involving external parties should be identified and appropriate controls implemented before granting access. If there is a need to provide an external party with access to the information-processing facilities or information of an enterprise, a risk assessment should be carried out to identify any requirements for specific controls. The identification of risk related to external party access should take into consideration the issues depicted in **figure 2.25**.

Figure 2.25—Risk Related to External Party Access

- The information-processing facilities an external party is required to access
- The type of access the external party will have to the information and information-processing facilities
  - Physical access (e.g., to offices, computer rooms and filing cabinets)
  - Logical access (e.g., to an organization's databases and information systems)
  - Network connectivity between the organization's and the external party's networks (e.g., permanent connection and remote access)
  - Whether the access is taking place onsite or offsite
- The value and sensitivity of the information involved and its criticality for business operations
- The controls necessary to protect information that is not intended to be accessible by external parties
- The external party personnel involved in handling the organization's information
- How the organization or personnel authorized to have access can be identified, the authorization verified, and how often it should be reconfirmed
- The different means and controls employed by the external party when storing, processing, communicating, sharing, exchanging and destroying information
- The impact of access not being available to the external party when required and the external party entering or receiving inaccurate or misleading information
- Practices and procedures to deal with information security incidents and potential damages, and the terms and conditions for the continuation of external party access in the case of an information security incident
- Legal and regulatory requirements and other contractual obligations relevant to the external party
- How the interests of any other stakeholders may be affected by the arrangements
- Audit monitoring costs of external parties including human resource hours and costs of independent audit firms

Source: ISACA, *CISA Review Manual*, 27th Edition, USA, 2019

Access by external parties to the enterprise's information should not be provided until the appropriate controls have been implemented and, where feasible, a contract has been signed defining the terms and conditions for the connection or access and the working arrangement. Generally, all security requirements resulting from work with external parties or internal controls should be reflected in the agreement with the external party.

Confirmation that the external party is aware of its obligations and accepts the responsibilities and liabilities involved in accessing, processing, communicating or managing the enterprise's information and information-processing facilities should be obtained.

External parties might put information at risk if their security management is inadequate. Controls should be identified and applied to administer external party access to information-processing facilities. For example, if there is a special need for confidentiality of information, nondisclosure agreements might be used. Enterprises may face risks associated with interorganizational processes, management and communication, if a high degree of outsourcing is applied, or it several external parties are involved.

Addressing Security When Dealing With Customers

All identified security requirements should be addressed before giving customers access to the enterprise's information or assets.

In addition to asset protection and access control policies, the items presented in **figure 2.26** should be considered to address security prior to giving customers access to any of the enterprise's assets. (Depending on the type and extent of access given, not all of them may apply.)

Figure 2.26—Customer Access Security Considerations
• Description of the product or service to be provided
• The different reasons, requirements and benefits for customer access
• Arrangements for reporting, notification and investigation of information inaccuracies (e.g., of personal details), information security incidents and security breaches
• The target level of service and unacceptable levels of service
• The right to monitor and revoke any activity related to the organization's assets
• The respective liabilities of the organization and the customer
• Responsibilities with respect to legal matters and ensuring that the legal requirements are met (e.g., data protection legislation), considering different national legal systems if the agreement involves cooperation with customers in other countries
• Intellectual property rights (IPRs), copyright assignment and protection of any collaborative work
Source: ISACA, *CISA Review Manual*, 27th Edition, USA, 2019

The security requirements related to customers accessing organizational assets can vary considerably depending on the information-processing facilities and information being accessed. Customer agreements can address all identified risk and security requirements.

Addressing Security in Third-party Agreements

Third-party agreements involving accessing, processing, communicating or managing the enterprise's information or information-processing facilities, or adding products or services to information-processing facilities should cover all relevant security requirements. Agreements should ensure clarification of policies and expectations of relevant security to reduce risk of misunderstanding between the enterprise and third parties. The enterprise should ensure that the agreements include adequate indemnification provisions to protect against potential losses caused by the actions of a third party.

The contract terms that are listed in **figure 2.27** should be considered for inclusion in third-party agreements to satisfy the identified securityrequirements.

Figure 2.27— Recommended Contract Terms for Third-Party Agreements

- Compliance with the organization's information security policy by the third party
- Controls to ensure asset protection, including:
  - Procedures to protect organizational assets, including information, software and hardware
  - Any required physical protection controls and mechanisms
  - Controls to ensure protection against malicious software
  - Procedures to determine whether any compromise of the assets (e.g., loss or modification of information, software and hardware) has occurred
  - Controls to ensure the return or destruction of information and assets at the end of or at an agreed point in time during the agreement
  - Confidentiality, integrity, availability and any other relevant property of the assets
  - Restrictions on copying and disclosing information, and using confidentiality agreements
- User and administrator training in methods, procedures and security
- A means to ensure user awareness of information security responsibilities and issues
- Provision for the transfer of personnel, where appropriate
- Responsibilities regarding hardware and software installation and maintenance
- A clear reporting structure and agreed reporting formats
- A clear and specified process for change management
- Access control policy, covering:
  - The different reasons, requirements and benefits that make the access by the third party necessary
  - Permitted access methods and the control and use of unique identifiers such as user IDs and passwords
  - An authorization process for user access and privileges
  - A requirement to maintain a list of individuals authorized to use the services being made available and what their rights and privileges are with respect to such use
  - A statement that all access that is not explicitly authorized is forbidden
  - A process for revoking access rights or interrupting the connection between systems
- Arrangements for reporting, notification and investigation of information security incidents and security breaches, and violations of the requirements stated in the agreement
- A description of the product or service to be provided and a description of the information to be made available, with its security classification
- The target level of service and unacceptable levels of service
- The definition of verifiable performance criteria, their monitoring and reporting
- The right to monitor and revoke any activity related to the organization's assets
- The right to audit responsibilities defined in the agreement, to have those audits carried out by a third party, and to enumerate the statutory rights of auditors (and, where appropriate, the provision of a service auditor's report)

Figure 2.27— Recommended Contract Terms for Third-Party Agreements *(cont.)*

- The establishment of an escalation process for problem resolution
- Service continuity requirements, including measures for availability and reliability, in accordance with an organization's business priorities
- The respective liabilities of the parties to the agreement
- Responsibilities with respect to legal matters and ensuring that the legal requirements are met (e.g., data protection legislation), considering different national legal systems if the agreement involves cooperation with organizations in other countries
- Intellectual property rights (IPRs) and copyright assignment and protection of any collaborative work
- Involvement of the third party with subcontractors, and the security controls the subcontractors need to implement
- Conditions for renegotiation/termination of agreements such as:
  - A contingency plan in case either party wishes to terminate the relationship before the end of the agreements
  - A provision for renegotiation of agreements if the security requirements of the organization change
- Current documentation of asset lists, licenses, agreements or rights relating to them
- Non-assignability of the contract

Source: ISACA, *CISA Review Manual*, 27th Edition, USA, 2019

In general, it is very difficult to ensure the return or destruction of confidential information disclosed to a third party at the end of the agreement. To prevent unauthorized copies or use, printed documents should be consulted on site. Using technical controls, such as digital rights management (DRM)—access control technologies used by publishers, copyright holders and individuals to impose limitations on the usage of digital content and devices—should be considered to set up desired constraints on actions such as printing the document, copying it, authorizing readers, or using it after a certain date.

Agreements can vary considerably for different enterprises and among different types of third parties. Therefore, care should be taken to include all identified risk and security requirements in the agreements. If necessary, the required controls and procedures can be expanded in a security management plan.

If information security management is outsourced, the agreements should address how the third party will guarantee that adequate security, as defined by the risk assessment, will be maintained, and how security will be adapted to identify and deal with changes to risk. Some differences between outsourcing and other forms of third-party service provision include the question of liability, planning the transition period and potential disruption of operations, contingency planning arrangements, due diligence reviews, and collection and management of information on security incidents. It is important that the enterprise plan and manage the transition to an outsourced arrangement, and have suitable processes in place to manage changes and the renegotiation/termination of agreements.

The procedures for continuing processing in the event that a third party becomes unable to supply its services need to be considered in the agreement to avoid any delay in arranging replacement services. Agreements with third parties may also involve other parties. Agreements granting third-party access should include allowances for designation of other eligible parties, and conditions for their access and involvement. A requirement for the third party to have certified compliance with recognized security standards (e.g., ISO 27001) may be advisable.

Generally, agreements are primarily developed by the enterprise. In some circumstances an agreement may be developed and imposed upon an enterprise by a third party. The enterprise needs to ensure that its own security is not unnecessarily impacted by third-party requirements stipulated in imposed agreements.

Human Resources Security and Third Parties

Proper information security practices should be in place to ensure that employees, contractors and third-party users understand their responsibilities and are suitable for their assigned roles. These practices can reduce the risk of theft, fraud or misuse of facilities.

Specific security practices:

- Security responsibilities should be addressed prior to employment in adequate job descriptions, and in terms and conditions of employment.
- All candidates for employment, contractors and third-party users should be adequately screened, especially for sensitive jobs.
- Employees, contractors and third-party users of information-processing facilities should sign an agreement on their security roles and responsibilities, including the need to maintain confidentiality.

Security roles and responsibilities of employees, contractors and third-party users should be defined and documented in accordance with the enterprise's information security policy.

Screening

All candidates for employment, contractors or third-party users should be subject to background verification checks. These checks should be carried out and documented in accordance with relevant laws, regulations and ethics, and be proportional to the business requirements, the classification of the information to be accessed, and the perceived risk. When an enterprise uses an agency to provide contractors, the contract with the agency should clearly specify the agency's responsibilities for screening and the notification procedures it needs to follow if screening has not been completed, or if the results give cause for doubt or concern. In the same way, the agreement with the third party should clearly specify all responsibilities and notification procedures for screening.

Removal of Access Rights

The access rights of all employees, contractors and third-party users to information and information-processing facilities should be removed upon termination of their employment, contract or agreement, or adjusted upon change. The access rights that should be removed or adapted include physical and logical access, keys, identification cards, information-processing facilities, subscriptions, and removal from any documentation that identifies them as a current member of the enterprise. This should include notifying partners and relevant third parties if a departing employee has access to the third-party premises.

If a departing employee, contractor or third-party user has known passwords for accounts remaining active, these should be changed upon termination or change of employment, contract or agreement. Access rights for information assets and information-processing facilities should be reduced or removed before the employment terminates or changes, depending on the evaluation of risk factors, such as:

- Whether the termination or change is initiated by the employee, contractor or third-party user or by management, and the reason of termination
- The current responsibilities of the employee, contractor or any other user
- The value of the assets currently accessible

Procedures should be in place to ensure that information security management is promptly informed of all employee movements, including employees leaving the enterprise.

1 Techopedia, "IT Infrastructure," www.techopedia.com/definition/30134/managed-data-center

2 Doig, C.; "Calculating the total cost of ownership for enterprise software," *CIO*, 19 November 2015, www.cio.com/article/3005705/calculating-the-total-cost-of-ownership-for-enterprise-software.html

3 National Institute of Standards and Technology, *NIST Special Publication SP 800-145: The NIST Definition of Cloud Computing*, USA, 2011

4 *Ibid.*

5 TechTarget, "Scale-out storage," 2016, https://whatis.techtarget.com/definition/scale-out-storage

6 Mougue, E.; "SSDLC 101: What Is the Secure Software Development Life Cycle?" *DZone,* 25 July 2017, https://dzone.com/articles/ssdlc-101-what-is-the-secure-software-development

7 Romeo, C.; "Secure Development Lifecycle: The essential guide to safe software pipelines," TechBeacon, https://techbeacon.com/security/secure-development-lifecycle-essential-guide-safe-software-pipelines

8 *Op cit* ISACA 2016

9 *Op cit* Romeo

10 Rajendran, S.; "Safeguarding Mobile Applications With Secure Development Life Cycle Approach," *ISACA Journal,* Vol. 3, 1 May 2017

11 *Op cit* Romeo

12 *Ibid.*

13 *Ibid.*

14 Cavoukian, A.; *Privacy by Design: The 7 Foundational Principles*, Information and Privacy Commissioner of Ontario, Canada, 2011

15 *Ibid.*

16 Information Commissioner's Office, "Guide to the General Data Protection Regulation (GDPR)," https://ico.org.uk/for-organisations/guide-to-data-protection/guide-to-the-general-data-protection-regulation-gdpr/

17 Digital.ai, "Application Hardening," https://www.arxan.com/resources/technology/application-hardening

18 Russell, N.; F. Schaub; A. McDonald; W. Sierra-Rocafort; *APIs and Your Privacy,* Fordham Center on Law and Information Policy/University of Michigan, USA, 2019

19 Virgillito, D.; "3 Tracking Technologies and Their Impact on Privacy," INFOSEC*,* 17 August 2018, https://resources.infosecinstitute.com/3-tracking-technologies-and-their-impact-on-privacy/

20 *Op cit* ISACA 2016

21 Lapowsky, I.; "How Cambridge Analytica Sparked the Great Privacy Awakening," *Wired,* 13 March 2019, www.wired.com/story/cambridge-analytica-facebook-privacy-awakening/

22 Koch, R.; "Cookies, the GDPR, and the ePrivacy Directive," GDPR.EU, https://gdpr.eu/cookies

23 Beal, V.; "The 7 Layers of the OSI Model," Webopedia, www.webopedia.com/quick_ref/OSI_Layers.asp

24 National Institute for Standards and Technology, *SP 800-153: Guidelines for Securing Wireless Local Area Networks (WLANs),* USA, 2012

25 Ito, K.; J. Kogure; T. Shimoyama; H. "Tsuda: De-identification and Encryption Technologies to Protect Personal Information," *FUJITSU Scientific and Technical Journal,* Vol. 52, July 2016

26 TechTarget, "Encryption," https://searchsecurity.techtarget.com/definition/encryption

27 Townsend Security, *The Definitive Guide to Encryption Key Management Fundamentals,* USA, 2016

28 Appdynamics, "What's the Difference? Logging vs Monitoring," www.appdynamics.com/product/how-it-works/application-analytics/log-analytics/monitoring-vs-logging-best-practices

Page intentionally left blank

Chapter 3:

Data Life Cycle

Overview

Part A: Data Purpose

Part B: Data Persistence

Overview

Between data creation/collection and destruction are typical phases in the stewarding of the data, which collectively are referred to as the data lifecycle. Data management frameworks typically differ in their description of the data life cycle: create, read, update and delete.

Data creation/collection employs many processes to achieve its objectives. Therefore, data are persisted or maintained to enable reuse by separate processes that are collectively deployed to achieve the purpose for which the data were collected.

Data persistence refers to data that outlives the process that created it. Data assets are persisted by storing them for reuse in databases, data marts, data warehouses and data lakes. Regardless of the data scope and storage technology used, data persistence follows data design principles that guide but do not necessarily dictate the structure of the physical database.

After the purpose for which data were created/collected is achieved, the data should be destroyed. Data destruction is principally guided by external laws and guidelines that emphasize sensitive data such as personally identifiable information (PII) and personal health information (PHI).

This domain represents 30 percent (36 questions) of the exam.

Domain 3: Exam Content Outline

Part A: Data Purpose

1. Data Inventory and Classification
2. Data Quality and Accuracy
3. Data Flow and Usage Diagrams
4. Data Use Limitation
5. Data Analytics

Part B: Data Persistence

1. Data Minimization
2. Data Migration
3. Data Storage
4. Data Warehousing
5. Data Retention and Archiving
6. Data Destruction

Learning Objectives/Task Statements

Within this domain, the data privacy practitioner should be able to:

- Identify the internal and external requirements for the organization's privacy programs and practices.
- Participate in the evaluation of privacy policies, programs and policies for their alignment with legal requirements, regulatory requirements and/or industry best practices.
- Coordinate and perform a privacy impact assessment (PIA) and other privacy-focused assessments.
- Participate in the development of procedures that align with privacy policies and business needs.

- Implement procedures that align with privacy policies.
- Participate in the management and evaluation of contracts, service level agreements, and practices of vendors and other external parties.
- Participate in the privacy incident management process.
- Collaborate with cybersecurity personnel on the security risk assessment process to address privacy compliance and risk mitigation.
- Collaborate with other practitioners to ensure that privacy programs and practices are followed during the design, development and implementation of systems, applications and infrastructure.
- Evaluate the enterprise architecture and information architecture to ensure it supports privacy by design principles and considerations.
- Evaluate advancements in privacy-enhancing technologies and changes in the regulatory landscape.
- Identify, validate and implement appropriate privacy and security controls according to data classification procedures.
- Design, implement and monitor processes and procedures to keep the inventory and dataflow records current.
- Develop and implement a prioritization process for privacy practices.

Suggested Resources for Further Study

Ambler, S.; *The Object Primer: Agile Model-Driven Development With UML 2.0,* 3rd Edition, Cambridge University Press, USA, 2004

Chrissis, M.; M. Konrad; S. Shrum; *CMMI for Development,* Third Edition, Addison-Wesley, USA, 2011

CMMI Institute, *Data Management Maturity Model,* USA, 2019

European Parliament and Council of the European Union, *General Data Protection Regulation (GDPR), Article 5, 1 (c)*, Official Journal of the European Union, 2016

Hoberman, S.; *Data Modeling Made Simple: A Practical Guide for Business and IT Professionals,* 2nd Edition, Technics Publications, USA, 2016

ISACA, *COBIT 2019: Introduction and Methodology,* USA, 2018

ISACA, *ISACA Privacy Principles and Program Management,* USA, 2016

Page intentionally left blank

Self-assessment Questions

CDPSE self-assessment questions support the content in this manual and provide an understanding of the type and structure of questions that typically appear on the exam. Often a question will require the candidate to choose the **MOST** likely or **BEST** answer among the options provided. Note that these questions are not actual or retired exam items. See the "About This Manual" section for more guidance regarding practice questions.

1. Which of the following would contain a unique list of terms to link defined concepts to data assets?

   A. Data inventory
   B. Business glossary
   C. Data dictionary
   D. Privacy policy

2. An organization is migrating from a legacy system to an enterprise resource planning system. While reviewing the data migration activity, the **MOST** important concern is to determine that there is a:

   A. Correlation of semantic characteristics of the data migrated between the two systems.
   B. Correlation of arithmetic characteristics of the data migrated between the two systems.
   C. Correlation of functional characteristics of the processes between the two systems.
   D. Relative efficiency of the processes between the two systems.

3. Which of the following is the **BEST** way to erase confidential information stored on a universal serial bus (USB) drive?

   A. Performing a low-level format
   B. Rewriting with zeros
   C. Burning
   D. Degaussing them

Answers on page 144

Chapter 3 Answer Key

Self-Assessment Questions

1. A. A data inventory is a list of data assets and can be driven out of IT, information security or data governance through manual or automated tools. The business glossary can be a key input into the data inventory.
   B. The business glossary is a unique list of defined concepts that connect common data in applications under shared meaning. Since policies and classifications refer to concepts pertaining to data, the business glossary is the ideal place to establish a formal link to data assets. That way, when privacy and other data requirements change, the impact of changes can be efficiently assessed and implemented.
   C. A data dictionary is a data inventory at the application level and would not contain definitions of concepts and how they link to the data.
   D. A privacy policy may influence the creation of tools such as a business glossary. The business glossary may be used to provide context to the privacy policy.

2. **A. Due to the fact that the two systems could have a different data representation, including the database schema, the main concern would be to verify that the interpretation of the data (structure) is the same in the new as it was in the old system.**
   B. Arithmetic characteristics represent aspects of data structure and internal definition in the database and, therefore, are less important than the semantic characteristics.
   C. A review of the correlation of the functional characteristics between the two systems is not relevant to a data migration review.
   D. A review of the relative efficiencies of the processes between the two systems is not relevant to a data migration review.

3. A. Performing a low-level format may be adequate but is a slow process, and with the right tools, data can still be recovered.
   B. . Rewriting with zeros will not overwrite information located in the disk slack space.
   C. Burning destroys the drive and does not allow reuse.
   D. Degaussing the universal serial bus (USB) drive would quickly dispose of all information because the magnetic domains are thoroughly scrambled and would not allow reuse.

Part A: Data Purpose

The purpose of data is to represent facts. Data collection is the result of performing procedures to achieve something through a process.[1] While automation is used to implement processes, systems rarely address all requirements. As a result, manual procedures are performed to compensate for required activities not supported by the application. Both automated and manual processes collect, organize and use structured and unstructured data to achieve their purposes.

Structured data processes align representations of facts with labeled fields, such as "first name," "last name," etc. Examples of structured data processes include forms, templates and models. Unstructured data processes contain facts expressed in natural language. Examples range from comment fields to entire documents.

The personal data to be collected should be documented along with the purpose for collecting personal data, as well as the consent the person has given to have the data collected for that purpose. It is important to understand that the purposes for which personal data are collected usually involve more than one process and each process involves several procedures.

Each procedure involved in data collection is performed to achieve specific purposes in support of the process. The specific purposes should be:

- Defined when developing requirements used for designing processes
- Documented in the metadata repository.

When the privacy and data quality issues are dealt with after the fact, the issues are typically found within the application when a data breach or defect is identified.

Consequently, undocumented data processes are full of privacy vulnerabilities and prone to workarounds. Thus, the motivation behind privacy by design, which was conceived in Canada, further developed in the UK[2], and is expressed in the European Union's Global Data Protection Regulation (GDPR).[3]

Privacy by design promotes a privacy-first approach to implementing new processes or systems to ensure privacy compliance. The concept has evolved into a global privacy standard. The UK information Commissioner's Office (ICO) has adopted the GDPR, which promotes privacy-by-design.[4] In essence, enterprises are required to integrate data protection into their processing activities and business practices, from the design stage and throughout the life cycle. See section 2.6 Secure Development Life Cycle for more information.

While privacy by design is not a legal requirement in many countries, its practice is becoming established since managing privacy risks are increasingly important to enterprises globally. ISACA's *Privacy Principles and Program Management Guide* details fourteen privacy principles common across standards and authoritative frameworks[5] as described in **figure 3.1.**

Figure 3.1—ISACA Privacy Principles and Related Frameworks and Standards

ISACA Privacy Principle	Organization for Economic Corporation (OECD) 2013	International Organization for Standardization (ISO) 29100:2011	Asia-Pacific Economic Cooperation (APEC)	Generally Accepted Privacy Principles (GAPP)
1. Choice and consent	N/A	Consent and choice	Choice	Choice and consent
2. Legitimate purpose specification and use limitation	Purpose specification and use limitation	Purpose legitimacy and specification and use, retention and disclosure limitation	Use of personal information	Use, retention and disposal
3. Personal information and sensitive information life cycle	Collection limitation	Collection limitation and data minimization	Collection limitations	Collection
4. Accuracy and quality	Data quality	Accuracy and quality	Integrity of personal information	Quality
5. Openness, transparency and notice	Openness	Openness, transparency and notice	N/A	N/A
6. Individual participation	Individual participation	Individual participation and notice	Access and correction	Access
7. Accountability	Accountability	Accountability	Accountability	Management
8. Security safeguards	Security safeguards	Information security	Security safeguards	Security for privacy
9. Monitoring, measuring and reporting	N/A	Privacy compliance	N/A	Privacy compliance
10. Preventing harm	N/A	N/A	Preventing harm	N/A
11. Third party/vendor management	N/A	N/A	N/A	Disclosure to third parties
12. Breach management	N/A	N/A	N/A	N/A
13. Security and privacy by design	N/A	N/A	N/A	N/A
14. Free flow of information and legitimate restriction	Free flow of information	N/A	N/A	N/A

Consistent with privacy regulations, privacy principles should be integrated into an enterprise's information systems implementation processes as well as, including in the enterprise's data life cycle. **Figure 3.2** provides guidance on how enterprises may integrate ISACA's Privacy Principles, ISACA's Information Lifecycle[6] and the relevant data management process areas in the Data Management Maturity Model (DMM).[7]

Figure 3.2—ISACA Privacy Principles and the Data Maturity Model

ISACA Privacy Principle	Build	Operate	Monitor	Dispose
Choice and consent	Data Governance			
Legitimate purpose specification and use limitation	Data Strategy Business Glossary Metadata Management Data Requirements Data Improvement	Data Life Cycle Management	Data Life Cycle Management	Data Life Cycle Management
Personal information and sensitive information life cycle		Data Life Cycle Management	Data Quality Assessment Data Profiling	Historical, Retention, Archiving
Accuracy and quality				
Openness, transparency and notice	Data Governance			
Individual participation				
Accountability		Data Governance	Data Governance	Data Governance
Security safeguards				
Monitoring, measuring and reporting	Data Governance			
Preventing harm				
Third party/vendor management	Data Management Platform	Data Provider Management	Data Provider Management Data Quality Assessment	Data Provider Management
Breach management				
Security and privacy by design	Data Strategy Data Requirements			
Free flow of information and legitimate restriction		Data Life Cycle Management	Data Life Cycle Management	Data Life Cycle Management

The DMM is a measurement tool that uses practices that represent the organic path of an enterprise toward a mature management of its data assets. The DMM has organized 25 data management process areas into five categories of data management (**figure 3.3**). Each process area identifies and describes an array of practices that characterize the behavior of enterprises in five ascending levels of capability.

Figure 3.3—CMMI Data Management Maturity Model Process Areas

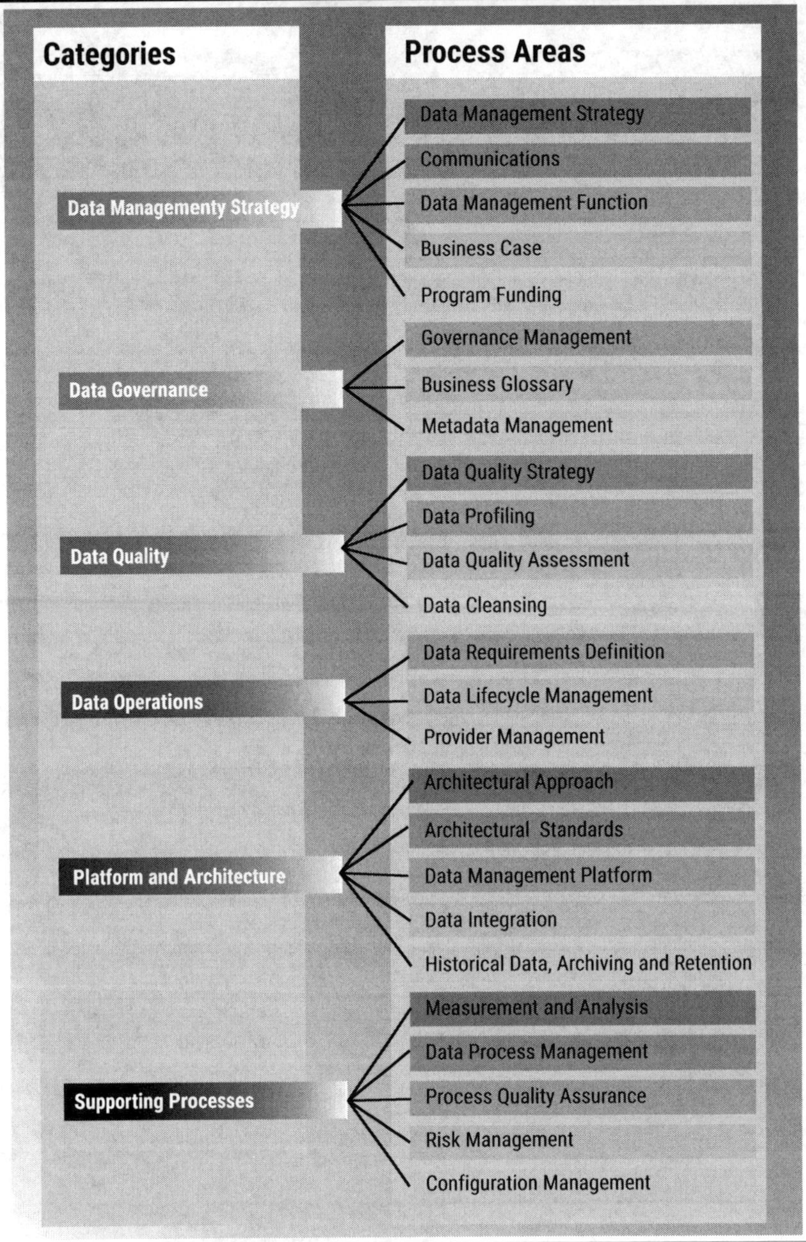

Categories	Process Areas
Data Managementy Strategy	Data Management Strategy
	Communications
	Data Management Function
	Business Case
	Program Funding
Data Governance	Governance Management
	Business Glossary
	Metadata Management
Data Quality	Data Quality Strategy
	Data Profiling
	Data Quality Assessment
	Data Cleansing
Data Operations	Data Requirements Definition
	Data Lifecycle Management
	Provider Management
Platform and Architecture	Architectural Approach
	Architectural Standards
	Data Management Platform
	Data Integration
	Historical Data, Archiving and Retention
Supporting Processes	Measurement and Analysis
	Data Process Management
	Process Quality Assurance
	Risk Management
	Configuration Management

Source: CMMI Institute, *Data Management Maturity Model*, USA, 2019, table 1

Based on this maturity model, an enterprise's DMM evaluation reveals capabilities that support each of the privacy principles along the data life cycle, exposing areas of strength and weakness in their ability to support sustainable privacy compliance.

3.1 Data Inventory and Classification

A fully specified and populated data inventory and classification is the most important resource for conducting a privacy impact assessment (PIA), because the master inventory covers all sensitive data. The data inventory includes the types of personal information collected and the information necessary to ensure privacy compliance.[8] The scope of the data inventory and classification must be enterprise-wide and up to date to ensure a PIA confirms adequate controls and identifies vulnerabilities.

The content and scope of the data inventory for sensitive information is largely consistent with a metadata repository which is implemented and managed by data governance. As part of enterprise metadata management, the privacy data inventory should be collaboratively managed between privacy and data governance.

According to the DMM, the purpose of metadata management is to:[9]

> *Establish the processes and infrastructure for specifying and extending clear and organized information about the structured and unstructured data assets under management, fostering and supporting data sharing, ensuring compliant use of data, improving responsiveness to business changes, and reducing data-related risks.*

3.1.1 Data Inventory

A data inventory is a list of data assets and can be driven out of IT, information security or data governance through manual or automated tools. While more than one inventory may exist within the enterprise, it is best to bring them into a common framework to stay up to date.

The data inventory should be part of an end-to-end process from data requirements definition through post-production maintenance. While data inventory templates differ, they all contain metadata. According to the DMM, "Metadata is a category of information that identifies, describes, explains, and provides content, context, structure, and classifications pertaining to an organization's data assets and enables effective retrieval, usage, and management of these assets."[10]

Moreover, metadata represents knowledge about data assets. Metadata artifacts include data dictionaries, data models, business glossaries[11] and data flow and usage diagrams.

A data dictionary is a data inventory at the application level. Ideally, all data dictionaries are managed collectively by the data governance enterprise within a single metadata repository. At a minimum, each data dictionary should contain information about the data in the application or system for each data element. It is important for each data element to be linked to a governance-approved business term within the business glossary.

The business glossary is a unique list of defined concepts that connects common data in applications under a shared meaning. Because policies and classifications refer to concepts pertaining to data, the business glossary is the ideal place to establish a formal link to data assets. That way, when privacy and other data requirements change, the impact of changes can be efficiently assessed and implemented.

Change management protocols also need to be defined and supported to keep applications and procedures aligned to ensure compliance with changes in policies and requirements. Change management protocols should also ensure applications using the same data are coordinated. For example, personal data on an individual is directly and indirectly collected by various applications. Lacking a fully annotated business glossary that is linked to data dictionaries results in data defects and privacy issues, which accumulate until replacing the system becomes the only practical solution.

The data inventory should serve as the master for the alignment of the uses, purposes, consents and privacy requirements of personal and sensitive data. Data inventory should be managed centrally through a metadata repository so that any changes to the policies that govern privacy compliance can be effectively monitored, implemented and controlled at any time, as needed.

Creating a Data Inventory

If the enterprise does not have nor does not intend to establish a metadata repository, then a data inventory must be created to perform a PIA. There are some basic steps enterprises can follow to create a data inventory suggested by the Open Data Institute (**figure 3.4**).[12]

Figure 3.4—Steps to Creating a Data Inventory

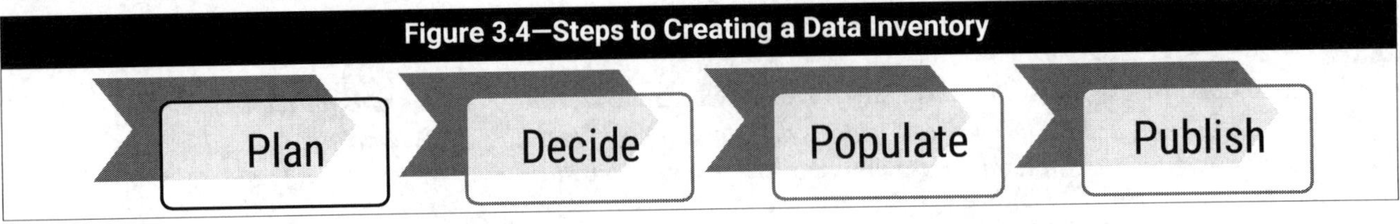

Plan

It is important to determine the purpose and the scope of the data inventory before starting to catalog items. Regulations or standards may help in establishing the scope of the data inventory project. Some considerations include:[13]

- The enterprise's definition of data and what to include: The business glossary should include the enterprise's definition of data. From there, determine what should be included in the inventory. Is information on physical/paper copies of data to be included? Are datasets and data created by vendors to be included?
- Relevant metadata: Appropriate metadata will help in narrowing down the data inventory being created. For example, it will be important to identify what datasets included personally identifiable information (PII) for compliance purposes.
- What level of detail is necessary: In general, it is recommended to gather more detail that can be filtered or summarized for specific audiences.
- How long the inventory will be maintained: As noted, data inventories should be kept current, so including updates in the process is key.

Decide

After there is a plan in place, the enterprise should determine what attributes to use to describe the data collected. **Figure 3.5** includes a recommended list of attributes.

Figure 3.5—Data Attributes

Attribute	Description
ID	Unique identifier for the dataset
Title	The name of the data asset
Description	A description of the data asset
Purpose	Why was the data collected or produced?
Data creator	Who created the data?
Data manager/owner	Who manages the data?

Figure 3.5—Data Attributes (cont.)	
Attribute	Description
Subject/keywords	What subjects/topics does this dataset cover? This will help discovery for users searching for this data. It is recommended to use a controlled vocabulary for this attribute (and others where possible) to improve future search and data linking potential (e.g., finding related datasets)
Location	Where is the data located or stored?
Creation date	When was the data created?
Update frequency	How often is the data updated?
Type	What type of data is it? Text, numbers, statistics, images, a database?
Format	What format is the data in (e.g., MS Excel, CSV, JPEG, SQL DB)?
Rights and restrictions	What are the access and usage rights and restrictions? If you are publishing the data, what can users do with the data? Include a link to the relevant license for use of the data (e.g., Creative Commons or a bespoke license).
Source: The Open Data Institute, *How to Create a Data Inventory*, USA, 2018	

The Data Catalog Vocabulary[14] can be useful for defining attributes to collect.

Populate

After the scope is determined and the enterprise has decided on what information to collect begin collecting the information to populate the data inventory. Some techniques for collecting data include:[15]

- Ask existing data owners to populate the data inventory.
- Conduct interviews with data owners and related stakeholders.
- Use surveys and questionnaires.
- Create automated processes. For example, add a basic metadata form to be completed when creating a new asset in a content management system to automatically add the data to the inventory.

Publish

After the metadata are collected, the information can be collated and published. Collating and publishing may be as simple as a spreadsheet or it could be as formal as a database, depending on the size of the inventory. Consider the criticality and sensitivity of data included in the inventory before publishing. It may be useful for users to see a listing of all assets, but note that some assets may not be freely accessible to all users without completing an agreement or requesting permission.

3.1.2 Data Classification

Data classifications enrich the data inventory, as they enable the determination of the sensitivity and criticality of data assets Since data classification depends on enterprises and various industry standards, the variety of classifications for data is virtually unlimited. **Figure 3.6** describes typical data classifications.

Figure 3.6—Typical Data Classifications

Data Classification	Critical data elements (CDEs)
Critical data elements (CDEs)	Not all data are equally important. Data considered highly effective to the enterprise should be tagged and tracked through the data life cycle to concentrate data quality efforts to optimize data usage. Identifying critical data often starts with client-facing content, such as statements, reports, account portals, etc., and data considered to highly affect business-critical processes. Identifying critical data this way results in thousands of critical data elements. To make critical data information manageable, critical data elements should be mapped to an approved, annotated business glossary. A business glossary entry can tie its many instances throughout the enterprise under one concept.
Data security level	Most enterprises tag data according to the domain where it is intended to be used. While data security classifications vary, typical classifications include public, internal use and confidential or restricted.
Data sensitivity type	Within the confidential or restricted domain are specific types of sensitive data, which typically include PII and protected health information (PHI). While existing laws and regulations identify PII by concept (for example, full name, date of birth and social security number), these names are only indicative. PII data is likely be labelled differently in applications. In addition, laws and regulations are not meant to be exhaustive. Therefore, usage rules and restrictions should be defined where non-PII designated data can be used in specific contexts to effectively emphasize PII.

The classifications used should adhere to a common internal standard and be developed collaboratively between privacy and data governance. The internal standard must be enterprisewide and consistent with external requirements to ensure adequate control over access and usage of sensitive data by the enterprise and the data it shares with third parties.

3.2 Data Quality

Data governance is responsible for defining and managing the vision, mission, goals and structure for data life cycle management. Chief among the goals for data governance is ensuring adequate data quality. Accordingly, enterprises without data governance struggle to achieve data quality and privacy goals, resulting in widespread inefficiencies, confusion and privacy vulnerabilities. Privacy strongly depends on data quality and data governance to ensure compliance with internal and external privacy requirements.

Data is considered high quality to the degree it is fit for the purposes data consumers require. It is important for data to be understandable and satisfactory within and beyond its system of record. The purpose of data is to represent facts, and facts should be generally understandable and efficiently usable. The business glossary will help to establish the metadata needed for data quality management.[16]

Data quality is a widely misunderstood concept that is concerned with more than data accuracy. Data quality embraces a multi-dimensional approach to ensuring the data under management is fit for purpose.

Data access is a dimension of data quality which is of increasing concern for all enterprises. How data should be accessed to perform business processes and analytics is just as much a privacy concern as it is a quality concern. Since data quality is concerned with fit-for-purpose, access methods and policies must ensure data are being used appropriately.

Data access defects point to a deeper issue in the enterprise. Users, especially data analysts, are relentless in their pursuit of data. Accordingly, inadequate data access invariably results in workarounds. Workarounds are non-standard, semi-automated processes that are not only inefficient, but are prone to human error.

Data analysts are more often than not forced to work around the problem of finding and using data for their models. Eventually, the right data is found and appropriately used, but not without a considerable amount of trial and error. While analytics is intrinsically iterative, problems with data access result in the unintended exposure and persistence of personal data. Consequently, data quality and data life cycle management are mutually supportive process areas that are critical to ensuring privacy.

Data quality is a discipline encompassing four process areas that guide an enterprise towards a full understanding of the nature and quality of the data under management. To understand the essential practices needed to identify, evaluate, prevent and remediate defects so that the quality of the data meets consumer requirements, internal and external. The discipline can be seen broadly as four process areas:

- Data quality strategy: Defines the goals, objectives, and plans for improving data integrity
- Data profiling: Includes data discovery tasks performed to quantitatively analyze the contents of databases to improve understanding as well as to identify potential defects
- Data quality assessment: Is the systematic measurement and evaluation of the data fitness for use
- Data cleansing: Includes mechanisms, rules, processes and methods performed to validate and improve data quality

3.2.1 Data Quality Dimensions

While data quality is often equated with accuracy, there are many measurable aspects of quality that are beneficial and advisable to adopt. Just as there is no standard set of business metrics, the same can be said for data quality. While there is no universal agreement on one set of data quality metrics, there is the common concept of data quality dimensions and it is important for an enterprise to standardize official nomenclature and methods. Although the following are authoritative examples of data quality dimensions, the examples are by no means exhaustive.

The DAMA UK Working Group on Data Quality Dimensions identified the following six key dimensions for measuring data quality:[17]

1. Completeness: The proportion of stored data against the potential of "100 percent complete"
2. Uniqueness: No thing will be recorded more than once based upon how that thing is identified
3. Timeliness: The degree to which data represent reality from the required point in time
4. Validity: Data are valid if it conforms to the syntax (format, type, range) of its definition
5. Accuracy: The degree to which data correctly describe the "real world" object or event being described
6. Consistency: The absence of difference, when comparing two or more representations of a thing against a definition

ISACA's *COBIT 2019* identifies fifteen dimensions (**figure 3.7**).

Figure 3.7—Information Reference Model: Quality Criteria for Information

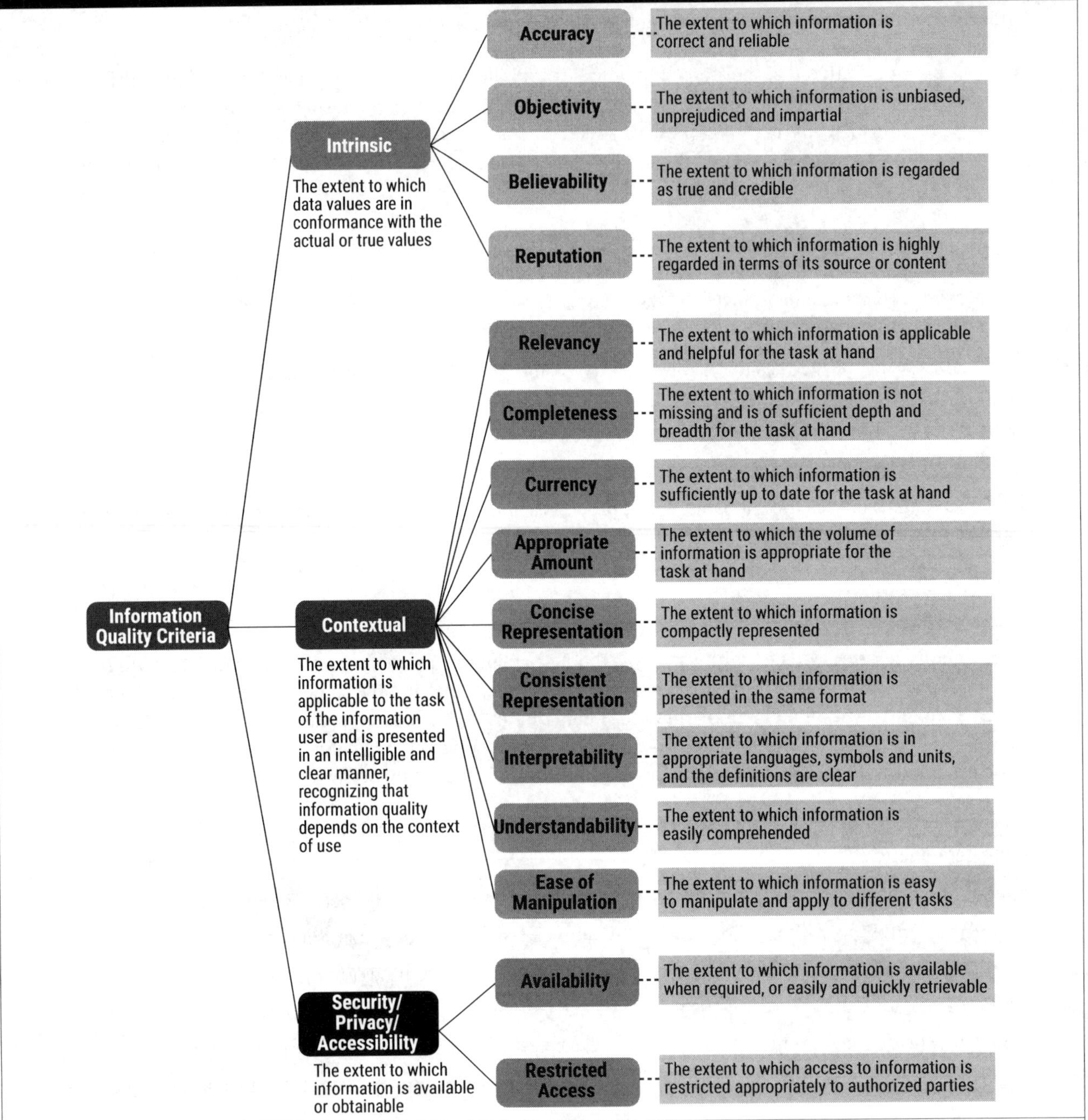

- **Information Quality Criteria**
  - **Intrinsic** — The extent to which data values are in conformance with the actual or true values
    - **Accuracy** — The extent to which information is correct and reliable
    - **Objectivity** — The extent to which information is unbiased, unprejudiced and impartial
    - **Believability** — The extent to which information is regarded as true and credible
    - **Reputation** — The extent to which information is highly regarded in terms of its source or content
  - **Contextual** — The extent to which information is applicable to the task of the information user and is presented in an intelligible and clear manner, recognizing that information quality depends on the context of use
    - **Relevancy** — The extent to which information is applicable and helpful for the task at hand
    - **Completeness** — The extent to which information is not missing and is of sufficient depth and breadth for the task at hand
    - **Currency** — The extent to which information is sufficiently up to date for the task at hand
    - **Appropriate Amount** — The extent to which the volume of information is appropriate for the task at hand
    - **Concise Representation** — The extent to which information is compactly represented
    - **Consistent Representation** — The extent to which information is presented in the same format
    - **Interpretability** — The extent to which information is in appropriate languages, symbols and units, and the definitions are clear
    - **Understandability** — The extent to which information is easily comprehended
    - **Ease of Manipulation** — The extent to which information is easy to manipulate and apply to different tasks
  - **Security/ Privacy/ Accessibility** — The extent to which information is available or obtainable
    - **Availability** — The extent to which information is available when required, or easily and quickly retrievable
    - **Restricted Access** — The extent to which access to information is restricted appropriately to authorized parties

Source: ISACA, *COBIT 2019: Introduction and Methodology*, USA, 2018

The DMM identifies the following eight examples of commonly applied dimensions:[18]

- **Accuracy**—Criteria related to affinity with original intent, veracity as compared to an authoritative source, and measurement precision
- **Completeness**—Criteria related to the availability of required data attributes
- **Coverage**—Criteria related to the availability of required data records
- **Conformity**—Criteria related to alignment of content with required standards

- **Consistency**—Criteria related to compliance with required patterns and uniformity rules
- **Duplication**—Criteria related to redundancy of records or attributes
- **Integrity**—Criteria related to the accuracy of data relationships (parent and child linkages)
- **Timeliness**—Criteria related to the currency of content and availability to be used when needed

While availability and restricted access pertain to privacy directly, most aspects of data quality are relevant to privacy. Whether phone calls, letters, email or text messages, all forms of communication rely on the quality of personal data. Personal data defects negatively affect consumer communications, resulting in privacy vulnerabilities. Examples include communicating protected health information to a foster child's former family members or sending financial statements to the wrong address.

3.3 Data Flow and Usage Diagrams

After creation, data are often passed along interdependent procedures within an application and then read into other applications. Practically speaking, data flows through an enterprise via the path of least resistance. Enterprises use the path of least resistance because they tend to view data as a means to an end rather than as an organizational asset to be managed and protected. However, even if the enterprise values data as an asset requiring protection, without internal standards and controls, capabilities for monitoring and controlling data for quality and privacy will be inconsistent and incomplete. Privacy and quality requirements must be intentional, internally consistent across applications, in conformance with privacy-by-design principles, and managed top-down using a fully annotated and populated metadata repository.

Detailed knowledge of what data is flowing within and across applications is critical to root cause analysis and contributes substantially to increased understanding of the data involved. Data flow and usage diagrams are methods for defining the flow of data, usually for a given application.

A data flow diagram is a functional model of the flow of data internally and externally through a process or a system. Its structure is generally expressed in terms of input, process and output (**figure 3.8**).[19]

Data flow diagrams emphasize data movement horizontally from sources to targets.

Figure 3.8—Data Flow Diagram

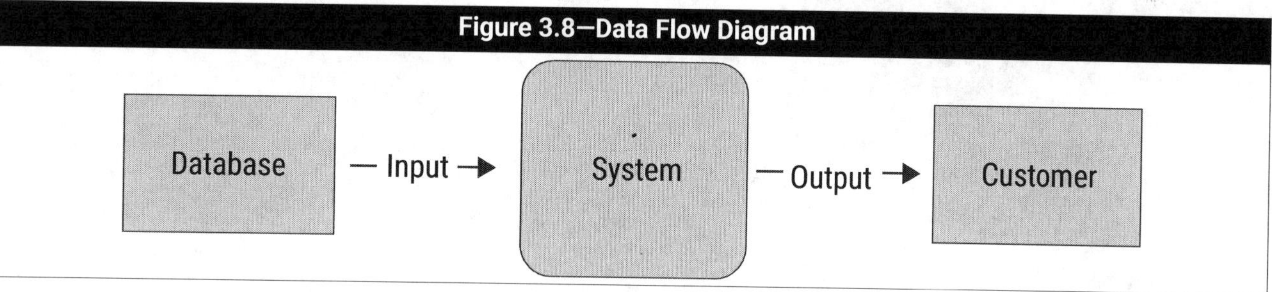

Alternatively, usage or activity diagrams emphasize a vertical view of data movement through each of the procedures involved in the data life cycle (**figure 3.9**). A usage diagram illustrates the steps and actions taken by each procedure within an application.

Figure 3.9—Usage Diagram

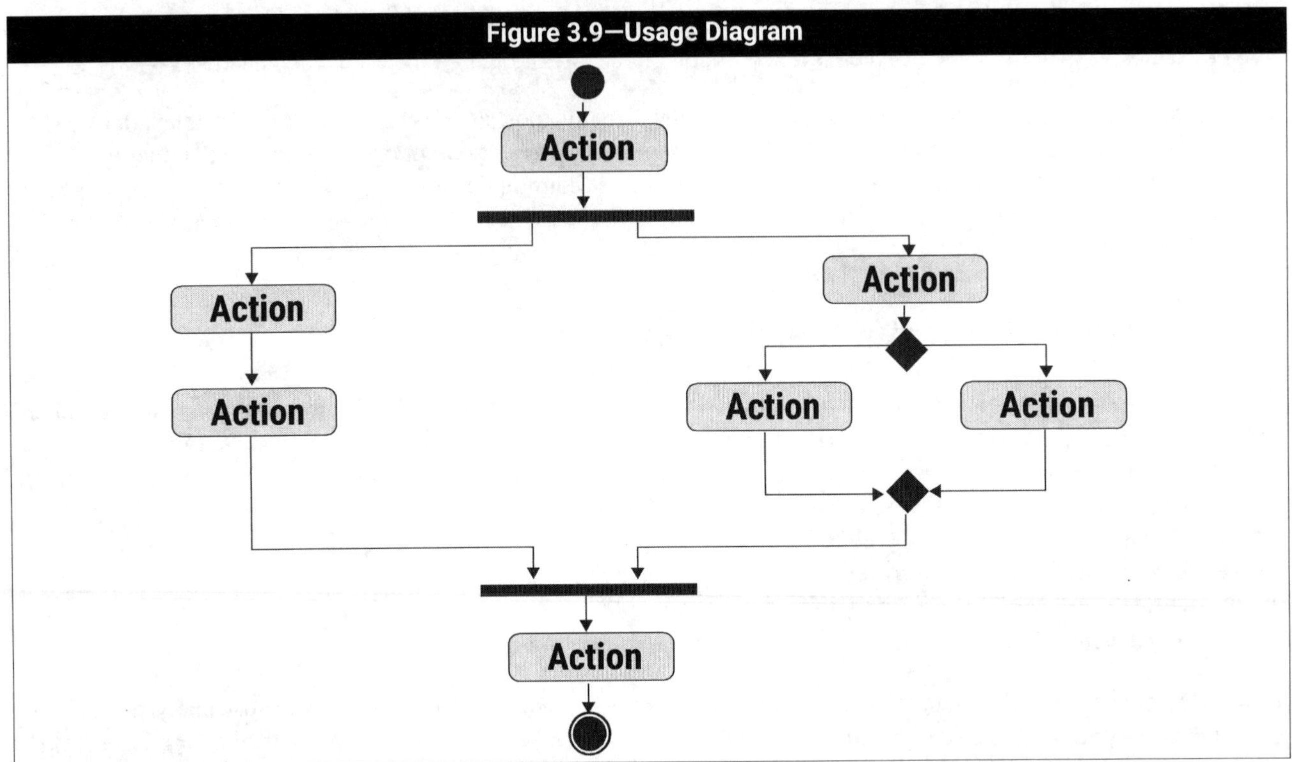

Each approach may be made considerably more useful to data management generally, and to privacy specifically, if the data and users involved in each of these steps are identified. Data may be indicated in varying levels of abstraction, from data domain—such as client, product, transaction, etc.—down to each data element involved, e.g., first name, last name, address, etc. Users can be modeled by adding swim lanes that divide processes in user groups, such as teams, departments, divisions, business units, etc., along a value stream, as shown in **figure 3.10**.

Figure 3.10—Value Stream Model with Swim Lanes

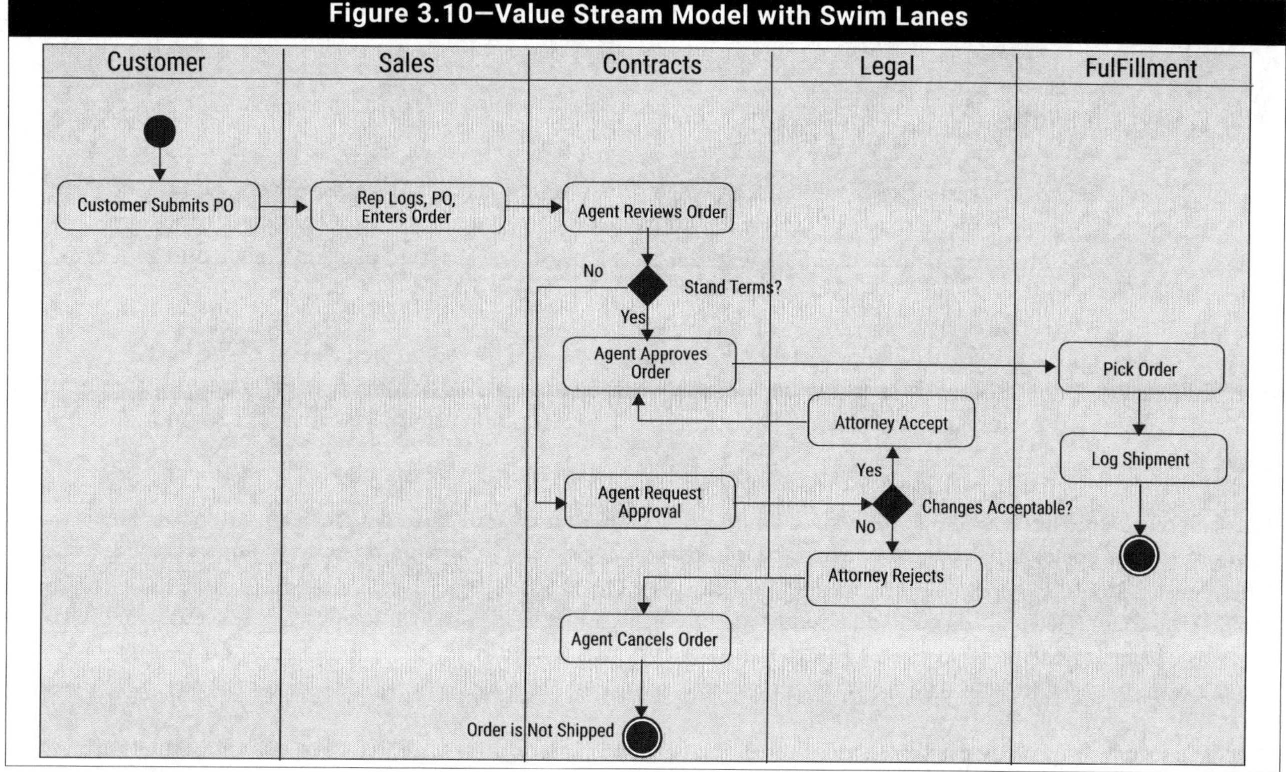

While both methods model data movement and can be similarly elaborated to model data and users, their orientations are more complementary than duplicative. Usage diagrams are better for illustrating the details of a complex workflow to implement, monitor and control data according to data quality and privacy policies. Data flow diagrams are better for illustrating data flow at a high level of abstraction, which is often extended to model the movement of data between systems across the enterprise.

GDPR states requirements explicitly for controlling workflows, thus emphasizing the need for usage diagrams. However, the regulation taken as a whole cannot be met without managing the horizontal flow of data internally and externally. See section 3.7 Data Migration for more information.

3.3.1 Data Lineage

Modeling the flow of data beyond its system of record is called data lineage. Data lineage is crucial to identifying the ultimate source of data in a downstream application, and it enables the identification of the application responsible for data defects detected downstream. This capability is essential for monitoring and controlling privacy compliance. Combined with the metadata repository, tracing the flow of PII and PHI can be more comprehensively managed through dynamic monitoring.

Due to the enormity of the scope and the complexity of changes that occur, data lineage is difficult to document and maintain manually. Therefore, the use of purpose-built tools that automate the detection and illustration of data flows within specified environments is recommended. When starting a data lineage program, it is important to restrict the scope of data lineage to the most important applications to the enterprise, working backward from downstream to upstream in the context of a business value stream.[20]

The value stream is a user group model that interacts with data in the delivery of products and services. The value stream usually represents a different view of data flow from the technology perspective. However, both the value

stream and the system architecture data flow diagrams are necessary for ensuring that the flow of data is compliant with privacy policies.

3.4 Data Use Limitation

Limiting data use often feels like limiting the use of water. Personal data is highly sensitive and should be treated with care, but even data designated for public use may not be considered a commodity. Personal data is one's identity, which is a formal recognition of a person in the world, insofar as it serves as a key to perform actions restricted to that person.

Data limitation requirements are guided by data purpose, which should be established as part of the data requirements definition process. Where practical, privacy stewards should develop, reuse and manage standard rules for data limitation in the metadata repository. See section 3.1 Data Inventory and Classifications for more information.

The data requirements process should adhere to and contribute standard rules for data usage for all new systems, built or bought. The data life cycle is comprised of automated and semiautomated processes. Understanding these processes is essential to grasping the meaning and ensuring the correct usage of data. Therefore, modeling processes should be documented and linked to data requirements.[21] Usage diagrams are best for designing and documenting the allowable usage of data in processes, while data flow diagrams are best for documenting and implementing high-level control over the flow of data from system to system.

Consistent with the privacy principles mentioned, the European Union's General Data Protection Regulation (GDPR), Article 5 (1) (b) states:[22]

> *Personal data shall be [...] collected for specified, explicit and legitimate purposes and not further processed in a manner that is incompatible with those purposes; further processing for archiving purposes in the public interest, scientific or historical research purposes or statistical purposes shall, in accordance with Article 89(1), not be considered to be incompatible with the initial purposes.*

3.5 Data Analytics

Data analytics is a quickly emerging function in many enterprises. Increases in global competition threaten an enterprise's status quo and reduce its returns on risky bets. Analytic insights are used to increase its probability of success. At the same time, global regulation is on the rise, pressuring enterprises otherwise resistant to data analytics to develop these capabilities.

Functionally, analytics is the formalization of asking business questions that result in quantifiable answers. Whether directed by a regulator or guided by business savvy, analytics has become a valuable resource for optimizing and altering an enterprise's ability to deliver its valued products and services. However, analytics depends on reliable and consistent access to a wide variety of data sets that are persisted to support their function. Data sets such as databases, data marts, data warehouses and data lakes can provide data for data analytics.

The quality of data analytics depends on the consistency of answers provided to similarly asked questions, regardless of the persons involved in the asking and answering. However, in practice this is often not the case. Moreover, analytics often exposes data quality issues whose magnitude persisted unnoticed long before the formation of the analytics function.

For example, it is important to determine the number of an enterprise's active clients and then to analyze their attributes and activities to better understand drivers for demand and identify cross-selling opportunities. Since analytics is typically concerned with clients, ensuring privacy protection is always a concern. Attributes that are used to classify groups of clients and better anticipate demand can reveal identities, even if the persons' names are excluded. While many such combinations can be controlled in applications, analysts often have more latitude. Therefore, ensuring privacy compliance in analytics requires training.

Analysts encounter many impediments that a data management program can help them avoid. **Figure 3.11** illustrates the relationships between common analyst pain points and the areas of data management that could reduce them.

Figure 3.11—Relationship Between Analyst Problems and DMM Process Areas

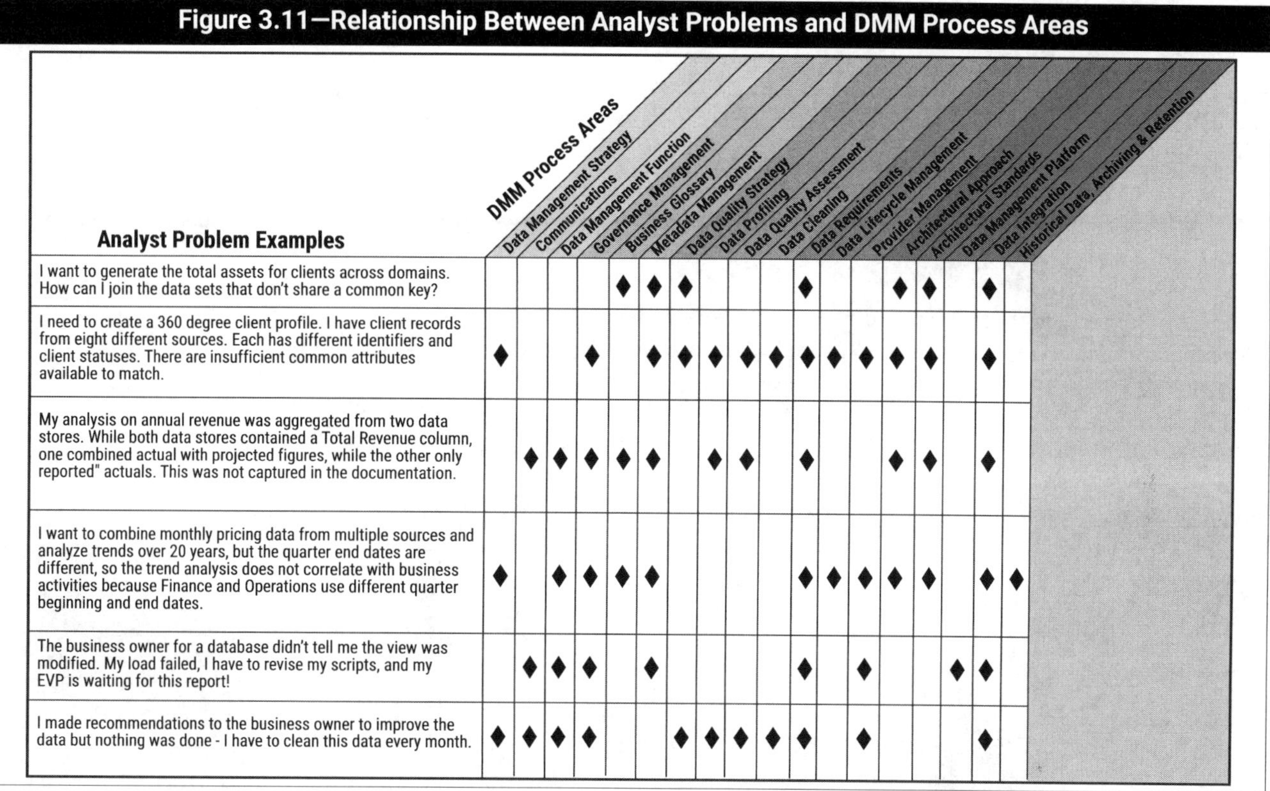

Analyst Problem Examples	Data Management Strategy	Communications	Data Management Function	Governance Management	Business Glossary	Metadata Management	Data Quality Strategy	Data Profiling	Data Quality Assessment	Data Cleaning	Data Requirements	Data Lifecycle Management	Provider Management	Architectural Approach	Architectural Standards	Data Management Platform	Data Integration	Historical Data, Archiving & Retention
I want to generate the total assets for clients across domains. How can I join the data sets that don't share a common key?					♦	♦	♦				♦			♦	♦		♦	
I need to create a 360 degree client profile. I have client records from eight different sources. Each has different identifiers and client statuses. There are insufficient common attributes available to match.	♦			♦		♦	♦	♦	♦	♦	♦	♦	♦	♦	♦		♦	
My analysis on annual revenue was aggregated from two data stores. While both data stores contained a Total Revenue column, one combined actual with projected figures, while the other only reported" actuals. This was not captured in the documentation.		♦	♦	♦	♦	♦		♦	♦		♦			♦	♦		♦	
I want to combine monthly pricing data from multiple sources and analyze trends over 20 years, but the quarter end dates are different, so the trend analysis does not correlate with business activities because Finance and Operations use different quarter beginning and end dates.	♦		♦	♦	♦	♦					♦	♦	♦	♦	♦		♦	♦
The business owner for a database didn't tell me the view was modified. My load failed, I have to revise my scripts, and my EVP is waiting for this report!		♦	♦	♦		♦					♦		♦			♦	♦	
I made recommendations to the business owner to improve the data but nothing was done - I have to clean this data every month.	♦	♦	♦	♦			♦	♦	♦	♦	♦		♦				♦	

Trusted insights depend on trusted data. Consequently, data analysts are shouldering onerous and unstated responsibilities to preserve their credibility. Responsibilities to preserve data include finding the right data, formatting data for analysis, and identifying and correcting inaccuracies. These responsibilities are absolutely necessary for producing trusted insights for decision makers. However, taxing analysts with the performance of these responsibilities reduces analytic throughput, and their efforts often do more harm than good.

Data analysts typically fix data defects only for their models and reports, not only for expediency, but also because they do not have the capability to report defects upstream. Since there is typically more than one user of a data source, allowing data to remain defective in the source can result in analysts delivering contradicting reports.

In general, without the coordinating function of data governance, analytics lacks the specific resources needed to reliably sustain data quality. Ensuring trusted data is ultimately the purview of data quality, which the research on analysts shows is a job unto itself. Moreover, data quality is a discipline that should be managed as a separate supporting function. Data quality's success depends on an effective data management program. See section 3.2 Data Quality and Accuracy for more information.

Apart from the problem of managing data quality within the analytics function, there is the challenge of consistently enforcing privacy policies and practices. The process of producing final analytic outputs requires a dynamic and iterative engagement with subject matter experts. Data is typically shared through spreadsheets and email, with minimal policy controls. Analytics is a prime example of how data tend to follow the path of least resistance, which rarely results in adequate capabilities for monitoring and controlling data for quality and privacy. See section 3.1 Data Inventory and Classification.

3.5.1 User Behavior Analytics

An area of data analytics of interest to privacy engineers is user behavior analytics (UBA), which focuses on gathering information on what the user is actually doing, such as opening applications, accessing files and engaging in network activity.[23] UBA and associated technologies can help enterprises find unusual usage patterns that could point to malicious behavior or breaches.

UBA works in two ways:[24]

1. Establishes a baseline of normal activities specific to the enterprise and its users
2. Uncovers deviations from the baseline activities

UBA software can process large amounts of user file and email activity by analyzing key metadata and activities across these data sources.[25]

While similar to security and information event management, UBA looks beyond the perimeter systems and logs and at the users themselves, rather than an event.[26] This is important as what is insignificant in one incident may be evidence of malicious behavior in another instance.[27]

Password guessing, phishing, structure query language (SQL) injection and advance persistent threats are all techniques hackers and malicious users employ to try to obtain data in an enterprise's system. UBA can help identify potential instances of these attacks. See section 1.12.1 Problematic Data Actions for more information.

Part B: Data Persistence

Data persistence refers to data that outlives the process that created it. Data persistence is most often necessary because the purpose for which personal data are collected often is not fully completed by the process that created or collected it. Data are persisted to enable reuse by other processes, avoiding the unnecessary redundancy of data collection. Unless planned and coordinated, redundant data entry is inefficient and error prone. While persisting personal data is necessary, it must be limited by retention schedules and guarded by access controls.

Data retention schedules prohibit the persistence of data beyond the purpose for which it was created/collected. Data access controls must be established and managed to ensure that persisted personal data is used appropriately by appropriate users. Unauthorized internal access to personal data is considered a breach of privacy policy, and it may result in loss of employment, legal action, and fines to the enterprise.

Data are persisted through storage in databases, data marts, data warehouses and data lakes. Regardless of the data scope and storage technology used, data persistence follows data design principles that guide but do not necessarily dictate the structure of the physical database.

Data modeling is the practice of defining data requirements in a structured model. The result is a logical data model, but it should not be confused with the final physical design of the data within the database. The goals of the logical data model are primarily to evoke unstated requirements and to ensure that there is no unnecessary duplication of data collection. Logical data models, due to their abstraction, are meant to be a reusable asset that not only improves the efficiency of requirements definition, but also ensures data consistency across databases. An example of a logical data model is shown in **figure 3.12.**

Figure 3.12—High-Level Logical Data Model for Information on a Business Card

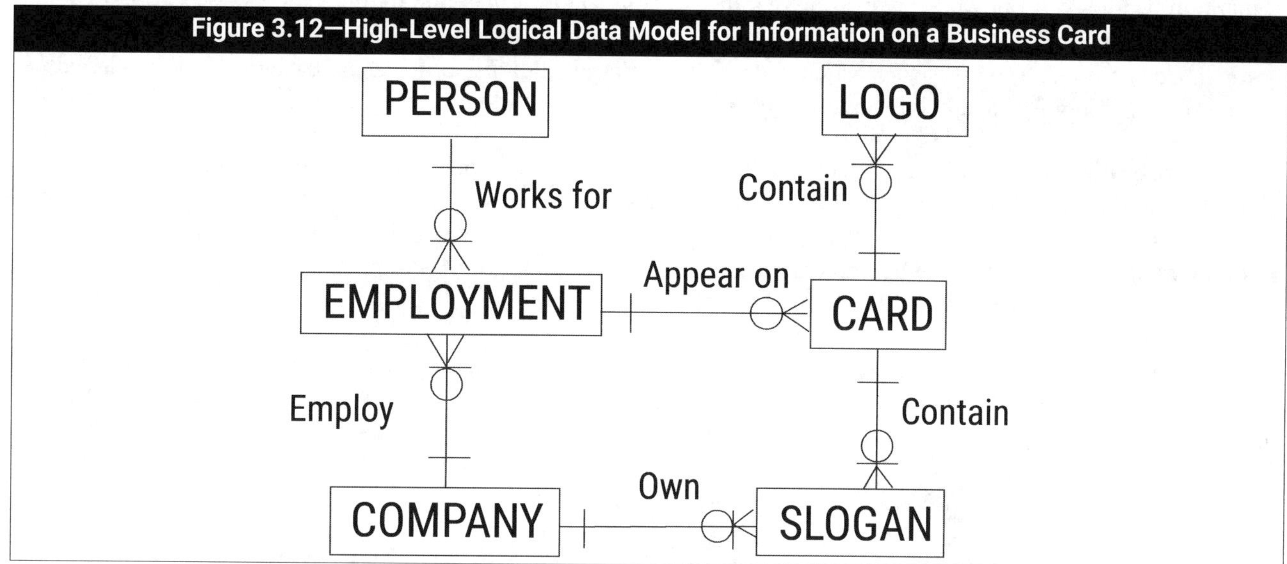

Technology has made persisting data easy, for example in spreadsheets, servers, etc., which results in many copies of data that are unplanned from an enterprise perspective. Unplanned duplication of data sets is a root cause of data quality issues at an enterprise level. Unplanned duplication creates unnecessary confusion for analytics, especially if no authoritative sources for data have been established. Adding to the analytics confusion, consumers of analytics get different answers to the same questions, depending on the analyst. See section 3.5 Data Analytics for more information.

Unplanned copies of data introduce heightened privacy risk. While the enormity of the problem is so great that many enterprises turn a blind eye to these risks, the inherent challenges of fragmented persistent data form the rationale for enterprise data management. Moreover, the purpose of data management is to establish and maintain an enterprise-

wide data infrastructure that ensures data quality for critical business objectives, including customer trust and efficiency. Privacy breaches undermine not only reputation, but also performance.

Privacy breaches reveal vulnerabilities. Vulnerabilities require workarounds and rework, which drag down efficiency and efficacy. An enterprise-wide data management infrastructure supports the entire life cycle of data to enable better risk management and to support data quality.[28]

Due to the inherent risks of unplanned data silos and uncoordinated redundant copies of data, the GDPR has established data portability as a right of individuals whose personal data has been collected.

Article 20 of the GDPR states:[29]

> *The data subject shall have the right to receive the personal data concerning him or her, which he or she has provided to a controller, in a structured, commonly used and machine-readable format and have the right to transmit those data to another controller without hindrance from the controller to which the personal data have been provided.*

Moreover, it is important to understand data minimization, which is the guiding principle for addressing unplanned data persistence. Data minimization should be established as an enterprise-wide policy built into the processes for implementing and maintaining systems for data movement and storage. Likewise, a data minimization policy should guide the archival and destruction of data.

3.6 Data Minimization

Data minimization is the practice of ensuring that the collection of data is explicitly relevant and necessary to accomplish a specified purpose. Data minimization is an important data management principle that is required to ensure adequate privacy controls over personal data. Data minimization has become increasingly challenging with the rapid accumulation of data within enterprises.

An enterprise will typically collect a person's data through more than one process, because a person may have multiple relationships with the enterprise. Different products and services are often supported by different accounts or memberships with business units or departments that operate in silos. If a person has more than one relationship, and each relationship is supported by processes that do not interact, the result is duplicate data from an enterprise perspective. Data silos result in data inconsistencies across the enterprise.

When consumers discover inconsistencies through their various interactions with an enterprise, a common reaction is frustration over having to fill out redundant forms and experiencing the disconnected delivery of service support. Internal users, especially analytics and decision makers, are likewise frustrated when they encounter personal data that is pooled into a commonly accessible environment but has not been logically integrated, e.g., database, data warehouse, data lake. See section 3.8 Data Storage for more information.

The EU's GDPR, Article 5 (1) (c) includes data minimization among its principles relating to processing of personal data:[30]

> *Personal data shall be [...] adequate, relevant and limited to what is necessary in relation to the purposes for which they are processed ('data minimisation')*

While the GDPR's scope is not wholly global, its reach extends to any enterprise dealing with personal data on EU citizens. The GDPR's position on data minimization is pervasive. It is invoked in five separate sections, re-emphasizing its importance in practice. Since data minimization is informed by data use limitation and ultimately by data purpose and consent, GDPR essentially requires data minimization rules and processes throughout the data life cycle.

The requirement to apply data minimization underscores the importance of centrally mastering privacy requirements from an enterprise metadata repository. Within the metadata repository, it is essential to have a comprehensive, approved and annotated business glossary, because complete data integration is a highly improbable result without one.

3.7 Data Migration

Data migration is the permanent transfer of data from a source to a target system. Data migration occurs for a variety of reasons, including:

- Server or storage equipment replacement
- Maintenance or upgrades
- Application migration
- Website consolidation
- Disaster recovery
- Data center relocation

Typical examples of data migration are an enterprise implementing a new chart of accounts, or sending data to a third party for processing.

Another form of data migration is data portability. The right to data portability allows individuals to obtain and reuse their personal data for their own purposes across different services. It allows them to move, copy or transfer personal data easily from one IT environment to another in a safe and secure way, without affecting its usability.

From a privacy perspective, moving data out of the enterprise does not provide the enterprise with relief from accountability, thereby necessitating implementation and monitoring of service level agreements (SLAs).[31] A mature data management infrastructure includes SLAs at critical points of data movement along the life cycle across the enterprise. The points of criticality can fluctuate, because the enterprise and its use of data are dynamic. SLAs implemented at critical junctures should contain expectations and requirements for data quality and privacy. These expectations and requirements should be guided by policies and business objectives.

Since data migration is a specific case of data movement, specific policies, standards, processes and systems should be defined and established. A thorough and annotated data inventory enables the top-down capability to precisely monitor and control personal data treated within SLAs not just with third parties, but with respect to permanent data transfers conducted internally. See section 3.1 Data Inventory and Classification.

3.7.1 Data Conversion

A data conversion, also known as data porting, is required if the source and target systems use different field formats or sizes, file/database structures, or coding schemes. For example, a number may be stored as text, floating point or binary-coded decimal.

Conversions are often necessary when the source and target systems are on different hardware or OS platforms, or use different file or database structures, e.g., if relational databases, flat files and virtual storage access methods are used.

The objective of data conversion is to convert existing data into the new required format, coding and structure, while preserving the meaning and integrity of the data. The data conversion process must provide some means, such as audit trails and logs, to allow for the verification of the accuracy and completeness of the converted data. This

verification of accuracy and completeness may be performed through a combination of manual processes, system utilities, vendor tools and one-time-use special applications.

A large-scale data conversion can potentially become a project within a project as considerable analysis, design and planning are required. Among the steps necessary for a successful data conversion:

- Determining what data should be converted using programs and what, if any, should be converted manually
- Performing any necessary data cleansing ahead of the conversion
- Identifying the methods to be used to verify the conversion, such as automated file comparisons that compare record counts and control totals, accounting balances, and individual data items on a sample basis
- Establishing parameters for a successful conversion (e.g., Is 100 percent consistency between the old and new systems necessary, or will some differences within defined ranges be acceptable?)
- Scheduling the sequence of conversion tasks
- Designing audit trail reports to document the conversion, including data mappings and transformations
- Designing exception reports to record any items that cannot be converted automatically
- Establishing responsibility for verifying and signing off on individual conversion steps and accepting the overall conversion
- Developing and testing conversion programs, including functionality and performance
- Performing one or more conversion dress rehearsals to familiarize persons with the sequence of events and their roles, and testing the conversion process end to end with real data
- Controlling the outsourcing of the conversion process with a proper agreement covering nondisclosure, data privacy, data destruction and other warranties
- Running the actual conversion with all necessary personnel on site or on call

3.7.2 Refining the Migration Scenario

In order to determine the scope of the implementation project, module analysis should be undertaken to identify the affected functional modules and data entities. The plan of the implementation project should be refined based on this information and on an analysis of business requirements.

The next step is to develop a migration plan. This is a detailed listing of tasks for the production deployment of a new system. Within this plan decision points are defined to make “go” or “no-go” decisions. The following processes require decision points:

- Support migration process—A support process to administer the enterprise repository must be implemented. Because this repository should be used on completion of the project to manage the software components of the new architecture, this process should be capable of supporting future development processes. The enterprise repository administration and report generation support the migration by supporting the reverse engineering of changes in the legacy architecture and facilitating the creation of impact analysis reports.
- Migration infrastructure—The project develops specifications for the infrastructure of the migration project. This approach ensures consistency and increases confidence in the functionality of the fallback scenario. The migration project team completes a high-level analysis of the legacy and new data models to establish links that will be refined later. The migration infrastructure is the basis for specifying the following components:
    - Data redirector (temporary adapters)—Good practices suggest the staged deployment of applications to minimize the end-user impact of their implementation and limit the risk by having a fallback scenario with minimum impact. For this reason, an infrastructure component is needed to handle distributed data on different platforms within distributed applications. The design of a data redirector on the new architecture corresponds to service-oriented architectures and should cover features such as access to the not-yet-

migrated legacy data during run time, data consistency due to the usage of standards such as X/Open XA interface, and a homogeneous new architecture.

- Data conversion components—The need to create an enterprise data model to eliminate data redundancies and inconsistencies often is identified. For this reason, infrastructure components to transform the legacy data model to the new data model must be provided. These components can be described as follows:
  - Unload components to copy the data (either as is or suitably modified to align with the data format of target system) in legacy databases that have been identified for migration
  - Load components to execute the load of the data into the new database

Software packages that support data migration, such as ERP and document management software, should be acquired as soon as the software evaluation is done. The data conversion plan should be based on the available databases and migration tools provided by the selected vendors.

Deciding which method to use for data conversion should be part of the implementation project and should be based on transaction volume and change degree of the data model.

Fallback (Rollback) Scenario

New system deployments do not always go as planned. To mitigate the risk of downtime for mission-critical systems, good practices dictate that the tools and applications required to reverse the migration are available prior to attempting the production cutover.

Some or all of these tools and applications may need to be developed as part of the project.

Components have to be delivered that can back out all changes and restore data to the original applications in the case of nonfunctioning new applications. Two types of components should be considered as part of a fallback contingency plan.

The first type consists of:

- Unload components to execute the unloading of the data from the new data structures
- Transfer components for the data conversion
- Load components to execute the loading of the data into the legacy data structures

The second type consists of:

- A log component to log the data modifications within the new data model during runtime within the service layer
- Transfer components for the data conversion
- Load components to execute the load of the data into the legacy data structures

Another important consideration is the new system's data structure. This can be determined by reading the software user guides, analyzing the entity relationship diagrams, understanding the relationships between data elements, and reviewing definitions of key terms (such as "entity" and "record") in the new system.

Next, it is important to review the decisions on how business processes should be conducted in the new system. Changes are identified, and the output of this exercise is a table of new data terminology against current definitions of data elements. In this step, the project team identifies how current data are defined in the new system. Following this step, a data cleanup is completed to eliminate inconsistencies in the current database, if possible, and discover and resolve duplications of data sets. The rules of conversion are defined and documented, with the objective of ensuring that the business processes executed in the new system yield results that maintain data integrity and relationships.

3.7.3 Post-Data Migration

A successful data migration delivers the new system on time, on budget, and with the required quality. The data migration project should be carefully planned and use appropriate methodologies and tools to minimize risk of the following:

- Disruption of routine operations
- Violation of the security and confidentiality of data
- Conflicts and contention between legacy and migrated operations
- Data inconsistencies and loss of data integrity during the migration process

The data model and the new application model should be stored in an enterprise repository. Using a repository allows a simulation of the migration scenario and traceability during the project. An enterprise repository enables an overview of the reengineering and data migration process, for example which modules and entities are in which stage, such as in service or already migrated. These models will be modified in the course of carrying out the processes described in the following sections.

Data conversion rules are programmed by the software development team. Data conversion scripts are created to convert the data from the old database to the new database. These are tested on a discrete selection of data that is carefully selected to include all cases. This process is referred to as "program" or "unit testing." Following the sign-off of data conversion scripts by programmers, the scripts are run on a test copy of the production database. The values of data are verified by executing assessments, including business process tests. Users and developers complete cycles of testing until conversion scripts are fine-tuned. After testing has been completed, the next step is to promote the converted database to production.

The key points to be taken into consideration in a data conversion project are to ensure:

- Completeness of data conversion
- Integrity of data
- Storage and security of data under conversion
- Consistency of data
- Continuity of data access

The last copy of the data before conversion from the old platform and the first copy of the data after conversion to the new platform should be maintained separately in the archive for future reference.

3.8 Data Storage

Technologies for data storage continue to have a powerful effect on data management in general and on privacy specifically. Big data, as the label implies, refers to very large data sets.

The increased need for bigger data sets is driven by a number of factors:

- Competition and compliance with respect to more data on everything relevant to the enterprise's performance and risk objectives
- Growth of the global population
- Growth in enterprise sizes
- Expanded usage of mobile devices, social media and the Internet of Things
- Advances in data storage

With constraints on volume, variety, velocity and veracity removed, and with "big" (more) data more readily available, it is now possible to analyze all types of data. These constraints are not taken away by new big data technologies. Instead they are removed through a synergy between new technologies and the extended capabilities provided by cloud computing.

Limitless volume availability and variety allow enterprises to reuse their "old" data for new purposes.

Furthermore, big data technology allows enterprises to examine their current data to find patterns that influence their way of doing business.

Along with advice from experienced people, enterprises receive decision-making support from big data analysis. Big data analysis produces real-time reporting and predictive analysis.

Unfortunately, advances in data storage have not addressed the added challenge of integrating data under common storage and access. In other words, enabling easier solutions for data access and storage alone increases the risk of poor data quality and privacy breaches.[32]

In the public domain, there has been a reluctance to store personal and protected data centrally at a macro level. This reluctance is fueled by the fear that a single data store represents a single point of failure, increasing the risks for massive data breaches and system outages. In spite of these concerns, centralization remains a cornerstone for economies of scale, and data warehousing is one approach.

Standardization represents a different approach from centralization, and it is especially key to managing data quality and privacy. Data standards represent a centralization of knowledge about shared data, allowing distributed storage to function as an integrated system. Metadata management is effectively data standardization, further emphasizing the importance of establishing and managing a data inventory. See section 3.1 Data Inventory and Classification for more information.

To ensure that standards represented in the metadata repository are implemented and followed, a reference data platform is needed. Reference data encompass a wide range of data that are not entirely static but tend to change slowly over time.

Standard codes and values defined in the metadata repository are prime examples of reference data. Reference data platforms are designed to store and manage deploying standard codes and values in a distributed storage environment from a central repository. A reference data platform enables efficient and controlled operationalization of metadata standards.

Even though standards enable improved interoperability along supply and demand chains, many enterprises resist cooperating to develop industry standards for shared data. While many reasons have been asserted, this resistance is primarily due to the difficulty in quantifying a return on investment. New standards require massive system changes that are complex, and in rare cases, changes may be impossible to implement. Historically, industries have not developed data standards until a crisis of significant magnitude warranted the effort. Take, for example, Wall Street's paperwork crisis in the late 1960s, which resulted in CUSIP (unified standard identification procedures for traded securities).[33] Instead, duplicative storage occurs, and human resources are unnecessarily consumed in workarounds to manage the flow of data with third parties.

Tokenization and end-to-end encryption are techniques deployed in data storage environments to control access and use of sensitive data. Tokenization involves the use of randomly generated numbers (tokens) as replacements for sensitive data. Similarly, encryption converts sensitive data (plaintext), but it converts it into ciphertext rather than numbers. See section 2.11 Encryption, Hashing and De-identification for more information.

The increase in data storage technologies supporting data security capabilities is closing the risk gap in both centralized and distributed storage environments. However, the increase in data storage technologies does not

address the lack of integration and standards in data warehouses. As a result, enterprises remain unnecessarily vulnerable to operational and privacy risk. Likewise, privacy standards change over time. Without metadata management, efforts to monitor and control changes at the data level are cumbersome and lack transparency. See section 3.1 Data Inventory and Classification for more information.

3.9 Data Warehousing

While data warehousing is often synonymous with large databases, it is actually a discipline of data integration methods that are not restricted by specific technologies or resulting designs. Data warehousing methods involve a layering of the integration of independent data sources into an organized delivery of data to many users. This process is broken down into at least two fundamental parts: staging and presentation.

3.9.1 Extract, Transform, Load

The process of moving data through layers from end to end is commonly referred to as ETL (extract, transform and load):

- Data **extraction** is the process of capturing data from one or more sources.
- Data **transformation** is the process of converting extracted data from one or more sources in preparation for loading into the target system.
- Data **loading** is the process of inserting transformed data from one or more sources into the target system.

The ETL components each follow simple or complex rules, depending on the nature of the data source and the purpose of the target layer.

Staging Layer

The staging layer, or data ingestion, deals with data as inputs, whereas the presentation layer deals with data as outputs of the data warehouse.

In the staging layer, it is important for the data to be *as-is*. That is because its purpose is to mirror the data in the source system. Mirroring the data in the source system in this layer enables the identification and resolution of any defects that may occur upstream (or source system) or downstream (or target system).

Accordingly, the transformation rules for data ingestion are minimal, whereas the rules for managing extraction may be more complex. The data extraction process must be tailored to the methods supported by each source system. It is necessary to synchronize extraction with the source system to ensure that all the data have been captured.

Presentation Layer

The presentation layer requires more complex rules to conform to the *to-be* design to prepare it for the destination target. While transformation is minimal in the staging layer, the to-be design of the presentation (access) layer is highly refined and organized to optimize downstream user efficiency and effectiveness. Consequently, data transformation rules are typically more complex.

Many data quality errors result from neglecting data movement into and out of the warehouse. Data ingestion into the staging layer can go awry due to unexpected changes in the source system. Larger than normal data volumes may require more processing time, which in turn delays availability of the data. Data corrections performed after the normal batch process can go undetected if not watched for. Unanticipated format and code changes can compromise the extraction process. Conversely, downstream usage of the warehouse often lands in spreadsheets, where fixes are typically made to the data and metadata.

3.9.2 Additional Considerations

While data warehousing often stops at the presentation or access layer, mature data-driven enterprises apply lean manufacturing concepts to their data, where the primary concern is throughput with minimal rework.[34] In other words, it is not enough to declare the data warehouse as right, if the data is corrupted downstream.

From a business perspective, data is not restricted to what is in the warehouse. Data is perceived as an open system that either supports or inhibits the quality of business performance, necessitating the management of data throughout the life cycle, including a concern for data corruption beyond the warehouse. See Part A: Data Purpose for more information. Data corruption occurs outside the warehouse due to not knowing the data exist, inability to access the data, or the warehouse not having the data needed by the data consumers, etc.

As an implemented system, a data warehouse is generally built to serve the entire enterprise, whereas smaller data integration systems are called data marts. Data marts are built for narrower purposes, such as a business line or a specific set of business functions. Ideally, data marts are fed by the data warehouse. Even with their scope differences, data marts and data warehouses are designed to optimize data access to support optimal business performance.

Data warehousing offers greater control over data, which supports privacy goals. To ensure compliance with data quality and privacy policies, a data warehouse should be standardized, well documented, and managed end-to-end. See section 3.1 Data Inventory and Classification for more information.

3.10 Data Retention and Archiving

Data retention and archiving is the discipline of ensuring persistent data is stored in compliance with legal and business data archival requirements through policies, standards, processes and procedures.

GDPR Article 5 (1)(e) states:[35]

> *Personal data shall be [...]kept in a form which permits identification of data subjects for no longer than is necessary for the purposes for which the personal data are processed; personal data may be stored for longer periods insofar as the personal data will be processed solely for archiving purposes in the public interest, scientific or historical research purposes or statistical purposes in accordance with Article 89(1) subject to implementation of the appropriate technical and organisational measures required by this Regulation in order to safeguard the rights and freedoms of the data subject ('storage limitation')*

Data is retained and archived primarily for business and regulatory purposes. Data retention and archiving are performed according to established schedules, archival rules, data formats and the permissible means of storage, access and security protocols (tokenization, encryption and anonymization).

Data retention requirements are derived from various sources:

- Internal requirements should be consistent with data limitation policies.
- External requirements derived from regulations and laws will vary even for the same data.

Given the high degree of requirements overlap, data retention policies must provide practical guidance in satisfying all parties.

Retention policies tend to focus on sensitive data and provide guidance for retention schedules and archival rules. Retention policies and schedules tend to address classes of data, such as PII and PHI. Therefore, ensuring

compliance requires an authoritative and up-to-date identification of sensitive data in all applications. Standard approaches to data retention start with data inventory and classification. See section 3.1 Data Inventory and Classification for more information.

3.11 Data Destruction

Data destruction is performed when the need for data to persist has expired. Since data destruction depends on data retention, a clear understanding of the purpose and consent for the use of the data is required. See section 3.1 Data Inventory and Classifications for more information.

For example, notice that the specific conditions for GDPR Article 17 are elaborations on the requirements for consent and purpose.

GDPR Article 17 (1) states:[36]

The data subject shall have the right to obtain from the controller the erasure of personal data concerning him or her without undue delay and the controller shall have the obligation to erase personal data without undue delay where one of the following grounds applies:

A. *the personal data are no longer necessary in relation to the purposes for which they were collected or otherwise processed;*

B. *the data subject withdraws consent on which the processing is based according to point (a) of Article 6(1), or point (a) of Article 9(2), and where there is no other legal ground for the processing;*

C. *the data subject objects to the processing pursuant to Article 21(1) and there are no overriding legitimate grounds for the processing, or the data subject objects to the processing pursuant to Article 21(2);*

D. *the personal data have been unlawfully processed;*

E. *the personal data have to be erased for compliance with a legal obligation in Union or Member State law to which the controller is subject;*

F. *the personal data have been collected in relation to the offer of information society services referred to in Article 8(1).*

Different methods may be used for data erasure.

3.11.1 Data Anonymization

Data anonymization irreversibly removes personally identifiable information from data sets, so that the people whom the data describe remain anonymous. In other words, data anonymization is a form of tokenization that renders the original data completely unrecoverable. See 3.8 Data Storage for more information on tokenization. Data anonymization can be risky if data that was not anonymized could be arranged in a manner that could divulge the identity of the person (e.g., a phone number, account number or any collection of data that could be used to look up the person).

3.11.2 Deletion

Deletion is a method of erasing data that preserves the reusability of rewritable media. The risk of deleting records is that the methods of deletion often leave the data intact on the storage media. For example, data cleared from the desktop trash bin are not deleted immediately. The data are marked for deletion to be overwritten when new data are stored.

3.11.3 Crypt-shredding

Crypt-shredding is different from data deletion, because only the encryption keys are deleted. Without the encryption keys, the data are rendered inaccessible. Crypt-shredding requires that all data written to the disk be encrypted. Crypto-shredding is useful where there may be less control over how data are deleted, for example on cloud-based systems.

3.11.4 Degaussing

Degaussing is wiping data from magnetic-based media, rendering all but hard drives reusable. Degaussing permanently destroys data by altering the magnetic field of magnetic storage media. Degaussing is a preferred method for the destruction of data, because destroying the drive alone can leave fragments of media that contain readable data.

3.11.5 Destruction

Destruction is a brute force approach to retiring data from use. It involves the physical destruction of the storage media. Without degaussing, fragments of destroyed media can be rendered readable. Therefore, destruction is more effective when used in combination with degaussing.

Properly destroyed data leave no trace of their existence. While persons have a right to be forgotten, this right is not absolute. While it is true that hoarding data increases legal liability beyond statutes of limitation, what constitutes an important historical fact is often not clear until much later.

The trade-off between save and destroy is incalculable if the expected benefit of keeping the data is unknown. This would suggest data destruction should be performed more than it is in practice. Instead, gray areas in the guidelines result in a reluctance to destroy data. The principles of data purpose for the limitations on use of sensitive data (i.e., PII and PHI) provide a practical basis for making these determinations and defining them in policies.

---

1 Chrissis, M.; M. Konrad; S. Shrum; *CMMI for Development,* Third Edition, Addison-Wesley, USA, 2011
2 *Op cit* ISACA 2016
3 *Op cit* European Parliament
4 Information Commissioner's Office, "Data protection by design and default," https://ico.org.uk/for-organisations/guide-to-data-protection/guide-to-the-general-data-protection-regulation-gdpr/accountability-and-governance/data-protection-by-design-and-default/
5 *Op cit* ISACA 2016
6 *Ibid.*
7 CMMI Institute, *Data Management Maturity Model,* USA, 2019
8 *Op cit* ISACA2017
9 *Op cit* CMMI Institute
10 *Ibid.*
11 *Ibid.*
12 Beale, T.; F. Smith; L. Dodds; P. L'Henaff; D. Yates; *How to Create a Data Inventory,* The Open Data Institute, United Kingdom, 2018
13 *Ibid.*
14 *Data Catalog Vocabulary (DCAT) – Version 2,* 4 February 2020, www.w3.org/TR/vocab-dcat/
15 *Op cit* Beale
16 Profisee, "Data Quality—What, Why, How, 10 Best Practices & More!" https://profisee.com/data-quality-what-why-how-who/
17 Knight, M.; "What Is Data Quality?", Dataversity, 20 November 2017, www.dataversity.net/what-is-data-quality/
18 *Op cit* CMMI Institute
19 Ambler, S.; *The Object Primer: Agile Model-Driven Development With UML 2.0,* 3rd Edition, Cambridge University Press, USA, 2004
20 *Op cit* CMMI Institute
21 *Ibid.*
22 *Op cit* European Parliament
23 Green, A.; "What is User Behavior Analytics?" *Varonis,* 29 March 2020, www.varonis.com/blog/what-is-user-behavior-analytics/
24 Johnson, J.; "User behavioral analytics tools can thwart security attacks," *SearchSecurity, May 2015,* https://searchsecurity.techtarget.com/feature/User-behavioral-analytics-tools-can-thwart-security-attacks
25 *Op cit* Green
26 *Ibid.*

27 *Op cit* Johnson
28 *Op cit* CMMI Institute
29 *Op cit* European Parliament
30 *Ibid.*
31 *Op cit* CMMI Institute
32 Woods, D.; "How to Create a Moore's Law for Data," *Forbes,* 12 December 2013, www.forbes.com/sites/danwoods/2013/12/12/how-to-create-a-moores-law-for-data/#7239f3c544ca
33 "The Paperwork Crisis," *The Shareholder Service Optimizer,* 2008, https://optimizeronline.com/the-paperwork-crisis/
34 *Op cit* CMMI Institute
35 *Op cit* European Parliament
36 *Ibid.*

Appendix A: CDPSE Exam General Information

ISACA is a professional membership association composed of individuals interested in IS audit, assurance, control, security, governance and data privacy. The CDPSE Certification Working Group is responsible for establishing policies for the CDPSE certification program and developing the exam.

Note: Because information regarding the CDPSE examination may change, please refer to www.isaca.org/credentialing/certified-data-privacy-solutions-engineer for the most current information.

Requirements for Certification

The CDPSE designation is awarded to individuals who have met the following requirements: (1) achieve a passing score on the CDPSE exam, (2) adhere to the Code of Professional Ethics, (3) adhere to the continuing education policy, and (4) demonstrate the required minimum work experience supporting proper intergration of IT privacy solutions that mitigate risk.

Successful Completion of the CDPSE Exam

The exam is open to all individuals who wish to take it. Successful exam candidates are not certified until they apply for certification (and demonstrate that they have met all requirements) and receive approval from ISACA.

Experience in Data Privacy

CDPSE candidates must meet the stated experience requirements to become certified. Please refer to *www.isaca.org/credentialing/certified-data-privacy-solutions-engineer/get-cdpse-certified* for experience requirements and a list of experience waivers.

Experience must have been gained within the 10-year period preceding the application date for certification, or within five years from the date of initially passing the exam. A completed application for certification must be submitted within five years from the passing date of the CDPSE exam. All experience must be independently verified with employers.

Description of the Exam

The CDPSE Certification Working Group oversees the development of the exam and ensures the currency of its content. Questions for the CDPSE exam are developed through a multitiered process designed to enhance the ultimate quality of the exam.

The purpose of the exam is to evaluate a candidate's knowledge and experience in data privacy. The exam consists of 120 multiple-choice questions, administered during a 3.5-hour session.

Registration for the CDPSE Exam

The CDPSE exam is administered on a continuous basis at qualifying test sites Please refer to the ISACA Exam Candidate Information Guide at *www.isaca.org/credentialing/certified-data-privacy-solutions-engineer/cdpse-exam* for specific exam registration information including registration, scheduling and languages, and important key

information for exam day. Exam registrations can be made online at *www.isaca.org/credentialing/certified-data-privacy-solutions-engineer/cdpse-exam*.

CDPSE Program Accreditation Renewed Under ISO/IEC 17024:2012

The American National Standards Institute (ANSI) has voted to continue the accreditation for the CISA, CISM, CGEIT, CRISC and CDPSE certifications, under ISO/IEC 17024:2012, General Requirements for Bodies Operating Certification Systems of Persons. ANSI, a private, nonprofit organization, accredits other organizations to serve as third-party product, system and personnel certifiers.

ISO/IEC 17024 specifies the requirements to be followed by organizations certifying individual against specific requirements. ANSI describes ISO/IEC 17024 as "expected to play a prominent role in facilitating global standardization of the certification community, increasing mobility among countries, enhancing public safety, and protecting consumers."

ANSI's accreditation:

- Promotes the unique qualifications and expertise ISACA's certifications provide
- Protects the integrity of the certifications and provides legal defensibility
- Enhances consumer and public confidence in the certifications and the people who hold them
- Facilitates mobility across borders or industries

Accreditation by ANSI signifies that ISACA's procedures meet ANSI's essential requirements for openness, balance, consensus and due process. With this accreditation, ISACA anticipates that significant opportunities for CISAs, CISMs, CGEITs, CRISCs and CDPSEs will continue to open in the United States and around the world.

Scheduling the Exam

The CDPSE exam can be scheduled directly from your My ISACA Certification Dashboard. Please see the Exam Candidate Scheduling Guide for complete instructions. Exams can be scheduled for any available time slot. Exams may be rescheduled a minimum of 48 hours prior to the originally scheduled appointment. If you are within 48 hours of your original appointment, you must take your exam or forfeit the exam registration fee.

Sitting for the Exam

Prior to the day of the exam make sure you:

- Locate the test center and confirm the start time
- Plan to arrive 15 minutes prior to exam start time
- Plan to store personal belongings
- Review the exam day rules

You must present an acceptable form of identification (ID) in order to enter the testing center. Please see the *Exam Candidate Information Guide* for acceptable forms of ID.

You are prohibited from bringing the following into the test center:

- Reference materials, paper, notepads or language dictionaries
- Calculators

- Any type of communication, surveillance or recording devices such as:
  - Mobile phones
  - Tablets
  - Smart watches or glasses
  - Mobile devices
- Baggage of any kind including handbags, purses or briefcases
- Weapons
- Tobacco products
- Food or beverages
- Visitors

If exam candidates are viewed with any such communication, surveillance or recording devices during the exam administration, their exam will be voided, and they will be asked to immediately leave the exam site.

Personal items brought to the testing center must be stored in a locker or other designated area until the exam is completed and submitted.

Avoid activities that would invalidate your test score.

- Creating a disturbance
- Giving or receiving help; using notes, papers or other aids
- Attempting to take the exam for someone else
- Possession of communication, surveillance or recording devices, including but not limited to cell phones, tablets, smart glasses, smart watches, mobile devices, etc., during the exam administration
- Attempting to share test questions or answers or other information contained in the exam (as such are the confidential information of ISACA), including sharing test questions subsequent to the exam
- Leaving the testing area without authorization. (You will not be allowed to return to the testing room.)
- Accessing items stored in the personal belongings area before the completion of the exam

Budgeting Your Time

The exam is administered over a three-hour period. This allows for a little more than 1.5 minutes per question. Therefore, it is advisable that candidates pace themselves to complete the entire exam.

Grading the Exam

Candidate scores are reported as a scaled score. A scaled score is a conversion of a candidate's raw score on an exam to a common scale. ISACA uses and reports scores on a common scale from 200 to 800.

A candidate must receive a score of 450 or higher to pass the exam. A score of 450 represents a minimum consistent standard of knowledge as established by ISACA's CDPSE Certification Working Group. A candidate receiving a passing score may then apply for certification if all other requirements are met.

Passing the exam does not grant the CDPSE designation. To become a CDPSE, each candidate must complete all requirements, including submitting an application and receiving approval for certification.

The CDPSE examination contains some questions that are included for research and analysis purposes only. Those questions are not separately identified, and the candidate's final score will be based only on the common scored questions. There are various versions of each exam but only the common questions are scored for your results.

A candidate receiving a score less than 450 is not successful and can retake the exam by registering and paying the appropriate exam fee. To assist with future study, the result letter each candidate receives will include a score analysis by content area.

You will receive a preliminary score on screen immediately following the completion of your exam. **Your official score will be emailed to you and available online within 10 working days**. Question-level results cannot be provided.

In order to become CDPSE-certified, candidates must pass the CDPSE exam and must complete and submit an application for certification (and must receive confirmation from ISACA that the application is approved). The application is available on the ISACA website at *www.isaca.org/credentialing/certified-data-privacy-solutions-engineer/get-cdpse-certified.* Once the application is approved, the applicant will be sent confirmation of the approval. The candidate is not CDPSE-certified, and cannot use the CDPSE designation, until the candidate's application is approved. A processing fee must accompany CDPSE applications for certification.

Candidates receiving a failing score on the exam may request a rescoring of their exam within 30 days following the release of the exam results. All requests must include a candidate's name, exam identification number and mailing address. A fee of US $75 must accompany this request.

Appendix B: CDPSE Job Practice

Knowledge Subdomains

Domain 1: Privacy Governance (34%)

A. Governance

1. Personal Data and Information
2. Privacy Laws and Standards Across Jurisdictions
3. Privacy Documentation
4. Legal Purpose, Consent and Legitimate Interest
5. Data Subject Rights

B. Management

1. Roles and Responsibilities Related to Data
2. Privacy Training and Awareness
3. Vendor and Third-Party Management
4. Audit Process
5. Privacy Incident Management

C. Risk Management

1. Risk Management Process
2. Privacy Impact Assessment
3. Threats, Attacks and Vulnerabilities Related to Privacy

Domain 2: Privacy Architecture (36%)

A. Infrastructure

1. Technology Stacks
2. Cloud-Based Services
3. Endpoints
4. Remote Access
5. System Hardening

B. Applications and Software

1. Secure Development Life Cycle
2. Applications and Software Hardening
3. APIs and Services
4. Tracking Technologies

C. Technical Privacy Controls

1. Communication and Transport Protocols
2. Encryption, Hashing and De-identification
3. Key Management
4. Monitoring and Logging
5. Identity and Access Management

Domain 3: Data Life Cycle (30%)

A. Data Purpose

1. Data Inventory and Classification
2. Data Quality and Accuracy
3. Dataflow and Usage Diagrams
4. Data Use Limitation
5. Data Analytics

B. Data Persistence

1. Data Minimization
2. Data Migration
3. Data Storage
4. Data Warehousing
5. Data Retention and Archiving
6. Data Destruction

Task Statements

1. Identify the internal and external requirements for the organization's privacy programs and practices.
2. Participate in the evaluation of privacy policies, programs and policies for their alignment with legal requirements, regulatory requirements, and industry best practices.
3. Coordinate and/or perform privacy impact assessment (PIA) and other privacy-focused assessments.
4. Participate in the development of procedures that align with privacy policies and business needs.
5. Implement procedures that align with privacy policies.
6. Participate in the management and evaluation of contracts, service levels, and practices of vendors and other external parties.
7. Participate in the privacy incident management process.
8. Collaborate with cybersecurity personnel on the security risk assessment process to address privacy compliance and risk mitigation.
9. Collaborate with other practitioners to ensure that privacy programs and practices are followed during the design, development and implementation of systems, applications and infrastructure.
10. Evaluate the enterprise architecture and information architecture to ensure that it supports privacy by design principles and considerations.
11. Evaluate advancements in privacy-enhancing technologies and changes in the regulatory landscape.
12. Identify, validate and/or implement appropriate privacy and security controls according to data classification procedures.
13. Design, implement and/or monitor processes and procedures to keep the inventory and dataflow records current.
14. Develop and/or implement a prioritization process for privacy practices.
15. Develop, monitor and/or report performance metrics and trends related to privacy practices.
16. Report on the status and outcomes of privacy programs and practices to relevant stakeholders.
17. Participate in privacy training and promote awareness of privacy practices.
18. Identify issues requiring remediation and opportunities for process improvement.

Glossary

A

Acceptable Use policy—A policy that establishes an agreement between users and the enterprise and defines for all parties' the ranges of use that are approved before gaining access to a network or the Internet.

Access control—The processes, rules and deployment mechanisms that control access to information systems, resources and physical access to premises.

Access control list (ACL)—An internal computerized table of access rules regarding the levels of computer access permitted to logon IDs and computer terminals.

Scope Notes: Also referred to as access control tables.

Access control table—An internal computerized table of access rules regarding the levels of computer access permitted to logon IDs and computer terminals.

Access Method—The technique used for selecting records in a file, one at a time, for processing, retrieval or storage. The access method is related to, but distinct from, the file organization, which determines how the records are stored.

Access path—The logical route that an end user takes to access computerized information.

Scope Notes: Typically includes a route through the operating system, telecommunications software, selected application software and the access control system.

Access rights—The permission or privileges granted to users, programs or workstations to create, change, delete or view data and files within a system, as defined by rules established by data owners and the information security policy.

Accountability—The ability to map a given activity or event back to the responsible party.

Address— 1. A number, character or group of characters that identifies a given device or a storage location, which may contain data or a program step.

2. To refer to a device or storage location by an identifying number, character or group of characters.

Addressing—The method used to identify the location of a participant in a network.

Scope Notes: Ideally, specifies where the participant is located rather than who they are (name) or how to get there (routing).

Administrative access—Elevated or increased privileges granted to an account for that account to manage systems, networks and/or applications. Administrative access can be assigned to an individual's account or a built-in system account.

Administrative control—The rules, procedures and practices dealing with operational effectiveness, efficiency and adherence to regulations and management policies.

Advanced Encryption Standard (AES)—A public algorithm that supports keys from 128 bits to 256 bits in size

Anonymity—The quality or state of not being named or identified.

Anonymization—Irreversible severance of a data set from the identity of the data contributor to prevent any future reidentification, even by the organization collecting the data under any condition.

Application programming interface (API)—A set of routines, protocols and tools referred to as building blocks used in business application software development

Architecture—Description of the fundamental underlying design of the components of the business system, or of one element of the business system (e.g., technology), the relationships among them, and the manner in which they support enterprise objectives.

Artificial intelligence—Advanced computer systems that can simulate human capabilities, such as analysis, based on a predetermined set of rules

Assurance—Pursuant to an accountable relationship between two or more parties, an IT audit and assurance professional is engaged to issue a written communication expressing a conclusion about the subject matters for which the accountable party is responsible. Assurance refers to a number of related activities designed to provide the reader or user of the report with a level of assurance or comfort over the subject matter.

Scope Notes: Assurance engagements could include support for audited financial statements, reviews of controls, compliance with required standards and practices, and compliance with agreements, licenses, legislation and regulation.

Asymmetric cipher—Most implementations of asymmetric ciphers combine a widely distributed public key and a closely held, protected private key. A message that is encrypted by the public key can only be decrypted by the mathematically related, counterpart

Asymmetric key (public key)—A cipher technique in which different cryptographic keys are used to encrypt and decrypt a message Scope Notes: See public key encryption.

Audit—Formal inspection and verification to check whether a standard or set of guidelines is being followed, records are accurate, or efficiency and effectiveness targets are being met.

Scope Notes: May be carried out by internal or external groups.

Audit trail— Data in the form of a logical path linking a sequence of events, used to trace the transactions that have affected the contents of a record

Source : ISO

Authentication—1. The act of verifying identity, i.e., user, system.

Scope Notes: Risk: Can also refer to the verification of the correctness of a piece of data.

2. The act of verifying the identity of a user, the user's eligibility to access computerized information.

Scope Notes: Assurance: Authentication is designed to protect against fraudulent logon activity. It can also refer to the verification of the correctness of a piece of data.

Authenticity—Undisputed authorship

Authorization—The process of determining if the end user is permitted to have access to an information asset or the information system containing the asset.

Availability—Ensuring timely and reliable access to and use of information

Awareness—Being acquainted with, mindful of, conscious of and well informed on a specific subject, which implies knowing and understanding a subject and acting accordingly.

B

Binding corporate rules (BCRs)—A set of rules that allow multinational organizations to transfer personal data from the EU to their affiliates outside of the EU.

Biometric data—Personal data resulting from specific technical processing relating to the physical, physiological or behavioral characteristics of a natural person, which allow or confirm the unique identification of that natural person, such as facial images or dactyloscopic data.

Block cipher—A public algorithm that operates on plaintext in blocks (strings or groups) of bits

Bridge—Data link layer device developed in the early 1980s to connect local area networks (LANs) or create two separate LAN or wide area network (WAN) network segments from a single segment to reduce collision domains.

Scope Notes: A bridge acts as a store-and-forward device in moving frames toward their destination. This is achieved by analyzing the MAC header of a data packet, which represents the hardware address of an NIC.

Bring your own device (BYOD)—An enterprise policy used to permit partial or full integration of user-owned mobile devices for business purposes

Brouter—Device that performs the functions of both a bridge and a router.

Scope Notes: A brouter operates at both the data link and the network layers. It connects same data link type LAN segments as well as different data link ones, which is a significant advantage. Like a bridge, it forwards packets based on the data link layer address to a different network of the same type. Also, whenever required, it processes and forwards messages to a different data link type network based on the network protocol address. When connecting same data link type networks, it is as fast as a bridge and is able to connect different data link type networks.

Bulk data transfer—A data recovery strategy that includes a recovery from complete backups that are physically shipped offsite once a week.

Scope Notes: Specifically, logs are batched electronically several times daily, and then loaded into a tape library located at the same facility as the planned recovery.

C

Certificate (Certification) authority (CA)—A trusted third party that serves authentication infrastructures or enterprises and registers entities and issues them certificates.

Certification practice statement (CPS)—A detailed set of rules governing the certificate authority's operations. It provides an understanding of the value and trustworthiness of certificates issued by a given certificate authority (CA).

Scope Notes: In terms of the controls that an enterprise observes, the method it uses to validate the authenticity of certificate applicants and the CA's expectations of how its certificates may be used.

Challenge/response token—A method of user authentication that is carried out through use of the Challenge Handshake Authentication Protocol (CHAP).

Scope Notes: When a user tries to log into the server using CHAP, the server sends the user a "challenge," which is a random value. The user enters a password, which is used as an encryption key to encrypt the "challenge" and return it to the server. The server is aware of the password. It, therefore, encrypts the "challenge" value and compares it with the value received from the user. If the values match, the user is authenticated. The challenge/response activity continues throughout the session and this protects the session from password sniffing attacks. In addition, CHAP is not vulnerable to "man-in-the-middle" attacks because the challenge value is a random value that changes on each access attempt.

Check digit—A numeric value, which has been calculated mathematically, is added to data to ensure that original data have not been altered or that an incorrect, but valid match has occurred.

Scope Notes: Check digit control is effective in detecting transposition and transcription errors.

Check digit verification (self-checking digit)—A programmed edit or routine that detects transposition and transcription errors by calculating and checking the check digit.

Checksum—A checksum value is generated by an algorithm and associated with an input value and/or whole input file. The checksum value can be used to assess its corresponding input data or file later and verify that the input has not been maliciously altered. If a subsequent checksum value no longer matches the initial value, the input may have been altered or corrupted.

Cipher—An algorithm to perform encryption

Ciphertext—Information generated by an encryption algorithm to protect the plaintext and that is unintelligible to the unauthorized reader.

Circuit-switched network—A data transmission service requiring the establishment of a circuit-switched connection before data can be transferred from source data terminal equipment (DTE) to a sink DTE.Scope Notes: A circuit-switched data transmission service uses a connection network.

Cleartext—Data that is not encrypted. Also known as plaintext.

Cloud computing—Convenient, on-demand network access to a shared pool of resources that can be rapidly provisioned and released with minimal management effort or service provider interaction

Community strings—Authenticate access to management information base (MIB) objects and function as embedded passwords.

Scope Notes: Examples are:

- Read-only (RO)- Gives read access to all objects in the MIB except the community strings, but does not allow write access
- Read-write (RW)- Gives read and write access to all objects in the MIB, but does not allow access to the community strings
- Read-write-all - Gives read and write access to all objects in the MIB, including the community strings (only valid for Catalyst 4000, 5000 and 6000 series switches)

Simple Network Management Protocol (SNMP) community strings are sent across the network in cleartext. The best way to protect an operating system (OS) software-based device from unauthorized SNMP management is to build a standard IP access list that includes the source address of the management station(s). Multiple access lists can be defined and tied to different community strings. If logging is enabled on the access list, then log messages are generated every time that the device is accessed from the management station. The log message records the source IP address of the packet.

Comparison program—A program for the examination of data, using logical or conditional tests to determine or to identify similarities or differences.

Completeness check—A procedure designed to ensure that no fields are missing from a record.

Compliance—Adherence to, and the ability to demonstrate adherence to, mandated requirements defined by laws and regulations, as well as voluntary requirements resulting from contractual obligations and internal policies

Compliance documents—Policies, standard and procedures that document the actions that are required or prohibited. Violations may be subject to disciplinary actions.

Computer sequence checking—Verifies that the control number follows sequentially and that any control numbers out of sequence are rejected or noted on an exception report for further research.

Concurrent access—A fail-over process, in which all nodes run the same resource group (there can be no [Internet Protocol] IP or [mandatory access control] MAC address in a concurrent resource group) and access the external storage concurrently.

Confidentiality—Preserving authorized restrictions on access and disclosure, including means for protecting privacy and proprietary information.

Consent—Any freely given, specific, informed and unambiguous indication of the data subject's wishes by which he or she, by a statement or by a clear affirmative action, signifies agreement to the processing of personal data relating to him or her.

Consequence—The result of a realized risk. A consequence can be certain or uncertain and can have positive or negative direct or indirect effects on objectives. Consequences can be expressed qualitatively or quantitatively.

Consumer—One who utilizes goods

Containment—Actions taken to limit exposure after an incident has been identified and confirmed

Continuous availability—Nonstop service, with no lapse in service; the highest level of service in which no downtime is allowed.

Control—The means of managing risk, including policies, procedures, guidelines, practices or organizational structures, which can be of an administrative, technical, management, or legal nature.

Scope Notes: Also used as a synonym for safeguard or countermeasure. See also Internal control.

Controller—The natural or legal person, public authority, agency or other body which, alone or jointly with others, determines the purposes and means of the processing of personal data.

Cookie—A message kept in the web browser for the purpose of identifying users and possibly preparing customized web pages for them.

Scope Notes: The first time a cookie is set, a user may be required to go through a registration process. Subsequent to this, whenever the cookie's message is sent to the server, a customized view based on that user's preferences can be produced. The browser's implementation of cookies has, however, brought several security concerns, allowing breaches of security and the theft of personal information (e.g., user passwords that validate the user identity and enable restricted web services).

Critical infrastructure—Systems whose incapacity or destruction would have a debilitating effect on the economic security of an enterprise, community or nation.

Criticality—The importance of a particular asset or function to the enterprise, and the impact if that asset or function is not available

Cross-border data transfers—The transfer of personal data to recipients outside of the territory in which the data originate

Cross-border processing—Processing of personal data which takes place in the context of the activities of establishments in more than one country of a controller or processor, where the controller or processor is established in more than one country; or processing of personal data which takes place in the context of the activities of a single establishment of a controller or processor union but which substantially affects or is likely to substantially affect data subjects in more than one country.

Cryptography—The study of mathematical techniques related to aspects of information security, such as confidentiality, data integrity, entity authentication and data origin authentication

Cryptosystem—General term referring to a set of cryptographic primitives that are used to provide information security services. Most often, the term is used in conjunction with primitives providing confidentiality, i.e., encryption.

D

Data accuracy—A component of data quality and refers to whether the data values stored for an object are the correct value and represented in a consistent and unambiguous form.

Data analysis—Obtaining an understanding of data by considering samples, measurement and visualization. Data analysis can be particularly useful when a data set is first received, before one builds the first model. It is also crucial in understanding experiments and debugging problems with the system.

Data anonymization—The protection of private or sensitive information by encrypting or removing personally identifiable information from data sets to keep the people whom the data represent anonymous.

Data classification—The assignment of a level of sensitivity to data (or information) that results in the specification of controls for each level of classification. Levels of sensitivity of data are assigned according to predefined categories as data are created, amended, enhanced, stored or transmitted. The classification level is an indication of the value or importance of the data to the enterprise.

Data classification scheme—An enterprise scheme for classifying data by factors such as criticality, sensitivity and ownership.

Data communications—The transfer of data between separate computer processing sites/devices using telephone lines, microwave and/or satellite links.

Data concerning health—Personal data related to the physical or mental health of a natural person, including the provision of healthcare services, which reveal information about his or her health status.

Data controller—See controller

Data custodian—The individual(s) and department(s) responsible for the storage and safeguarding of computerized data.

Data destruction—The elimination, erasure or clearing of data

Data dictionary—Stores all the details that correspond to the data flow diagram (DFD) stores, processes and flows. It may be called a database that contains the name, type, range of values, source and authorization for access for each data element in a system. It also indicates which application programs use those data so that when a data structure is contemplated, a list of the affected programs can be generated.

Data Encryption Standard (DES)—A legacy algorithm for encoding binary data that was deprecated in 2006. DES and its variants have been replaced by the Advanced Encryption Standard (AES).

Data flow—The flow of data from the input (in Internet banking, ordinarily user input at his/her desktop) to output (in Internet banking, ordinarily data in a bank's central database). Data flow includes travel through the communication lines, routers, switches and firewalls as well as processing through various applications on servers, which process the data from user fingers to storage in a bank's central database.

Data governance—Setting direction on data use through prioritization and decision making and ensuring alignment with agreed-on direction and objectives.

Data integrity—The degree to which a collection of data is complete, consistent and accurate

Data leakage—Unauthorized transmission of data from an organization either electronically or physically

Data life cycle—The sequence of steps data go through, beginning with its collection/generation and ending with archiving or deleting it at the end of its useful life

Data loss prevention—Detecting and addressing data breaches, exfiltration or unwanted destruction of data

Data minimization—Data are adequate, relevant and limited to what is necessary in relation to the purposes for which they are processed

Data normalization—A structured process for organizing data into tables in such a way that it preserves the relationships among the data.

Data owner—The individual(s) who has responsibility for the integrity, accurate reporting and use of computerized data

Data portability—The ability to transmit a data subject's data from one controller to another.

Data processing—Any operation or set of operations which is performed on personal data or on sets of personal data, whether or not by automated means, such as collection, recording, organization, structuring, storage, adaptation or alteration, retrieval, consultation, use, disclosure by transmission, dissemination or otherwise making available, alignment or combination, restriction, erasure or destruction.

Data processor—A natural or legal person, public authority, agency or other body that processes personal data on behalf of the controller.

Data protection authority—Independent authorities that monitor and supervise the application of a data protection law.

Data protection officer—Under the GDPR, some organizations need to appoint a data protection officer who is responsible for informing them of and advising them about their data protection obligations and monitoring their compliance with them.

Data recipient—Any person, public authority, agency or another body, to which the personal data are disclosed, whether a third party or not.

Data retention—Refers to the policies that govern data and records management for meeting internal, legal and regulatory data archival requirements

Data security—Those controls that seek to maintain confidentiality, integrity and availability of information.

Data structure—A particular arrangement of units of data, such as an array or a tree

Data subject—A natural person whose personal data are collected, held or processed

Data warehouse—A generic term for a system that stores, retrieves and manages large volumes of data.

Scope Notes: Data warehouse software often includes sophisticated comparison and hashing techniques for fast searches as well as for advanced filtering.

Data-oriented systems development—Focuses on providing ad hoc reporting for users by developing a suitable accessible database of information and to provide useable data rather than a function.

Database—A collection of data, often with controlled redundancy, organized according to a schema to serve one or more applications. The data are stored so that they can be used by different programs without concern for the data structure or organization. A common approach is used to add new data and to modify and retrieve existing data. See Archival database.

Database administrator (DBA)—An individual or department responsible for the security and information classification of the shared data stored on a database system. This responsibility includes the design, definition and maintenance of the database.

Database management system (DBMS)—A software system that controls the organization, storage and retrieval of data in a database.

Database replication—The process of creating and managing duplicate versions of a database.

Scope Notes: Replication not only copies a database but also synchronizes a set of replicas so that changes made to one replica are reflected in all of the others. The beauty of replication is that it enables many users to work with their own local copy of a database, but have the database updated as if they were working on a single centralized database. For database applications in which, geographically users are distributed widely, replication is often the most efficient method of database access.

Database specifications—These are the requirements for establishing a database application. They include field definitions, field requirements and reporting requirements for the individual information in the database.

Decision support systems (DSS)—An interactive system that provides the user with easy access to decision models and data, to support semi structured decision-making tasks.

Decryption—A technique used to recover the original plaintext from the ciphertext so that it is intelligible to the reader. The decryption is a reverse process of the encryption.

Decryption key—A digital piece of information used to recover plaintext from the corresponding ciphertext by decryption.—A digital piece of information used to recover plaintext from the corresponding ciphertext by decryption.

Defense in depth—The practice of layering defenses to provide added protection. Defense in depth increases security by raising the effort needed in an attack. This strategy places multiple barriers between an attacker and an enterprise's computing and information resources.

Digital certificate—Electronic credentials that permit an entity to exchange information securely via the internet using the public key infrastructure (PKI).

Digital code signing—The process of digitally signing computer code to ensure its integrity.

Digital signature—An electronic identification of a person or entity using a public key algorithm that serves as a way for the recipient to verify the identity of the sender, integrity of the data and proof of transaction

Disk mirroring—The practice of duplicating data in separate volumes on two hard disks to make storage more fault tolerant. Mirroring provides data protection in the case of disk failure because data are constantly updated to both disks.

Due care—The level of care expected from a reasonable person of similar competency under similar conditions.

Due diligence—The performance of those actions that are generally regarded as prudent, responsible and necessary to conduct a thorough and objective investigation, review and/or analysis.

Due professional care—Diligence that a person, who possesses a special skill, would exercise under a given set of circumstances.

E

Editing—Ensures that data conform to predetermined criteria and enable early identification of potential errors.

Electronic data interchange (EDI)—The electronic transmission of transactions (information) between two enterprises. EDI promotes a more efficient paperless environment. EDI transmissions can replace the use of standard documents, including invoices or purchase orders.

Elliptical curve cryptography (ECC)—An algorithm that combines plane geometry with algebra to achieve stronger authentication with smaller keys compared to traditional methods, such as RSA, which primarily use algebraic factoring.

Scope Notes: Smaller keys are more suitable to mobile devices.

Encryption—The process of taking an unencrypted message (plaintext), applying a mathematical function to it (encryption algorithm with a key) and producing an encrypted message (ciphertext).

Encryption algorithm—A mathematically based function or calculation that encrypts/decrypts data. May be block or stream ciphers.

Encryption key—A piece of information, in a digitized form, used by an encryption algorithm to convert the plaintext to the ciphertext.

End-user computing—The ability of end users to design and implement their own information system utilizing computer software products.

Endpoints—A device that can communicate with a connected network.

Enterprise architecture (EA)—Description of the fundamental underlying design of the components of the business system, or of one element of the business system (e.g., technology), the relationships among them, and the manner in which they support the enterprise's objectives.

Erasure—Also called the right to be forgotten, the data subject's ability to obtain from the controller the erasure of personal data concerning him or her

Event—Something that happens at a specific place and/or time

Exception reports—An exception report is generated by a program that identifies transactions or data that appear to be incorrect.

Scope Notes: Exception reports may be outside a predetermined range or may not conform to specified criteria.

External storage—The location that contains the backup copies to be used in case recovery or restoration is required in the event of a disaster.

F

Fail-over—The transfer of service from an incapacitated primary component to its backup component.

False enrollment—Occurs when an unauthorized person manages to enroll into the biometric system.

Scope Notes: Enrollment is the initial process of acquiring a biometric feature and saving it as a personal reference on a smart card, a PC or in a central database.

False negative—In intrusion detection, an error that occurs when an attack is misdiagnosed as a normal activity.

False positive—A result that has been mistakenly identified as a problem when, in reality, the situation is normal.

Filing system— Structured set of personal data which are accessible according to specific criteria, whether centralized, decentralized or dispersed on a functional or geographical basis.

Foreign key—A value that represents a reference to a tuple (a row in a table) containing the matching candidate key value.

Scope Notes: The problem of ensuring that the database does not include any invalid foreign key values is known as the referential integrity problem. The constraint that values of a given foreign key must match values of the corresponding candidate key is known as a referential constraint. The relation (table) that contains the foreign key is referred to as the referencing relation and the relation that contains the corresponding candidate key as the referenced relation or target relation. (In the relational theory it would be a candidate key, but in real database management systems (DBMSs) implementations it is always the primary key.)

Framework— A framework is a basic conceptual structure used to solve or address complex issues. An enabler of governance. A set of concepts, assumptions and practices that define how something can be approached or understood, the relationships among the entities involved, the roles of those involved and the boundaries (what is and is not included in the governance system).See Control framework and IT governance framework.

G

Genetic data—Personal data relating to the inherited or acquired genetic characteristics of a natural person which give unique information about the physiology or the health of that natural person and which result, in particular, from an analysis of a biological sample from the natural person in question.

Geographical information system (GIS)—A tool used to integrate, convert, handle, analyze and produce information regarding the surface of the earth.

Scope Notes: GIS data exist as maps, tri-dimensional virtual models, lists and tables

H

Harden—To configure a computer or other network device to resist attacks.

Hash—A cryptographic hash function takes an input of an arbitrary length and produces an output (also known as a message digest) that is a standard-sized binary string. The output is unique to the input in such a way that even a minor change to the input results in a completely different output. Modern cryptographic hash functions are also resistant to collisions (situations in which different inputs produce identical output); a collision, while possible, is statistically improbable. Cryptographic hash functions are developed so that input cannot be determined readily from the output.

Hash function— 1. An algorithm that maps or translates one set of bits into another (generally smaller) so that a message yields the same result every time the algorithm is executed using the same message as input

2. Fixed values derived mathematically from a text message

Hash total—The total of any numeric data field in a document or computer file. This total is checked against a control total of the same field to facilitate accuracy of processing.

Hashing—Using a hash function (algorithm) to create hash valued or checksums that validate message integrity

Hierarchical database—A database structured in a tree/root or parent/child relationship.

Scope Notes: Each parent can have many children, but each child may have only one parent.

Horizontal defense-in depth—Controls are placed in various places in the path to access an asset (this is functionally equivalent to concentric ring model above).

I

Identifiability—Condition that results in a personally identifiable information (PII) principal being identified, directly or indirectly, on the basis of a given set of PII

Identifiable natural person—Someone who can be identified, directly or indirectly, in particular by reference to an identifier, such as a name, an identification number, location data, an online identifier or to one or more factors specific to the physical, physiological, genetic, mental, economic, cultural or social identity of that natural person.

Identifier—Set of attribute values that unambiguously distinguish one entity from another one, in a given context total list of attribute values of an entity that allows this entity to be unambiguously distinguished from all other entities within a context and to be recognized as a single identity in that specific context

Identity and access management (IAM)—Encapsulates people, processes and products to identify and manage the data used in an information system to authenticate users and grant or deny access rights to data and system resources. The goal of IAM is to provide appropriate access to enterprise resources.

Imaging—A process that allows one to obtain a bit-for-bit copy of data to avoid damage of original data or information when multiple analyses may be performed.

Scope Notes: The imaging process is made to obtain residual data, such as deleted files, fragments of deleted files and other information present, from the disk for analysis. This is possible because imaging duplicates the disk surface, sector by sector.

Impersonation—An entity that mimics a system, process or person in an attempt to manipulate the user into an action that can cause an unexpected or unwanted event to a system

Incident—A violation or imminent threat of violation of computer security policies, acceptable use policies, guidelines or standard security practices

Indexed Sequential Access Method (ISAM)—A disk access method that stores data sequentially while also maintaining an index of key fields to all the records in the file for direct access capability.

Indexed sequential file—A file format in which records are organized and can be accessed, according to a pre-established key that is part of the record.

Information—An asset that, like other important business assets, is essential to an enterprise's business. It can exist in many forms. It can be printed or written on paper, stored electronically, transmitted by post or by using electronic means, shown on films, or spoken in conversation.

Scope Notes: COBIT 5 and COBIT 2019 perspective

Information architecture—Information architecture is one component of IT architecture (together with applications and technology).

Information criteria—Attributes of information that must be satisfied to meet business requirements.

Information engineering—Data-oriented development techniques that work on the premise that data are at the center of information processing and that certain data relationships are significant to a business and must be represented in the data structure of its systems.

Information processing facility (IPF)—The computer room and support areas.

Information security—Ensures that, within the enterprise, information is protected against disclosure to unauthorized users (confidentiality), improper modification (integrity) and nonaccess when required (availability). Information security deals with all formats of information – paper documents, digital assets, intellectual property in people's minds, and verbal and visual communications.

Information security governance—The set of responsibilities and practices exercised by the board and executive management with the goal of providing strategic direction, ensuring that objectives are achieved, ascertaining that risk is managed appropriately and verifying that the enterprise's resources are used responsibly.

Information security program—The overall combination of technical, operational and procedural measures and management structures implemented to provide for the confidentiality, integrity and availability of information based on business requirements and risk analysis.

Ingestion—A process to convert information extracted to a format that can be understood by investigators.

Scope Notes: See also Normalization.

Inheritance (objects)—Database structures that have a strict hierarchy (no multiple inheritance). Inheritance can initiate other objects irrespective of the class hierarchy, thus there is no strict hierarchy of objects.

Integrity—The guarding against improper information modification or destruction, and includes ensuring information non-repudiation and authenticity

Intellectual property—Intangible assets that belong to an enterprise for its exclusive use. Examples include patents, copyrights, trademarks, ideas and trade secrets.

International organization—An organization and its subordinate bodies governed by public international law or any other body that is set up by, or on the basis of, an agreement between two or more countries

Interrogation—Used to obtain prior indicators or relationships, including telephone numbers, IP addresses and names of individuals, from extracted data

IT architecture—Description of the fundamental underlying design of the IT components of the business, the relationships among them, and the manner in which they support the enterprise's objectives.

IT user—A person who uses IT to support or achieve a business objective.

J

Joint PII controller—PII controller that determine the purposes and means of the processing of PII with one or more other PII controllers

K

Key length—The size of the encryption key measured in bits

Key management—The generation, exchange, storage, use, destruction and replacement of keys in a cryptosystem.

L

Legitimate interest—The basis for lawful processing of data.

Librarian—The individual responsible for the safeguard and maintenance of all program and data files.

Life cycle—A series of stages that characterize the course of existence of an organizational investment (e.g., product, project, program).

Likelihood—The probability of something happening

Log— 1. To record details of information or events in an organized record-keeping system, usually sequenced in the order in which they occurred

2. An electronic record of activity (e.g., authentication, authorization and accounting)

Logical access—Ability to interact with computer resources granted using identification, authentication and authorization.

Logical access controls—The policies, procedures, organizational structure and electronic access controls designed to restrict access to computer software and data files

Logoff—The act of disconnecting from the computer.

Logs/log file—Files created specifically to record various actions occurring on the system to be monitored, such as failed login attempts, full disk drives and email delivery failures.

Loss event—Any event during which a threat event results in loss.

Scope Notes: From Jones, J.; "FAIR Taxonomy," Risk Management Insight, USA, 2008

M

Magnetic card reader—Reads cards with a magnetic surface on which data can be stored and retrieved.

Main establishment—The place of central administration for a controller with establishments in more than one country

Mandatory access control—A means of restricting access to data based on varying degrees of security requirements for information contained in the objects and the corresponding security clearance of users or programs acting on their behalf.

Manual journal entry—A journal entry entered at a computer terminal.

Scope Notes: Manual journal entries can include regular, statistical, inter-company and foreign currency entries. See also Journal Entry.

Mapping—Diagramming data that are to be exchanged electronically, including how they are to be used and what business management systems need them. See also Application Tracing and Mapping.

Scope Notes: Mapping is a preliminary step for developing an applications link.

Masking—A computerized technique of blocking out the display of sensitive information, such as passwords, on a computer terminal or report.

Master file—A file of semi permanent information that is used frequently for processing data or for more than one purpose.

Media access control (MAC)—Lower sublayer of the OSI Model Data Link layer

Media access control (MAC) address—A 48-bit unique identifier assigned to network interfaces for communications on the physical network segment

Media oxidation—The deterioration of the media on which data are digitally stored due to exposure to oxygen and moisture.

Scope Notes: Tapes deteriorating in a warm, humid environment are an example of media oxidation. Proper environmental controls should prevent, or significantly slow, this process.

Memory dump—The act of copying raw data from one place to another with little or no formatting for readability.

Scope Notes: Usually, dump refers to copying data from the main memory to a display screen or a printer. Dumps are useful for diagnosing bugs. After a program fails, one can study the dump and analyze the contents of memory at the time of the failure. A memory dump will not help unless each person knows what to look for because dumps are usually output in a difficult-to-read form (binary, octal or hexadecimal).

Message authentication code—An American National Standards Institute (ANSI) standard checksum that is computed using Data Encryption Standard (DES).

Message digest—A cryptographic hash function takes an input of an arbitrary length and produces an output (also known as a message digest) that is a standard-sized binary string. The output is unique to the input in such a way that even a minor change to the input results in a completely different output. Modern cryptographic hash functions are also resistant to collisions (situations in which different inputs produce identical output); a collision, while possible, is statistically improbable. Cryptographic hash functions are developed so that input cannot be determined readily from the output. See hash

Message digest algorithm—One-way functions that serve as a way for the recipient to verify data integrity and sender identity. Common message digest algorithms are MD5, SHA256 and SHA512.

Multifactor authentication—A combination of more than one authentication method, such as token and password (or personal identification number [PIN] or token and biometric device).

N

Nonrepudiation—The assurance that a party cannot later deny originating data; provision of proof of the integrity and origin of the data and that can be verified by a third party.

Scope Notes: A digital signature can provide non-repudiation.

Normalization—The elimination of redundant data.

O

Offsite storage—A facility located away from the building housing the primary information processing facility (IPF), used for storage of computer media such as offline backup data and storage files.

Online data processing—Achieved by entering information into the computer via a video display terminal.

Scope Notes: With online data processing, the computer immediately accepts or rejects the information as it is entered.

Opt-in—A declaration or an active motion in which a data subject agrees to particular data processing; Process or type of policy whereby the personally identifiable information (PII) principal is required to take an action to express explicit, prior consent for their PII to be processed for a particular purpose.

Opt-out—A choice that is made on behalf of a data subject, indicating the subject's desire to no longer receive unsolicited information

P

Personal data—Information relating to an identified or identifiable natural person.

Personal data breach—Any accidental or unlawful destruction, loss, alteration, unauthorized disclosure or access of a subject's data.

Personal identification number (PIN)—A type of password (i.e., a secret number assigned to an individual) that, in conjunction with some means of identifying the individual, serves to verify the authenticity of the individual.

Scope Notes: PINs have been adopted by financial institutions as the primary means of verifying customers in an electronic funds transfer (EFT) system.

Personal information—A synonym for personal data.

Personally identifiable information (PII)—Any information that can be used to establish a link between the information and the natural person to whom such information relates, or that is or might be directly or indirectly linked to a natural person

PII controller—Privacy stakeholder (or privacy stakeholders) who determines the purposes and means for processing personally identifiable information (PII) other than natural persons who use data for personal purposes

PII principal—Natural person to whom the personally identifiable information (PII) relates

Plaintext—Digital information, such as cleartext, that is intelligible to the reader.

Policy—A document that communicates required and prohibited activities and behaviors

Primary account number (PAN)—Unique payment card number (typically for credit or debit cards) that identifies the issuer and the particular cardholder account.

Principle of least privilege/access—Controls used to allow the least privilege access needed to complete a task

Privacy—The right of an individual to trust that others will appropriately and respectfully use, store, share and dispose of his/her associated personal and sensitive information within the context, and according to the purposes for which it was collected or derived.

Privacy by design—The integration of privacy into the entire engineering process

Privacy controls—Measures that treat privacy risk by reducing its likelihood or consequences. Privacy controls include organizational, physical and technical measures, e.g., policies, procedures, guidelines, legal contracts, management practices or organizational structures. Control is also used as a synonym for safeguard or countermeasure.

Privacy impact—Anything that has an effect on the privacy of a PII data subject and/or group of PII subjects.

Privacy impact assessment—The overall process of identifying, analyzing, evaluating, consulting, communicating and planning the treatment of potential privacy impacts with regard to the processing of personally identifiable information, framed within an organization's broader risk management framework.

Privacy incident management—The process by which an organization addresses a privacy breach.

Privacy information management system (PIMS)—Information security management system that addresses the protection of privacy as potentially affected by the processing of PII.

Privacy notice—A notification that provides individuals with information on how their personal data will be processed.

Privacy policy—Intention and direction, rules and commitment, as formally expressed by the personally identifiable information (PII) controller related to the processing of PII in a particular setting. Set of shared values governing the privacy protection of personally identifiable information (PII) when processed in information and communication technology systems.

Privacy preferences—Specific choices made by a personally identifiable information (PII) principal about how their PII should be processed for a particular purpose.

Privacy principles—Set of shared values governing the privacy protection of personally identifiable information (PII) when processed in information and communication technology systems.

Privacy risk—Any risk of informational harm to data subjects and/or organization(s) including deception, financial injury, health and safety injuries, unwanted intrusion, and reputational injuries which harm (or damage) that goes beyond economic and tangible losses.

Privacy risk assessment—A process used to identify and evaluate privacy-related risk and its potential effects.

Private key—A mathematical key (kept secret by the holder) used to create digital signatures and, depending on the algorithm, to decrypt messages or files encrypted (for confidentiality) with the corresponding public key.

Private key cryptosystems—Private key cryptosystems involve secret, private keys. The keys are also known as symmetric ciphers because the same key both encrypts message plaintext from the sender and decrypts resulting ciphertext for a recipient. See symmetric cipher.

Privilege—The level of trust with which a system object is imbued.

Privileged user—Any user account with greater than basic access privileges. Typically, these accounts have elevated or increased privileges with more rights than a standard user account.

Procedure—A document containing a detailed description of the steps necessary to perform specific operations in conformance with applicable standards. Procedures are defined as part of processes.

Process—Generally, a collection of activities influenced by the enterprise's policies and procedures that takes inputs from a number of sources, (including other processes), manipulates the inputs and produces outputs.

Scope Notes: Processes have clear business reasons for existing, accountable owners, clear roles and responsibilities around the execution of the process, and the means to measure performance.

Processing—Any operation or set of operations which is performed on personal data or on sets of personal data, whether or not by automated means, such as collection, recording, organization, structuring, storage, adaptation or alteration, retrieval, consultation, use, disclosure by transmission, dissemination or otherwise making available, alignment or combination, restriction, erasure or destruction.

Processing PII—Operation or set of operations performed upon personally identifiable information (PII). Examples of processing operations of PII include, but are not limited to, the collection, storage, alteration, retrieval, consultation, disclosure, anonymization, pseudonymization, dissemination or otherwise making available, deletion or destruction of PII.

Processor—A natural or legal person, public authority, agency or other body which processes personal data on behalf of the controller.

Professional competence—Proven level of ability, often linked to qualifications issued by relevant professional bodies and compliance with their codes of practice and standards.

Professional judgement—The application of relevant knowledge and experience in making informed decisions about the courses of action that are appropriate in the circumstances of the IS audit and assurance engagement

Professional standards—Refers to standards issued by ISACA. The term may extend to related guidelines and techniques that assist the professional in implementing and complying with authoritative pronouncements of ISACA. In certain instances, standards of other professional organizations may be considered, depending on the circumstances and their relevance and appropriateness.

Profiling— The automated processing of personal data to evaluate or make a decision about an individual. Any form of automated processing of personal data consisting of the use of personal data to evaluate certain personal aspects relating to a natural person, in particular to analyze or predict aspects concerning that natural person's performance at work, economic situation, health, personal preferences, interests, reliability, behavior, location or movements.

Protective measure— A measure intended to achieve adequate risk reduction.

Pseudonymization—The processing of personal data in such a manner that the personal data can no longer be attributed to a specific data subject without the use of additional information, provided that such additional information is kept separately and is subject to technical and organizational measures to ensure that the personal data are not attributed to an identified or identifiable natural person.

Public key—In an asymmetric cryptographic scheme, the key that may be widely published to enable the operation of the scheme.

Public key cryptosystem—Public key cryptosystems combine a widely distributed public key and a closely held, protected private key. A message that is encrypted by the public key can only be decrypted by the mathematically related, counterpart private key. Conversely, only the public key can decrypt data that was encrypted by its corresponding private key. See asymmetric cipher.

Public key infrastructure (PKI)—A series of processes and technologies for the association of cryptographic keys with the entity to whom those keys were issued.

Purpose limitation—Data are collected for specified, explicit and legitimate purposes and not further processed in a manner that is incompatible with those purposes.

R

Re-identification—Discovering the individual to which deidentified data belong by matching anonymous data with publicly available information or auxiliary data

Reasonableness check—Compares data to predefined reasonability limits or occurrence rates established for the data.

Recipient— Natural or legal person, public authority, agency or other body to which the personal data are disclosed, whether a third party or not. However, public authorities that may receive personal data in the framework of a particular inquiry in accordance with state law shall not be regarded as recipients; the processing of those data by those public authorities shall be in compliance with the applicable data protection rules according to the purposes of the processing.

Rectification—A data subject's ability to have any incorrect personal data be corrected.

Redundancy check—Detects transmission errors by appending calculated bits onto the end of each segment of data.

Registration authority (RA)—An authority in a network that verifies user requests for a digital certificate and tells the certificate authority (CA) to issue it

Regulation—Rules or laws defined and enforced by an authority to regulate conduct

Regulatory requirements—Rules or laws that regulate conduct and that the enterprise must obey to become compliant

Rekeying—Process of changing cryptographic keys. Periodic rekeying limits the amount of data encrypted by a single key.

Reliable information—Information that is accurate, verifiable and from an objective source.Scope Notes: Refer to COBIT 5 information quality goals

Remediation—Actions taken to mitigate or eliminate the vulnerability after vulnerabilities are identified and assessed

Remote access—An authorized user's ability to access a computer or network from anywhere through a network connection.

Repository—An enterprise database that stores and organizes data.

Repudiation—The denial by one of the parties to a transaction, or participation in all or part of that transaction, or of the content of communication related to that transaction.

Residual risk—The remaining risk after management has implemented a risk response.

Restriction of processing—The marking of stored personal data with the aim of limiting their processing in the future.

Risk—The combination of the likelihood of an event and its impact.

Risk analysis—1. A process by which frequency and magnitude of IT risk scenarios are estimated.

2. The initial steps of risk management: analyzing the value of assets to the business, identifying threats to those assets and evaluating how vulnerable each asset is to those threats.

Scope Notes: It often involves an evaluation of the probable frequency of a particular event, as well as the probable impact of that event.

Risk assessment—A process used to identify and evaluate risk and its potential effects.

Scope Notes: Risk assessments are used to identify those items or areas that present the highest risk, vulnerability or exposure to the enterprise for inclusion in the IS annual audit plan.Risk assessments are also used to manage the project delivery and project benefit risk.

Risk evaluation—The process of comparing the estimated risk against given risk criteria to determine the significance of the risk. [ISO/IEC Guide 73:2002].

Risk management—1. The coordinated activities to direct and control an enterprise with regard to risk

Scope Notes: In the International Standard, the term "control" is used as a synonym for "measure." (ISO/IEC Guide 73:2002)

2. One of the governance objectives. Entails recognizing risk; assessing the impact and likelihood of that risk; and developing strategies, such as avoiding the risk, reducing the negative effect of the risk and/or transferring the risk, to manage it within the context of the enterprise's risk appetite.

Scope Notes: COBIT 5 perspective

Risk source— Element that, alone or in combination, has the potential to give rise to risk.

RSA—A public key cryptosystem developed by R. Rivest, A. Shamir and L. Adleman used for both encryption and digital signatures.Scope Notes: The RSA has two different keys, the public encryption key and the secret decryption key. The strength of the RSA depends on the difficulty of the prime number factorization. For applications with high-level security, the number of the decryption key bits should be greater than 512 bits.

S

Secure development life cycle—The inclusion of security in the software development life cycle

Sensitive PII—Category of personally identifiable information (PII), either whose nature is sensitive, such as those that relate to the PII principal's most intimate sphere, or that might have a significant impact on the PII principal. It can consist of PII revealing the racial origin, political opinions or religious or other beliefs, personal data on health, sex life or criminal convictions, as well as other PII that might be defined as sensitive.

Sensitivity—A measure of the impact that improper disclosure of information may have on an enterprise.

Single factor authentication (SFA)—Authentication process that requires only the user ID and password to grant access

Standard—A mandatory requirement, code of practice or specification approved by a recognized external standards organization, such as International Organization for Standardization (ISO).

Storage limitation—The principle that personal data must be kept in a form which permits identification of data subjects for no longer than is necessary for the purposes for which the personal data are processed.

Subject access — The data subject's right to obtain from the data controller, on request, certain information relating to the processing of his/her personal data.

Supervisory authority— An independent public authority.

Symmetric cipher—A symmetric cipher is an algorithm that encrypts data using a single key. In symmetric cryptographic algorithms, a single key is used for encipherment (encrypting) and decipherment (decrypting).

Symmetric key encryption—System in which a different key (or set of keys) is used by each pair of trading partners to ensure that no one else can read their messages. The same key is used for encryption and decryption. See also Private Key Cryptosystem.

System hardening—A process to eliminate as many security risks as possible by removing all nonessential software programs, protocols, services and utilities from the system

T

Technology stack— The underlying elements used to build and run an application

Third party—A natural or legal person, public authority, agency or body other than the data subject, controller, processor and persons who, under the direct authority of the controller or processor, are authorized to process personal data.

Tolerable risk—Risk that is within a tolerable or acceptable range based on management's appetite.

Transparency—Refers to an enterprise's openness about its activities and is based on the following concepts:

- How the mechanism functions is clear to those who are affected by or want to challenge governance decisions
- A common vocabulary has been established
- Relevant information is readily available

Scope Notes: Transparency and stakeholder trust are directly related; the more transparency in the governance process, the more confidence in the governance.

Two-factor authentication—The use of two independent mechanisms for authentication, (e.g., requiring a smart card and a password) typically the combination of something you know, are or have.

U

User awareness—A training process in security-specific issues to reduce security problems; users are often the weakest link in the security chain.

V

Verification—Checks that data are entered correctly.

Vertical defense-in depth—Controls are placed at different system layers – hardware, operating system, application, database or user levels

Volatile data—Data that changes frequently and can be lost when the system's power is shut down